# THE CREATED SELF

Painted by W. Hogarth.

O THE ROAST BEEF OF OLD ENGLAND, &c.

Published according to Act of Parliament. March 6. 1749.

Engraved by W. Hogarth.

JOHN PRESTON

# *The Created Self*

## THE READER'S ROLE IN
## EIGHTEENTH-CENTURY FICTION

'Thou thy selfe art the subject of my Discourse.'
('Democritus Junior to the Reader',
Robert Burton, *The Anatomy of*
*Melancholy*, p. 2)

HEINEMANN

LONDON

Heinemann Educational Books Ltd
LONDON MELBOURNE TORONTO
SINGAPORE CAPE TOWN
AUCKLAND NEW DELHI
IBADAN HONG KONG NAIROBI


ISBN 0 435 18720 1 (cased)
ISBN 0 435 18721 X (paperback)

Published by
Heinemann Educational Books Ltd
48 Charles Street, London W1X 8AH

Printed by Butler & Tanner Ltd
Frome and London

FOR DOREEN

# ACKNOWLEDGMENTS

Two of the following chapters are revised versions of articles first published in *ELH*. I am grateful to the editors of that journal for their permission to reprint '*Tom Jones* and the "Pursuit of True Judgment" ' from *ELH*, Vol. 33, No. 3, Sept. 1966, pp. 315–326, and 'Plot as Irony: The Reader's Role in *Tom Jones*' from *ELH*, Vol. 35, No. 3, Sept. 1968, pp. 365–380.

# ILLUSTRATIONS

# CONTENTS

# CHAPTER 1

# *Introduction:* The Created Self

## I

I INTEND this book as an interpretation of four novels from one point of view. The novels chose themselves: that is to say, they were not chosen in order to provide a point of view. They hardly could be. Though they were published within a period of fifty years they have very little in common. I am writing about the eighteenth-century novel, but can hardly pretend that this in itself will give unity to what I have to say. On the other hand, it does seem that these novels, in which the modern concept of the novel (at least in England) first begins to take shape, give a very conspicuous position to some of the essential features of the novel's form and characteristic procedures. For instance, they are obviously rhetorical. It is not always, of course, their obvious rhetoric that is significant, as we shall see in considering *Tom Jones.* But it is clear that the novelists of this period were interested in exploring different ways of relating to their readers, and did not try to disguise their interest. Things have become very different since then and, as Wayne Booth notes, 'critics have often been troubled by this kind of overt, distinguishable rhetoric'.[1] Nevertheless the whole of his book is meant to controvert their view. 'It takes,' this is the basis of his argument, 'no very deep analysis to show that the same problems are raised, though in less obvious form, by the disguised rhetoric of modern

[1] *The Rhetoric of Fiction,* Preface (detailed bibliographical references are given in the bibliography, pp. 212–217)

fiction.'[1] In their different ways the novels I have chosen illuminate many aspects of this 'disguised rhetoric'.

One aspect which I shall be particularly concerned with in this book is the role of the reader. Wayne Booth again provides the terms of reference. They occur in his discussion of the question of belief in the reading of fiction. He notes that the novelist protects himself against our disbelief by inducing us to read in certain ways and from certain points of view. He defines the kind of reading he wants. In effect he defines his reader:

> The author creates, in short, an image of himself and another image of his reader; he makes his reader, as he makes his second self, and the most successful reading is one in which the created selves, author and reader, can find complete agreement.[2]

What interests me is this concept of the 'created self', the 'reader' invented by the author in order to make his fictional world work. He is in this sense a fictional reader; yet, as Booth notes, he is a fiction the real reader is willing to co-operate with. He represents what the reader will have to become in order to take possession of the whole fictional experience. He stands for a desired reading. Of course we may find it difficult to accept the desired role. Booth quotes in this connection an essay by Walker Gibson in which the created self is described as a 'mock reader', who may be 'a person we refuse to become, a mask we refuse to put on, a role we will not play'.[3] And Gibson raises the possibility that when a book proposes such a 'mock reader' we will be likely to reject it as a bad book. That is to say, the fictional situation devised for the real reader, the role intended for him, may be instrumental in our evaluation of the work. What we value in the novel may be closely related to what it asks us to do or who it asks us to be. Whether this is so or not, and what might be some other effects of creating a

---

[1] *The Rhetoric of Fiction*, loc. cit.    [2] Ibid., p. 138
[3] Ibid., loc. cit.

'self' for the reader are questions that I think I can answer best by looking closely at what happens in certain novels. I make no attempt to provide a 'rhetoric of reading', though no doubt this would be worth doing. Rather I trust that the rhetorical principles in question will provide a unifying point of view for these four novels, and yet not seem unduly arbitrary or restrictive. And I should be glad to feel that such an approach might prompt other more radical enquiries into the nature of the reader's role in fiction.

## II

Each of the writers we are concerned with makes it quite clear that the reader has a vital role to play. Defoe maintains, in the Preface to *Moll Flanders*, that the 'Work is chiefly recommended to those who know how to Read it'. He appears to refer to readers who know how to make 'good Uses of it' and who 'will be more pleased with the Moral than the Fable'. Yet, as we shall see, the story is overall an oblique criticism of a presumed reader. Defoe suppresses the 'mock reader's' image, but there is nothing in the novel which does not contribute to the ironic creation of a self for the reader. To 'know how to read it' is in effect to know how to read oneself.

Richardson also thinks that in his stories 'something . . . must be left for the reader to make out'.[1] The reader is important, and in *Clarissa* he is in fact represented in multiple reflected images. All the characters in the novel are readers; they are as much involved in reading letters as in writing them; the process of reading and writing is itself a significant part of the drama. Richardson is deeply involved in the paradox presented by reading and writing, the fact that they are at once the most intimate and most isolating of activities. *Clarissa* is the working out of a tragic conflict inherent in the medium itself; it has in the end to assert the

[1] *Selected Letters*, p. 296

reality of the kind of relationship which cannot be maintained by letters. The reader has therefore to understand that reading may be a process of estrangement, and he has to be prepared to go beyond this process to discover a concept of freedom.

Fielding takes much more lightly the fact that a lot must be left in the reader's hands. No question here of the mutual isolation of writer and reader. In fact it appears to be a situation which allows them to get on well together.

> Bestir thyself therefore on this Occasion; ... for thou art highly mistaken if thou dost imagine that we intended, when we begun this great Work, to leave thy Sagacity nothing to do, or that, without sometimes exercising this Talent, thou wilt be able to travel through our Pages with any Pleasure or Profit to thyself.
> (*Tom Jones*, XI, ix)

Fielding's humour represents an escape from the book. He translates the lonely process of reading into a friendly encounter; his art is concentrated on creating a sociable atmosphere. Yet there is in *Tom Jones* a lot of interest in the questions and ambiguities that crop up specifically in the process of reading. The reader is in effect being offered a variety of ways in which he may be a bad reader, on the assumption that this will bring him eventually to see what is needed for reading well. It is his ironic counterpart that he finds in the book, just as it is an ironic version of the real author that is to be found in 'Fielding-as-narrator'. Both writer and reader are asked for more discernment and subtlety than either of them is made to display in the novel itself.

Sterne in particular is aware of the reader's importance:

> The truest respect which you can pay to the reader's understanding, is to halve this matter amicably, and leave him something to imagine, in his turn, as well as yourself.
>
> For my own part, I am eternally paying him compliments of this kind, and do all that lies in my power to keep his imagination as busy as my own. (*Tristram Shandy*, II, xi)

Sterne asks deeper questions than any of the other novelists about the creative imagination and its relation to the act of reading. *Tristram Shandy* is an intricate picture of narrators and readers, of stories and stories within stories. It keeps in play the dazzling interchanges between fiction and reality. It discovers, in the complex operations of reading, an image of what is involved in the creating of fictions. The story-teller offers a 'reading' of reality; at the same time the reader has to rise to the imaginative level of the author. Sterne in fact offers the completest and most revealing portrait of the reader. He shows how, like an actor, the reader is simultaneously both involved and detached, intimately engaged in creating the fiction but coolly critical at the same time, taken out of himself yet in the end in a position to find himself.

## III

What Sterne makes very clear is what is sensed in different ways by all these novelists: the reader is involved in an activity much more complex and challenging than would be suggested by the notion of 'identification'. D. W. Harding comments on this activity in an illuminating essay on the 'Psychological Processes in the Reading of Fiction'. Like Sterne he understands reading as an ideal conversation. 'Fiction has to be seen', he writes, '. . . as a convention, a convention for enlarging the scope of the discussions we have with each other about what may befall.'[1] There is more to reading than vicarious experience or 'identification'. It is a matter of joining 'with the novelist or dramatist in the psychological act of giving them [i.e. our desires] statement in a social setting'.[2]

This suggests that the reader is in a pseudo-situation, but

[1] *British Journal of Aesthetics*, Vol. 2, No. 2, April 1962, p. 139
[2] Ibid., p. 144

a real relationship. He really does make contact with another mind, he does enter into a dialogue. He is not passive, at least at his best he is not: he brings his own experience and expectations to the work. At the same time he is making discoveries about a hypothetical, not a real, situation. He is improving his understanding of human nature by means of a fiction. He extends himself in play, in an action without consequences and in relationships without responsibility. What counts is the quality of the talk about these situations. The reality is in the discussion, the encounter between writer and reader. Novels enlarge the reader's experience by 'enlarging the scope of the discussions'.

Of course it looks as if there cannot be literally a discussion. After all, as we shall see, the writer cannot even predict his reader, still less converse with him. Similarly the reader can only be *creative* to the extent that the text will allow. Yet it does seem to me that the discourse is a real and not a fictional one. It is a strange one, certainly, in which the writer reaches out to an unseen and unforeseeable reader, and the reader wishes to respond to an absent writer who has already said his last word. Yet the text itself is something in which they both have a share. It faces both ways; for the writer it is an address to someone, for the reader it is a message from someone. It presumes both a writer and a reader; it really creates a writer and a reader. We are accustomed to asking about the kind of *writer* implied by this or that text. We are used to hearing about, say, 'Fielding-as-narrator', and we see the value of having the implied author identified for us (for instance, as Tristram or Yorick). It is clearly more difficult to introduce a comparable image of the reader into the text, for the reader will always want to separate himself from any image of himself; he will always be conscious, that is, of *himself*, as he cannot be of the writer, beyond the margins of the fiction. But I do not think it is inconceivable. Indeed my argument is that it is quite usual. As we have seen, these novelists, with more or less seriousness, invite the reader to participate. They are interested in creating a text which will, as it were, give instructions to the reader. They wish to keep the form open; they think of the novel as a process, not a product, and as a situation for the reader, not a received text. They want to create readers, just as the readers want to create writers. It is the created reader, the 'created self', and the work he is given to do, that we shall be looking for in the following chapters.

# CHAPTER 2

# Moll Flanders: *'The Satire of the Age'*

## I

DEFOE'S writings are a kind of action. They belong to his dealings in the practical world. They relate not to art but to prudence. As one critic puts it, not even the novels are 'aesthetic objects': Defoe wants the reader 'to participate in the experience he describes, not to contemplate it'.[1] He takes this to mean that Defoe is chiefly interested in problem-solving.[2] As Denis Donoghue says, his novels are not ethical or moral but 'strategic': they have to do with 'ways and means'.[3] But I think Defoe is intending something more subtle as well. He is an ironist and responsible to his society. He wants to re-route our thinking about social principles and motives. Irony is for him more than a literary mode, it is a way of life and a way of living to some effect. His books are meant to 'work' in the public mind; they are a kind of conscience.

In this sense what Taine asserts is true: 'Defoe is a man of action; effect not noise touches him.'[4] His fictions behave like life. And it is striking that, once at least, his life achieved

---

[1] Jonathan Bishop, 'Knowledge, Action and Interpretation in Defoe's Novels', *Journal of the History of Ideas*, xiii, 1952, p. 3

[2] Ibid., p. 4

[3] 'The Values of *Moll Flanders*', *Sewanee Review*, lxxi, Spring 1963, pp. 289, 288.

[4] *History of English Literature*, iii. 262

the effect of his art. In 1702 he published *The Shortest Way with the Dissenters*. As a parody of the language of religious intolerance it is devastatingly accurate, too accurate to work as irony. As Ian Watt says, Defoe's 'vicarious identification with the supposed speaker' left no room for the necessary contradictions and incongruities of irony. It was certainly 'a masterpiece, but a masterpiece not of irony but of impersonation'.[1] This is true: the pamphlet is not self-explanatory like Swift's *A Modest Proposal*. It is not a work of art: its meaning lies not in what it was but what it did.

In this sense, as an event which created a new situation, it was highly effective. The work produced an immediate and violent reaction. Defoe was imprisoned, tried and sentenced to stand three times in the pillory. He had provoked his judges into an act consistent with the attitudes parodied in the pamphlet. As Defoe wrote ten years later, 'the Case the Book pointed at, was to speak in the first Person of the Party, and then, thereby, not only to speak their language, but make them acknowledge it to be theirs, which they did so openly, that confounded all their Attempts afterwards to deny it, and to call it a Scandal thrown upon them by another'.[2] If the pamphlet was not in itself ironic, the situation certainly was, especially when Defoe came to be pilloried. The intended disgrace turned out to be a personal triumph. What is more, his condition had its own kind of eloquence: the spectators 'halloo'd him down from his wooden punishment, as if he had been Cicero that had made an excellent oration in it, rather than a Cataline that was exposed and declaimed against there'.[3] But Defoe did not in fact leave the situation to speak for itself. In *A Hymn to the Pillory*, he articulates the meaning of these events. The pillory, the

[1] *The Rise of the Novel*, p. 126

[2] *The Present State of the Parties* (1712), p. 24, quoted by M. E. Novak, 'Defoe's *Shortest Way with the Dissenters*', MLQ, xxvii, 1966, p. 407

[3] *The True-Born Hugonot; Or, Daniel de Foe. A Satyr* (1703), p. 25, quoted by M. Shinagel, *Daniel Defoe and Middle-Class Gentility*, p. 68

B

'*Hi'roglyphic* State *Machin*' is 'no Shame to Truth and Honesty':

> Shame, like the Exhalations of the Sun,
> Falls back where first the motion was begun:
> And he who for no Crime shall on thy Brows appear,
> Bears less Reproach than they who plac'd him there. (58–61)

In fact the pillory is 'the Satyr of the Age' (274), the instrument of a severe irony. 'Tell us, Great Engine, how to understand / Or reconcile the Justice of the Land' (39–40). Men like '*Bastwick, Pryn, Hunt, Hollingsby*, and *Pye*, / Men of unspotted Honesty' (41–2) have stood there; why not, then, all those whose 'Crimes are too remote / Whom leaden-footed Justice has forgot' (114–15), the magistrates, clergymen, lawyers, statesmen and above all the capitalists, 'the Authors of the Nations discontent, / And Scandal of a Christian Government' (162–3)? The pillory, which should expose crime, has become a way to conceal it; it is an ironic manifesto of the inverted values of a society where what 'pays' is what is right, and it is only wrong to be found out, where 'honesty' and plain dealing are an offence and virtue is foolish. Thus the pilloried man is

> an Example made,
> To make Men of their Honesty afraid,
> That for the Time to come they may
> More willingly their Friends betray;
> Tell 'em the m[en] that plac'd him here,
> Are sc[anda]ls to the Times,
> Are at a loss to find his Guilt,
> And can't commit his Crimes. (409–16)

It is the whole episode that is exemplary, not just the written texts. Defoe moves from word to event and back to the word again. The word has the force of an act, the event becomes a statement. The sequence is ironic and the irony is a social act, a way of improving the public conscience.

## II

This is the kind of irony there is in *Moll Flanders*. Or, rather, this is the ironic effect of *Moll Flanders*. For the irony is not *in* the novel. It seems to be wrong to describe the book either in Dorothy Van Ghent's way as a complex architectural organization of 'ironies and counterstresses'[1] or as an unmodulated 'realistic' narrative in which ironies happen to be lying around. Ian Watt, whose view this is, maintains that if there are such ironies, 'they are surely the ironies of social and moral and literary disorder'.[2] In these and other comments on Defoe's irony what appears to count is that it should be 'structural'. It is assumed that conscious and purposive irony must be lodged in some concept of the novel as a self-supporting fabric. Either Defoe uses irony structurally or his irony shows that he has no sense of structure. It comes to the same thing: irony that is not like Jane Austen's either has nothing to do with art or it is not irony. 'Later novelists such as Jane Austen and Flaubert', writes Ian Watt, '. . . created irony, and made novel readers sensitive to its effects. We cannot but approach Defoe's novels through the literary expectations which later masters of the form made possible'.[3] If this is so, we may have to admit that such expectations are unduly restrictive. They hardly allow for the variety of ways in which a novel may be told to someone.

The 'there was . . .' of narrative presents not a fact but a situation. It constitutes a bargain between teller and listener. The story exists as the precipitate of a relationship between them. Jane Austen's art consists in suppressing the signs of this relationship. It calls on irony to render the narrative intelligence as a kind of third dimension to the action, or as a colour filter, not visible itself but affecting all the tones in the scene. Thus the reader is conscious of the

---

[1] *The English Novel*, p. 36        [2] *The Rise of the Novel*, p. 129
[3] *The Rise of the Novel*, p. 130

play of mind rather as an enlargement of his own sensibility than as the mechanism of a narration. Nevertheless, though the story seems to be impersonal and free-standing as an object, it is in reality a transaction between author and reader. The good reader of Jane Austen, as Wayne Booth notes, values 'the sense of standing with the author', and 'we ordinary, less perceptive readers have by now been raised to a level suited to grasp the ironies'.[1] The situation is one in which we are taken beyond our usual capacities. But there are other ways of contriving this situation. It may even be that Jane Austen's way is effective not just because it is oblique, but because obliqueness of this kind is not really characteristic of the novel. (Allen Tate, writing of a similar effect in Flaubert, claims that 'it has been through Flaubert that the novel has at last caught up with poetry.'[2]) At any rate it is not at all certain that a more direct negotiation between narrator and reader (as, for instance, in George Eliot) is necessarily cruder or more primitive. Though it does not arise from irony the situation may well be ironic. In this way the irony can be said to be structural though it does not sustain an autonomous structure. For the form of the novel is at least partly to be explained as the form of the situation in which it is told. More than most literary modes it is influenced by the ways we get on with each other. It is involved in the social experience.

Thus it is not damaging to say that Defoe's novels are not 'aesthetic objects'. It means in fact that they demonstrate rather clearly something that is true of most novels. They remind us that the novel may display the formal clarity of a work of art elsewhere than in the configurations of the text. *Moll Flanders* is about social efficiency, about expediency and morality, and (as H. H. Andersen has shown[3]) about

[1] *The Rhetoric of Fiction*, p. 257
[2] 'Techniques of Fiction', *Sewanee Review*, 1944, reprinted in *Forms of Modern Fiction*, ed. W. V. O'Connor, p. 45
[3] 'The Paradox of Trade and Morality in Defoe', *MP*, xxxix, 1942

the necessary economic connection between private vice and public prosperity. But the story itself hardly persuades the reader that Defoe knows how to handle these contradictory issues. Andersen in fact concludes that he simply shelved them, putting trade and its necessities in one corner of his mind and morality in another. Jonathan Bishop argues that what looks like contradiction is a 'dialectical progression' in the narrative: Moll's development is from the innocent soul (the thesis) through experience (antithesis) to repentance (a synthesis of the whole).[1] More recently, George Starr has shown that a pattern of this kind would link *Moll Flanders* with a long tradition of religious self-analysis in the form of 'spiritual autobiography'. Many of the apparent contradictions could be 'owing not to any "double vision" on Defoe's part, but rather to a traditional conception of the sinner's progress, which Moll's portrayal largely embodies'.[2] But such readings do not dispel the sense of 'moral obtuseness' Denis Donoghue finds in Defoe's characterization.[3] In fact, since they allow for an element of the conventional, they tend to cut corners and to prune what Martin Price calls the 'untidy fullness of the book'. As he says, 'the stress is more upon the energy of impulse than upon its evil'. On the other hand to say so only strengthens the impression that Defoe will not declare himself: 'he does not seem to need to reduce these tensions to a moral judgment ... he is one of the artists who make our moral judgments more difficult.'[4]

I do not think this is right. It seems to be a position we get into because we dislike the alternative. But this need not happen if we are prepared to grant that for Defoe the story is not the whole story. His art does not end there, in *mimesis*. His subject looks untidy and inchoate if we regard only

---

[1] *Journal of the History of Ideas*, xiii, 1952, p. 16
[2] *Defoe and Spiritual Autobiography*, p. 161
[3] 'The Values of *Moll Flanders*', p. 292
[4] *To the Palace of Wisdom*, pp. 268, 276 and 267

what gets into the tale. But there are aspects of it that belong
to the area between fiction and reality in which the novel is
mediated. Defoe's art extends into *praxis*. That is not to say
that it encroaches on satire or propaganda; there is always
something in it that is not merely exemplary, that resists
formulation. It is an art that has the weight of action: it
displaces event. It is an art of the real, an art of rhetoric, a
traffic with the reader. This is what gives Defoe control of
irony and of moral judgment. It brings the whole of his
subject into focus by asking the reader to meet it as a
challenge to his own experience. It defines what the book is
about by defining the reader's response to it.


# III


Defoe's relationship with the reader has its basis in his
style. He has little interest in the dramatic possibilities of
what his characters say. All his narrators speak alike. Moll's
style, like Roxana's, is admitted in the Preface to be 'a little
altered'. Moll is supposed to have written 'more like one
still in Newgate than one grown penitent and humble, as she
afterwards pretends to be'; she is made to tell her tale 'in
modester words'. Defoe is drawing attention to the dullness
of the style. He will not be colourful even when the situation
demands it. His style is featureless. It has few adjectives; it
is non-figurative; it is without wit, exaggeration, emphasis
or emotion:

> I went boldly in, and was just going to lay my Hand upon a
> peice of Plate, and might have done it, and carried it clear off,
> for any care that the Men who belong'd to the Shop had taken
> of it; but an officious Fellow in a House, not a Shop, on the
> other side of the Way, seeing me go in, and observing that there
> was no Body in the Shop, comes running over the Street, and
> into the Shop, and without asking me what I was, or who, seizes
> upon me, and cries out for the People of the House.

I had not, as I said above, touch'd any thing in the Shop, and seeing a glimpse of some Body running over to the Shop, I had so much presence of Mind as to knock very hard with my Foot on the Floor of the House, and was just calling out too, when the Fellow laid Hands on me. (p. 309)

This is a recital of facts. The style hardly allows for any shading or adjustment. Words like 'boldly' and 'officious' carry no emphasis; they slip unnoticed into the file of events. The sequence puts the facts end to end and leaves no room for opinion.

Ian Watt relates this style on the one hand to the style of preaching recommended by Richard Baxter and on the other to the 'new values of the scientific and rational outlook of the late seventeenth century'.[1] That is to say, it is both a robust rhetorical medium and an instrument of scientific fact. It has, in Watt's view, 'a positive and wholly referential quality very well suited to carrying out the purpose of language as Locke had defined it, "to convey the knowledge of things" '. It renders the world in terms of the 'primary qualities' of objects—'their solidity, extension, figure, motion and number—especially number: there is very little attention to the secondary qualities of objects, to their colours, sounds or tastes.'[2] At this point it becomes easy to align Defoe with the beginnings of 'modern realism' in philosophy and the move towards a fiction 'concerned with the correspondence of words to things'.[3] But, as Dorothy Van Ghent notes, 'it is unfortunate that factual orientation in the novel should have come to determine the definition of realism in the novel.'[4] She would rather we looked for a 'hypothetical structure' in *Moll Flanders*, asking questions about its formal coherence and consistency with itself. And actually Ian Watt also assumes that facts alone do not establish an authentic world. Both are agreed that Defoe's style is 'factual' and both, from different points of view,

[1] *The Rise of the Novel*, p. 102     [2] Ibid., loc. cit.
[3] Ibid., p. 28     [4] *The English Novel*, p. 33

consider that this is not enough to establish him as an artist. As Leslie Stephen says:

> the praise which has been lavished upon De Foe for the verisimilitude of his novels seems to be rather extravagant. The trick would be easy enough, if it were worth performing. The storyteller cannot be cross-examined; and if he is content to keep to the ordinary level of commonplace facts, there is not the least difficulty in producing conviction.[1]

Indeed to him the factual style almost suggested incompetence. Defoe, he says,

> will accumulate any number of facts and details; but they must be such as will speak for themselves without the need of an interpreter. . . . He never seems to know his own strength. . . . He is decent or coarse, just as he is dull or amusing, without knowing the difference. . . . In short, the merit of De Foe's narrative bears a direct proportion to the intrinsic merit of a plain statement of the facts.[2]

Once more it appears that what is most characteristic of Defoe is just what obstructs our view of his 'peculiar merit', which says Stephen, must be elsewhere than in 'the circumstantial nature of his lying'.[3] What strikes every reader as evidence of his vitality, what Stephen calls 'the vigour naturally connected with an unflinching realism',[4] or Bonamy Dobrée the 'intensity of . . . realizing imagination',[5] turns out, in this view, to be the very thing which diminishes him as an artist.

The difficulty arises, I think, because we come to Defoe with the wrong expectations. The factual style is not only or even primarily 'realistic'. Ian Watt considers that Defoe, like Richardson, arrived at realism by breaking with 'the accepted canons of prose style.'[6] But I think Defoe was looking beyond realism to the possibilities in a way of writing free of any obligations to 'style'. He certainly wants

[1] *Hours in a Library*, i. 8    [2] *Hours in a Library*, i. 28–9    [3] Ibid., i. 9
[4] Ibid., i. 9    [5] *English Literature in the Early Eighteenth Century*, p. 411
[6] *The Rise of the Novel*, p. 29

above all not to be literary, and his 'realism' is a means to this end. It allows him to come close to what Roland Barthes calls 'le degré zéro' of writing. This 'neutral' mode, a 'transparent form of speech', tries to refuse the social and cultural implications of 'literature'. It wishes to be 'innocent', to achieve 'a style of absence which is almost an ideal absence of style'. If it could remain in this condition it would escape from the 'opacity of form', from the feeling that speech is an 'object' to 'receive treatment at the hands of a craftsman, a magician or a scriptor'. It would 'rediscover the primary condition of classical art: instrumentality'. But unlike classical art it would not be 'at the service of a triumphant ideology'. Barthes thinks that even this colour-less writing must turn into a habit: 'the writer, taking his place as a "classic", becomes the slavish imitator of his original creation, society demotes his writing to a mere manner, and returns him prisoner to his own formal myths.'[1] But Defoe's distinction is that he would not be tempted to become a 'classic'. He trusted the temporary style of journalism, a style which is no style, which 'deliberately forgoes any elegance of ornament'.[2]

To achieve this style is, says Barthes, to become 'irre-trievably honest': it is a moral as well as an existential necessity. And it is in such terms that Defoe justifies his faith in 'plainness'. What concerns him is not just truth to fact, but truth of discourse, truth in a man's dealings with other men. In the *Serious Reflections* he speaks, through Crusoe, of honesty 'as it regards mankind among themselves, as it looks from one man to another, in those necesssary parts of man's life, his conversation and negotiation, trusts, friendships, and all the incidents of human affairs' (p. 25). He goes on to make it clear that he regards writing as an extension of these social relationships.

The plainness I profess, both in style and method, seems to me to have some suitable analogy to the subject, *honesty*; and,

[1] *Writing Degree Zero*, pp. 83–4     [2] Ibid., p. 84

therefore, is absolutely necessary to be strictly follow'd. And I must own, I am the better reconcil'd, on this very account, to a natural infirmity of homely plain writing; in that I think the plainness of expression, which I am condemn'd to, will give no disadvantage to my subject, since honesty shews the most beautiful, and the more like *honesty*, when artifice is dismiss'd, and she is honestly seen by her own light only; likewise the same sincerity is required in the reader; and he that reads this essay without *honesty*, will never understand it right: *she must, I say, be view'd by her own light.* (p. 25)

Thus the plain style is really a test of good faith; it is an *exercise* in honesty, for the reader as well as the writer:

> If prejudice, partiality, or private opinions stand in the way, *the man's a reading knave*, he is not honest to the subject; and upon such an one all the labour is lost; this work is of no use to him, and by my consent, the bookseller should give him his money again. (p. 25)

What is needed is not goodness but candour. 'A man cannot be truly an honest man, without acknowledging the mistakes he has made; particularly, without acknowledging the wrong done to his neighbour; and why pray is justice less required in his acknowledgement to his Maker? He then that will be honest, must dare to confess he has been a knave' (p. 27). 'All shame is cowardise' (p. 26); the courage to be honest with ourselves is a matter of conscience, it is what we owe ourselves and God. It is also what is owing to our neighbours: 'I question much, whether a covetous, narrow, stingy man, as we call him, one who gives himself up to himself, as born for himself only, ... can be an honest man' (p. 18). Crusoe's experience goes to show that solitude as 'a retreat from human society, on a religious or philosophical account, is a meer cheat' (p. 10). Men need each other and are meant to help each other. Thus 'poor, wild, wicked *Robinson Crusoe*' (p. 25) can claim to be honest: he has been able to confess his errors and repent, and, more

important, this 'assists to qualify me for the present under-
taking, as well to recommend that rectitude of soul, which I
call *honesty* to others, as to warn those who are subject to
mistake it, either in themselves or others' (p. 26). Honesty is
a way of confronting ourselves and others; and so is Defoe's
plain style in the novels.

## IV

So the honesty of Moll's confession is an end in itself. No
doubt it implies that she is now repentant; but her repentance is not, I think, the point. George Starr, who thinks
that it is, concludes that the book is 'at a certain disadvantage' because this spiritual meaning cannot be enacted, as it
is in *Robinson Crusoe*, and Moll's narrative commentary
tends therefore to be too explicit, even 'bald'.[1] But really
this commentary is the important thing. What Moll does or is
matters less than what she says about it. Actually Defoe
once or twice indicates that she is not deeply repentant: in
the Preface she is said to be finally 'not so extraordinary a
penitent as she was at first'; and we recall that she is supposed to have written her story in a style more appropriate
to Newgate than to a state of repentance. In fact, as we
shall see, it is quite important to Defoe that Moll should not
live up to the 'honesty' of her narration. She has to be both
conscious of the meaning of her life and powerless to change
it, entirely open with herself yet out of touch with her own
knowledge of herself. Howard Koonce has written about
her from this point of view: 'Moll's sense of destiny (i.e., as
he later explains, her sense of 'necessity') not only was in
conflict with her circumstances, it is in conflict with her own
sense of morality.'[2] Moll is honest about her own dishonesty,

---

[1] *Defoe and Spiritual Autobiography*, p. 162
[2] 'Moll's Muddle: Defoe's Use of Irony in *Moll Flanders*', *ELH*, xxx,
1963, p. 382

but without any quickening of conscience. In fact she has an equal facility with truth and falsehood.

Bonamy Dobrée notes that she 'lied in life, but she never lies to herself, nor to us'.[1] This is not quite true, as we shall see, but it throws some light on the book. Defoe is interested in those traits of character that will secure a certain style, or more accurately, a contrast of styles. What he needs is someone who is capable of both candour and deceit. Moll is defined by the needs of the book even by the demands of language: 'the fable is always made for the moral, not the moral for the fable'.[2] As Howard Koonce says, the conflict in Moll's own sense of herself is 'thematic': Moll's character is an 'artistic creation' arising out of the book's thematic conflict and is 'so controlled that imagining her under any other circumstances at any time is plainly impossible'.[3] The book deals with the need for honesty and also the need for deceit. It is a study of the double standards society seems to expect, in the form principally of an examination of the way people speak.

The story of Moll's affair with the banker demonstrates this. Moll is looking for an honest man to take charge of her money. She is introduced to someone who might be taken to stand for the ideal of integrity society proposes for itself. 'And indeed,' Moll writes, 'as soon as I saw (him) . . . I was fully satisfied that I had a very honest Man to deal with, his Countenance spoke it, and his Character, as I heard afterwards, was everywhere so good, that I had no room for any more doubts upon me' (p. 152). But there is irony in their meeting, and at first it looks as if Defoe may develop it. Moll expects the banker to be honest, but she is not quite honest with him or with us. 'I entered more freely with him into my Case,' she reports; '*I told him* my Circumstances at large: that *I* was *a Widow* come over from *America* . . .' (p. 152). Yet only a few pages earlier she has been telling us

[1] *English Literature in the Early Eighteenth Century*, p. 422
[2] *Serious Reflections*, Preface          [3] 'Moll's Muddle', p. 386

of the linen-draper who was still legally her husband and of a gentleman at Bath with whom she had been 'no less than a Whore and an Adultress all this while' (p. 144). She will surely have to admit that it was ironic that the banker should go on to speak of his wife as a whore and to ask Moll, of all people, for her advice. And in fact her words leave a margin for irony: 'I wav'd the Discourse, and began to talk of my Business' (p. 156). But Defoe lets the opportunity slip. He seems unappreciative of the layers of equivocation in the episode. He is hardly prepared to consider that Moll should be difficult to pin down in her relationships with others and with her own past. He chooses to be unsubtle. Moll herself is made to tell us what we are meant to get out of the episode. Her 'frankness' is ironic, in a simple way, not because of any misalignment in the record, or any unconfessed motives, but because she was not intending to be frank: 'it was necessary to Play the Hypocrite a little more with him', 'I play'd with this Lover as an Angler does with a Trout' (p. 162). She thinks she behaved badly: she was deceiving him all the time; she keeps pointing to the difference between what she said and what she thought, what she said to him and what she said to herself. The banker objects that an honest woman would hardly consent to live with him, 'and for the other sort, *says he*, I have had enough of her to meddle with any more Whores'. Moll's real reaction, she recalls, was quite different from the one she pretended:

> It occurr'd to me presently, I would have taken your word with all my Heart, if you had but ask'd me the Question, But that was to myself; *to him I reply'd*, why, you shut the Door against any honest Woman accepting you, for you condemn all that should venture upon you at once, and conclude, that really a Woman that takes you now, can't be honest. (p. 158)

Later he proposes that she should marry him before he is divorced. Her response to this we have already seen: 'My

Heart said yes to this offer at first Word, but it was necessary to Play the Hypocrite a little more with him; so I seem'd to decline the Motion with some warmth' (p. 161). These candid accounts of double-dealing are quite unrealistic. They are a naïve version of what Moll was, yet their naïveté cannot really be said to reflect what she now is. Her narration simplifies and makes things look more shapely, as no doubt it would. But it is unnaturally impartial. She has an opinion about her past but no vital connection with it. She annotates but does not acknowledge it. Her experiences do not thicken into consciousness. She remains innocent, Martin Price observes, like 'those Puritans who scrutinize their motives as if they were spectators beholding a mighty drama'.[1] But if she has a point of view she has no character and no command of her destiny. Thus to say that she 'play'd with this Lover' really makes no sense: she lied from instinct and without any plan, just as she now tells truth. It is almost as an afterthought that she explains why she kept him dangling: '. . . and the Reason why I did it was because the Lady that had invited me so earnestly to go with her into *Lancashire* insisted so positively upon it, and promised me such great Fortunes, and such fine things there, that I was tempted to go and try' (p. 162). She has no deeper strategy than an eye to the main chance.

But Defoe is not concentrating on this. He has no interest in character, nor even in the absence of character. In fact he again shows that he is thinking about the geometry of the situation rather than the people involved in it. Its usefulness is that it allows him to test, almost as an abstract issue, the different ways of using language. The people are 'set up' in an experimental, even hypothetical, way in order to assess ways of speaking.

What emerges is unexpected. At least it contradicts Moll's inclination to blame herself. Her duplicity begins to look like honesty. On the other hand the banker's words

[1] *To the Palace of Wisdom*, p. 276

tend to become suspect. Of course this is partly because
Moll tells us what she really was thinking, whereas the
banker's words remain opaque: Moll has the advantage of
telling her own story. Yet there is in fact something odd
about the banker's behaviour. In the end, it is true, he is
found to have all the virtues: he is 'a Quiet, Sensible, Sober
Man, Virtuous, Modest, Sincere, and in his Business
Diligent and Just' (p. 218). But at this point he is made
to ask some impossible things, impossible to an 'honest'
woman at any rate. 'Why do you not get a head Steward,
Madam, that may take you and your Money together into
keeping?' 'I wish,' Moll remembers saying 'secretly' to
herself, 'I wish you would ask me the Question fairly, I
would consider very seriously on it before I said no' (p. 153).
Later, when he comes out with it—'*will you take me,*
Madam?'—Moll's reply is quite justified:

> That's not a fair question, *says I,* after what you have said;
> however, least you should think I wait only for a Recantation
> of it, I shall answer you plainly, NO, *not I*; my Business is of
> another kind with you, and I did not expect you would have
> turn'd my serious Application to you in my own distracted Case,
> into a Comedy.' (p. 158)

His words do have a built-in resistance to honesty. 'If your
case is so plain as you say it is', Moll tells him, 'you may be
legally Divorc'd, and then you may find honest Women enough
to ask the Question of fairly, the Sex is not so scarce that you
can want a Wife' (p. 158). 'Can you think so Ill of me,' she
adds, 'as that I would give any Answer to such a Question
beforehand? Can any Woman alive believe you in earnest,
or think you design anything but to banter her?' (p. 159.)
    Of course, the scene, as we have observed, hinges on the
fact that Moll would have taken his word. Her objections,
which seem to expose something discreditable in the
banker's motives, are in her own view hypocritical. They
aim to keep up the character of a 'very modest sober Body;
which whether true or not in the Main, yet you may see how

necessary it is, for all Women who expect anything in the World, to preserve the Character of their Virtue, even when perhaps they may have sacrificed the Thing itself' (p. 160). Yet it does not quite appear that she is dealing dishonestly with the banker. She meets him fairly on his own terms. Her objections do not camouflage her real intentions. They make sense and they are also sincere. If Moll 'expects anything in the world', if she is to make a good bargain, she must appear as a good business woman. She does not disguise this from him. His proposal to 'marry' her before he has obtained the divorce 'from the whore his wife' is not good business at all. Moll tells him so and stands out for a firm contract. 'Well then he went from it to another, and that was, that I would Sign and Seal a Contract with him, Conditioning to Marry him as soon as the Divorce was obtain'd, and to be void if he could not obtain it' (p. 162). Moll tells him this is 'more Rational', and it is in fact more use to her than his earlier proposals. The 'honest' language of calculation and mutual suspicion is one she believes in. But at the same time she is ashamed of it. It offends her natural feelings: 'my Heart said yes to this offer at first Word'. Her impulse is to take his word 'with all my Heart'. She is impulsive, imprudent, uncalculating; she assents without reflection to the banker's proposals. But she understands clearly enough that they are 'unfair', that they pre-judge anyone who would accept them. She sees the situation as one in which feelings must seem 'immoral' though to her they are natural, and business must seem 'honest' though to her it is hypocritical. She sees further into the situation than the banker does. She takes, as it were, the responsibility for the double-talk it demands. She knows her own history—she has no shame in calling herself a whore—and cannot help bringing it to bear on the present situation. Thus it appears that the language she is expected to use is deceitful, the language of truth is what she must conceal.

So there is in the episode almost a reversal of roles. An

honest man, a pillar of society, speaks a language which is recognized at once by an 'immoral' woman. And it is the immoral woman who can be honest about the real implications of that language. This is not to say that she is 'good', but that she is in a position from which all that is said must be revalued. To be what she would spontaneously be is to be what he would call immoral. But to be what is called honest is to her immoral also. It is her destiny to be immoral and admit it. And this is a kind of honesty Defoe particularly valued, as we have seen. 'All shame is cowardise.' It almost seems in fact that he values it above simple goodness. There comes a point when Moll has to realize that the banker really is without guile. His trusting nature is a reproach to her. Yet Defoe appears to think that she comes out of the situation creditably. What he wants is that she shall be honest with herself. That she is at the same time concealing the truth from the banker does not seem to matter. In fact as it adds to her guilt it also augments her candour. Defoe suggests that Moll has no responsibility for her behaviour, only for her unspoken thoughts. She is in a state of moral weightlessness:

> Then it occourr'd to me what an abominable Creature am I! and how is this innocent Gentleman going to be abus'd by me! How little does he think, that having Divorc'd a Whore, he is throwing himself into the Arms of another! that he is going to Marry one that has lain with two Brothers, and has had three Children by her own Brother! one that was born in *Newgate*, whose Mother was a Whore, and is now a transported Thief; one that has lain with thirteen Men, and has had a Child since he saw me! poor Gentleman! *said I*, What is he going to do? After this reproaching my self was over, it followed thus: Well, if I must be his Wife, if it please God to give me Grace, I'll be a true Wife to him, and love him suitably to the strange Excess of his Passion for me; I will make him amends, if possible, by what he shall see, for the Cheats and Abuses I put upon him, which he does not see. (pp. 210–11)

c

This extraordinary soliloquy is certainly a key passage. As the rendering of a moral crisis it is ludicrous. But that is not Defoe's intention at all. He wants to examine the relations between honesty and deceit, between candour and conceal-ment. And for this it is entirely necessary that Moll shall remain impervious to her own self-reproach. There is really no question of her reforming. Her usefulness is that it is in her nature to be both truthful and dishonest. And the irony is that the more dishonest she is the better she can adjust to the world in which she must establish herself: 'I'll be a true wife to him . . .'

## V

This is surely going to suggest that Moll's whole way of life is an irony, a 'satire of the age' like the pillory. The faults she discovers in herself are quite likely to be shared by the society she aspires to. The irony was there from the start: she wished to be a 'gentlewoman' and has actually been going the right way about it. At any rate she has got to a point where 'gentility' is easily seen through. She thinks she is in a position to censure apparently respectable people, and, as Defoe presents things, she is right. Take for instance the episode when she is picked up by a 'gentleman' who gets so drunk that she is able to rob him of his watch, his purse, his periwig and silver-fringed gloves, his sword and his snuffbox. It provokes in her what might seem an unlikely fit of moralizing:

> There is nothing so absurd, so surfeiting, so ridiculous, as a Man heated by Wine in his head, and a wicked Gust in his Inclination together; he is in the possession of two Devils at once, and can no more govern himself by his Reason than a Mill can Grind without Water; His Vice tramples upon all that was in him that had any good in it, if any such thing there was . . . (p. 260)

We cannot think that Moll is the person who ought to preach like this. But 'gentlemen' may be mortified to 'consider the contemptible thoughts which the very Women they are concern'd with, in such cases as these, have of them' (p. 262). Just because she is a whore she can see things which otherwise would remain hidden. The rest of the story deals with this gentleman's reputation. The 'governess' hears from a friend that he has been set upon by robbers.

> PSHAW! says my old Governess jeering, I warrant you he has got drunk now and got a Whore, and she has pick'd his Pocket, and so he comes home to his Wife and tells her he has been Robb'd; that's an old sham, a thousand such tricks are put upon the poor Women every Day. (p. 264)

Moll and the governess now have their man in full view: he is a hypocrite himself. It is true that Moll takes the blame for his conduct: 'had I not yielded to see him again, the corrupt desire in him had worn off, and 'tis very probable he had never fallen into it, with any Body, else as I really believe he had not done before'. (p. 273). But she also notes that the man blamed himself: 'he would often make just Reflections also upon the Crime itself, . . . and he made the Moral always himself' (p. 273).

Certainly the episode cannot be taken to mean that Moll is excusable, or that she is trying to justify herself. As Ian Watt says, it is a 'travesty of piety and morality' to see Moll and her governess preaching as they go to work on their victim. And, as he also says, it is 'very unlikely that Defoe is being ironical', at least about the incongruities between Moll's talk and her actions.[1] Defoe does not seem to notice what they are going to suggest about her character. In fact it seems clear that he is interested in another kind of irony. The episode may in fact be one of those 'examples of patent and conscious irony' that Ian Watt himself refers to. In the passage, he notes, where Moll determines she is going to be

[1] *The Rise of the Novel,* p. 123

a 'gentlewoman' there is a 'verbal emphasis' which drives home the 'difference between virtue and class, and the moral dangers of being taken in by external evidences of gentility'; and at another point there is 'a contrast between overt and actual moral norms'.[1] This is the kind of effect Defoe is working for in the scenes with the drunken gentleman. He is not getting confused about Moll: she remains simply what she is, and her moralizing is meant, bluntly and crudely, to make it clear what she is. But she is not worse than some people who have a better reputation. And there is a sustained irony in the fact that, though she feels she must confess to the things that other people are always trying to evade or conceal, this is not the way to succeed. She has to discover the social usefulness of hypocrisy. And Defoe is discovering that social behaviour may have its ironic reflection in the life of a criminal.

This is apparent from the start. Moll's affair with the two brothers sets the pattern. The younger brother does her no good by letting it be known that he loves her: it 'grew so publick that the whole House talk'd of it, and his Mother reprov'd him for it, and their Carriage to me appear'd quite Altered' (p. 37). But this suits the elder brother. He sees that it will draw off attention from his own affair with Moll. He even advises her to marry his brother: 'you may come into a safe Station, and appear with Honour, and with splendor at once, and the Remembrance of what we have done, may be wrapt up in an eternal Silence, as if it had never happen'd' (p. 45). The younger brother gets no credit for his frankness: 'if you are in Earnest you are Undone', his mother tells him (p. 54). But the elder brother builds his reputation on deceit: 'I dare answer for my Brother,' says the elder sister, 'he knows the World better' (p. 54). Moll has a 'great deal of Satisfaction' in telling him with 'honest Plainess' that she loves him. She thinks this must make it impossible for him to break his pledge as a

---

[1] *The Rise of the Novel*, p. 121

'gentleman' that he would marry her when he came into the estate. Yet she has already forced him to acknowledge what he really thinks of her. He has been telling her that she will always have his 'respect':

> you shall be my Dear Sister, as now you are my Dear ——
> and there he stop'd.
> Your Dear whore, *says I*, you would have said, if you had gone on; and you might as well have said it; but I understand you. (p. 45)

And in the end he is saying that what has happened between them 'may be buried and forgotten' (p. 64). So Moll agrees to marry the younger brother and the elder is secure: 'thus diligently did he cheat him, and had the Thanks of a faithful Friend for shifting off his Whore into his Brothers Arms for a Wife' (p. 67). Moll repents that she has become the 'instrument to abuse so honest a Gentleman'.

> But there was no Remedy, he would have me, and I was not oblig'd to tell him that I was his Brother's Whore, tho' I had no other way to put him off; so I came gradually into it, to his Satisfaction, and behold, we were Married. (p. 67)

Moll is becoming acclimatized. She finds that she need not be good in order to do well for herself: the social system favours the hypocrite and cheat. In fact Defoe makes it look as if goodness is slightly feeble. The younger brother does not get on. After his marriage his story continues for just two sentences: he gives Moll two children, lives five years and dies. Goodness is an irrelevance in the world Defoe is depicting. It withers away. But Moll is learning to survive.

That is, she is learning how to do wrong with impunity. She is learning how to adjust 'overt' to 'actual' moral norms. Defoe was quite clear that the struggle for economic survival did not necessarily bring out the best in people. It might do so, no doubt it should do so: in the chapter 'Of Projectors' in *An Essay upon Projects* he maintains that there are those who in necessity turn to 'Honest Invention'. They become

'honest projectors', working on 'fair and plain principles of
Sense, Honesty, and Ingenuity'. But there are also many
who are driven to despair and death, or to crime: they 'turn
open Thieves, House-breakers, Highwaymen, Clippers,
Coiners, &c. till they run the length of the Gallows, and
get a Deliverance the nearest way at St. *Tyburn.*' There are
yet others who find that society is actually tolerant of crime.

> Others being masters of more Cunning than their Neighbours,
> turn their Thoughts to Private Methods of Trick and Cheat, a
> Modern way of Thieving, every jot as Criminal, and in some
> degree worse than the other, by which honest men are gull'd
> with fair pretences to part from their Money, and then left to
> take their Course with the Author, who sculks behind the curtain
> of a Protection, or in the *Mint* or *Friars*, and bids defiance as
> well to Honesty as the Law.

# VI

But Defoe goes further, beyond the question of criminality
and social survival, to a more critical aspect of the way
truth is mixed up with deceit. The occasion is the story of
Moll's life in Virginia. She finds there, it is true, a society
which almost blatantly has its roots in criminality. Her
mother-in-law tells her how in this country 'many a *Newgate*
Bird becomes a great Man, and we have, *continued she,*
several Justices of the Peace, Officers of the Train Bands,
and Magistrates of the Towns they live in, that have been
burnt in the Hand' (p. 100). In fact she herself had been a
criminal 'but these Passages were long before your time,
and they give me no trouble at all now' (p. 102). Yet they do
turn out to have a bearing on Moll's own life. It is from
these reminiscences that she discovers who her husband
really is.

> Let any one judge what must be the Anguish of my Mind,
> when I came to reflect, that this was certainly no more or less

*than my own Mother*, and I had now had two Children, and was big with another by my own Brother, and lay with him still every Night. (p. 102)

She is now faced with a desperate need to conceal the truth; 'and thus I liv'd with the greatest Pressure imaginable for three Year more, but had no more Children' (p. 103). She maintains a hypocrisy that even to her seems monstrous, not because it is criminal—indeed she was 'not much touched with the Crime of it'—but because it called for an act that 'had something in it shocking to Nature'. She and her mother both assume that to bring the matter into the open would be social and economic ruin. But, after all, Moll cannot bring herself to accept her mother's advice:

> for my Mother's Opinion was, that I should bury the whole thing entirely, and continue to live with him as my Husband, till some other Event should make the discovery of it more convenient; ... that we might lie as we us'd to do together, and so let the whole matter remain a secret as close as Death, for Child, *says she*, we are both undone if it comes out. (p. 112)

The episode is important. Without it Defoe could be meaning the book to show that society is no more than systematized double-dealing. And this would not carry much conviction. It would be bound to have the rather feverish tone of *The Political History of the Devil* which makes something like this point. You can see the devil's cloven foot in all the affairs of men:

> ... The Cloven-Foot is an Emblem of the true *double Entendre* or divided Aspect, which the great Men of the World generally act with, and by which all their Affairs are directed; from whence it comes to pass that there is no such Thing as a single-hearted Integrity, or an upright Meaning to be found in the world; that Mankind, worse than the ravenous Brutes, preys upon his own Kind, and devours them by all the laudable Methods of Flattery, Whyne, Cheat and Treachery; *Crocodile like*, weeping over those it will devour, destroying those it smiles upon, and,

in a Word, devours its own Kind, which the very Beasts refuse,
and that by all the Ways of Fraud and Allurement that *Hell*
can invent; holding out a cloven divided Hoof, or Hand, pretending to save, when the very Pretence is made use of to ensnare and
destroy.

Thus the divided Hoof is the Representative of a divided
double Tongue, and Heart, an Emblem of the most exquisite
Hypocrisy, the most fawning and fatally deceiving Flattery . . .
(II, vi)

But in the Virginia episode Defoe puts in a more disturbing way the need for lying and the consequences of truth.
Here is a secret which cannot be kept, though it is too
appalling to be told. Concealment is intolerable and so is
frankness. Moll is here in a situation which demands deceit
because it is hardly possible to live with the truth; yet the
deceit too is impossible to live with. And for a time only
Moll has any experience of this dilemma. The situation is
obviously calculated to throw the whole weight of it on her
alone.

I was now the most unhappy of all Women in the World:
O had the story never been told me, all had been well; it had
been no Crime to have lain with my Husband, since as to his
being my Relation I had known nothing of it.

I had now such a load on my Mind that it kept me perpetually
waking; to reveal it, *which would have been some ease to me*, I
cou'd not find wou'd be to any purpose, and yet to conceal it
wou'd be next to impossible; nay, I did not doubt but I should
talk of it in my sleep, and tell my Husband of it whether I would
or no. (p. 102)

# VII

Her mother's advice expresses the social will, and it is
unthinkable. But Moll is not now concerned only with the
social will, or if so, then not only with its manifestations in

the action of the book. She confronts the reader. 'I leave it to
any Man to judge,' she says, 'what Difficulties presented
to my view' (p. 103). Moll does in fact stand in a closer
relationship to any one of her readers than to the characters
in the novel. She tells us what she hides from them. She is
hypocritical with them but not with us. She makes us attend
to the distance between the truth and her lies. What is more,
she compels us to accept her as a habitual liar. She does not
excuse this. And simply the fact that she does not endows
her with a kind of veracity. She thinks of herself as dishonest. But to think this is to be capable of unusual honesty.
She invites our censure and our approval simultaneously.
She is both better and worse than we are ourselves. When
we try to understand and value her we are faced with a
conflict in ourselves. We are, or are meant to be, uncomfor-
table in her presence.

   This seems to me to indicate that she has the qualities of
a picaresque heroine. Robert Alter notes that the picaroon is
able, indeed is compelled, to be both 'immoral' and candid.
He

> does not act according to 'official' morality because, observing
> how such morality is more frequently preached than practiced,
> he realizes that he must ignore much of it in order to get along
> in the world. Since he has no set place in society and is not
> committed to the established order, he is free from the tribute
> of lip service to conventional morality which most people feel
> is exacted from them. He can call a thief a thief and a whore a
> whore, even when he is the thief or his wife is a whore.[1]

Clearly this would allow us to take Moll, on my reading of
her character, as a picaroon. And Alter recognizes in Moll a
kind of candour: she

> has a habit of cutting sharply through all camouflaging phrase-
> ology and rapping out harsh realities in the short, unambiguous
> syllables of what she herself calls 'plain English'. . . . these

[1] *Rogue's Progress*, pp. 37–8

moments of unmitigated candour in Moll are by no means limited
to her judgments of other people. She is just as ready to put the
plainest label of condemnation on her own actions.[1]

Yet his opinion is that in some essential ways she differs
from the true picaroon. Her candour is really, he says, a
kind of 'verbal literalism': 'she calls a whore a whore not so
much out of moral honesty as out of moral literal-mindedness.'[2] Also she lacks 'the nimbleness of imagination' that is
characteristic of the picaroon;[3] she is, in a term borrowed
from E. A. Baker, 'a rogue who does not rejoice in her
rogueries'.[4] No doubt it is necessary, if terms like 'picaresque'
are to mean something, to see that they do not mean just
anything. If we are to stick to the categories, we may well
have to say that Moll does not get into this one. I do not
think that is such an important matter. But I do think that
it is useful to be able to interpret Moll in the light of our
experience of the picaresque. What we find there should
give a firmer edge to our sense of her character. The
picaresque novel, Northrop Frye says, is 'the story of the
successful rogue who, from Reynard the Fox on, makes
conventional society look foolish without setting up any
positive standard'.[5] The picaresque hero is a satirist without
credit. He finds society crooked but is a crook himself. He
rejects society yet he needs it and battens on it. He is not
admirable, yet we admire him—at least we admire his
realism and his truthfulness. Yet we cannot admire them
without noticing that they undermine his own position.
Conversely we feel sympathy and affection for him whilst
having to admit that his low estimate of our behaviour is
right. He makes us allies, not like the satirist against the
others, but against ourselves. We are both attracted and
repelled by him.

So it is with Moll. It is not that she is morally confused,

[1] *Rogue's Progress*, pp. 36 and 37        [2] Ibid., p. 43
[3] Ibid., p. 41        [4] Ibid., p. 46
[5] *Anatomy of Criticism*, p. 229

but that she establishes herself in that area of confusion which society finds it expedient to tolerate. It is not that she is confused but that she does not allow us to evade our own confusion. It is with us that she is honest, implying that we will not be honest with ourselves. In this sense some of her direct appeals to the reader take on an extra significance. It is true that at the crisis of the book, when Moll is face to face with herself in Newgate, the reader is asked to take particular note of her repentance. 'It would be a severe Satyr on such, to say they do not relish the Repentance as much as they do the Crime'; the repentance 'is really the best part of my Life, the most Advantageous to myself, and the most instructive to others' (p. 335). If this were really so the book would certainly have to be called naïve and confused. The word 'advantageous' would, for instance, be a give-away. We could not help noticing that Moll does not in fact forfeit any of the profits of her criminal life, nor does she lose her ability to make a good bargain. And she retains her instinct for deception:

> I launch'd out into a new World, as I may call it in the Condition (as to what appear'd) only of a poor, nak'd Convict, order'd to be Transported in respite from the Gallows, my Cloaths were poor and mean, but not ragged or dirty, and none knew in the whole Ship that I had anything of value about me. (p. 359)

'Value' remains what it was. So, we must conclude, repentance is what it was. Yet the fact that she makes an appeal to the reader does seem in keeping with her role in the book. She is putting into words what we have been conscious of all along, that her conduct is making us question our own conduct.

Actually she says 'I am not capable of reading Lectures of instruction to any Body, but I relate this [i.e. her experience in Newgate] in the very manner in which things then appear'd to me, as far as I am able, but infinitely short of the lively impressions which they made on my Soul at that time' (p. 331). But, precisely because she cannot really describe how she felt, the reader is called on to supplement her story from his own experience. 'It must be the Work of every sober Reader to make just Reflections on them, as their own Circumstances may direct' (p. 331). And surely this is what she has in mind when she claims that 'every Branch of my Story, if duly consider'd, may be useful to honest People'. In one sense she means 'don't get taken in': her story should be 'a due Caution to People of some sort, or other to Guard against the like Surprizes, and to have their Eyes about them when they have to do with Strangers of any kind, for 'tis very seldom that some Snare or other is not in their way' (p. 309). But she continues in more general terms:

> The Moral, indeed of all my Historys left to be gather'd by the Senses and Judgment of the Reader; I am not Qualified to preach to them, let the Experience of one Creature compleatly Wicked, and compleatly Miserable be a Store-house of useful Warning to those that read. (p. 309)

She is, we may say, a 'judge-penitent', like Camus's Jean-Baptiste Clamence. His profession begins with 'indulging in public confession as often as possible'.

> Then imperceptibly I pass from the 'I' to the 'we'. When I get to 'This is what we are', the game is over and I can tell them off. I am like them, to be sure; we are in the soup together. However, I have a superiority in that I know it and this gives me the right to speak. You see the advantage, I am sure. The more I accuse myself the more I have a right to judge you. Even better, I provoke you into judging yourself, and this relieves me of much of the burden.[1]

Clamence also has 'accepted duplicity instead of being upset about it'. He has found that the important thing is to permit oneself everything, even self-condemnation. 'I haven't

[1] *The Fall*, p. 103

changed my way of life; I continue to love myself and to make use of others. Only, the confession of my crimes allows me to begin again lighter in heart and to taste a double enjoyment, first of my nature and secondly of a charming repentance'.[1] Moll has a similar freedom and the energy that comes from being on good terms with herself. But she too has her real existence as the teller of her own story. It is not a story that has come to an end. It is concluded in the conscience of the listener, or reader.

'You say, you are an honest man, how do you know it?'[2] Defoe thinks that only someone who recognizes his own dishonesty can ask the question. In the *Serious Reflections* Crusoe is not slow to admit his faults. But this means he can expect the same of others.

> But let them be sure, they have been juster on their own parts; let them be positive, that their own integrity is untainted, and would abide all the tryals and racks, that a ruin'd fortune, strong temptations, and deep distresses, could bring it into; let them not boast till these dangers are past, and they put their armour off; and if they can do it then, I will freely acknowledge, they have less need of repentance than I.[3]

*Moll Flanders* provides a medium in which the reader can face himself. It offers an ironic experience, the approach to truth through deceit. But the irony is to be felt by the reader rather than by the narrator. It is an irony that can be expressed in Clamence's words: 'Yes, we have lost track of the light, the mornings, the holy innocence of those who forgive themselves.[4]

[1] Ibid., p. 104  [2] *Serious Reflections*, p. 37
[3] Ibid., p. 58  [4] *The Fall*, p. 106

# CHAPTER 3

# Clarissa *(i)*: *A Process of Estrangement*

## I

THE NARRATIVE of *Clarissa* is always at the point of crisis. This is what happens when you tell a story in a series of letters. As a means to 'inwardness' they cause a lot of trouble, mainly because, being articulate and a deliberate act, they are already at some distance from the inner life. The letter-writer is self-conscious rather than self-aware; he wants to state his case, to argue and impress. He is solitary, but not alone with himself. Yet it is 'inwardness' that many readers look for in *Clarissa*: 'we all know', as Leavis says, 'that if we want a more inward interest it is to Richardson we must go'.[1] And Ian Watt maintains that Richardson chose letters as a narrative medium because they come nearest in ordinary life to the 'minute-by-minute content of consciousness which constitutes what the individual's personality really is'; access to this consciousness is important to the reader who only thus 'can participate fully in the life of a fictional character'.[2] This follows Percy Lubbock's argument that Richardson is 'dramatising [Clarissa's] sensibility' so as 'to get into the closest touch with [her] life, and to set the reader in the midst of it'. Looked at like this the letters appear to be a clumsy way to write a Jamesian kind of novel. 'Richardson and Henry

[1] *The Great Tradition*, p. 4   [2] *The Rise of the Novel*, p. 19

James, they are both faced by the same difficulty; one of them is acutely aware of it, and takes very deep-laid precautions to circumvent it; the other, I suppose, does not trouble about the theory of his procedure, but he too adopts a certain artifice which carries him past the particular problem, though at the same time it involves him in several more'.[1] And, in fact, this reading of Richardson as a more primitive James does appear to be sanctioned by what he himself proposed for his method. Letters, he claims, lead 'farther into the Recesses of the human Mind, than the colder and more general Reflections suited to a continued and more contracted Narrative'. But he means this in a specific sense: letters reveal not 'the content of consciousness' in general but consciousness in emergency. They are, he thinks, 'the only natural Opportunity that could be had, of representing with any Grace those lively and delicate Impressions, which *Things present* are known to make upon the Minds of those affected by them'.[2] Letters belong to the immediate present, to the instant; and the instant is felt to be a point of crisis: 'The Events at the Time generally dubious:— So that they abound, not only with critical Situations: but with what may be called *instantaneous* Descriptions and Reflections'.[3] No doubt letters are an attempt to make the instant less perilous, to subdue it to the stable forms of literature. But letters lack the equilibrium of literature. They embody an emotional situation still in process; they are undetonated, on the brink. They are the true expression of crisis. They render, not only what a recent critic describes as 'the actual moment of experience' in 'a continuous present',[4] but the continuing experience of the present as a critical moment.

That is to say, the experiences in the novel are precisely

---

[1] *The Craft of Fiction*, pp. 153, 152
[2] *Hints of Prefaces* for *Clarissa*, p. 6          [3] *Clarissa*, 'Preface'
[4] Anthony Kearney, '*Clarissa* and the Epistolary Form', *Essays in Criticism*, xvi, i, 1966, p. 44

the experiences of letter-writers. Scott long ago observed that 'to the letter-writer every event is recent, and is described while immediately under the eye, without a corresponding degree of reference to its relative importance to what has past and is to come. All is, so to speak, painted in the foreground, and nothing in the distance'.[1] This is the source of Richardson's minuteness, which, however, is without amplitude or scale. Letter-writers are near-sighted, anxiously absorbed in details, unselective. 'Toute lettre', Jean Rousset says, 'a . . . une sorte de myopie, une attention extrême.'[2] Richardson was always claiming, in fact, that his readers were unwilling to give his work the kind of attention it needed. 'Ye World is not enough used to this way of writing, to the moment. It knows not that in the minutiae lie often the unfoldings of the Story, as well as of the heart; & judges of an action undecided, as if it were absolutely decided.'[3] In the terms proposed by Frank Kermode these letters are deprived of 'plot', of 'the sense of an ending', which will bestow upon the whole duration and meaning'.[4]

His argument, in so far as it relates to Richardson in particular, is that they actually stand outside the temporal. Everything in Richardson, he asserts, 'became *kairos* by virtue of the way in which letters coincided with critical moments'.[5] But, as we have seen, the crisis is something created in the process of letterwriting; they do not transcend time, they fill it with a sense of apprehension. *Kairos* is, in Kermode's definition, 'the season, a point in time filled with significance, charged with a meaning derived from its relation to the end'.[6] This is quite different from the anxiety we find in the letters, written 'while the heart is agitated by hopes and fears, on events undecided'.[7] Kermode elsewhere speaks of *kairos* as being like 'the experience of love,

---

[1] *Lives of the Novelists*, p. 41  [2] *Forme et Signification*, p. 71
[3] *Selected Letters*, p. 289  [4] *The Sense of an Ending*, p. 46
[5] Ibid., p. 51  [6] Ibid., p. 47
[7] Preface to *Sir Charles Grandison*

the erotic consciousness which makes divinely satisfactory
sense out of the commonplace person'.[1] But in this sense
also it appears to be wrong to intrepret the critical moment
in *Clarissa* as *kairos*. *Clarissa* is about love, of course. But
specifically it is about the need for love and the difficulty of
love, and the obstacles to it. Love enters the novel as something it can hardly tolerate, a current of feeling which
controverts everything established by the form.

For the form, or more properly the narrative method, of
*Clarissa* displays an existential crisis. The letters occur in
what Georges Poulet describes as the Cartesian moment:
'séparée à la fois du monde extérieure, du passé et du futur,
la conscience cartésienne ne peut exister que dans l'enceinte
la plus étroite, celle du moment présent'.[2] The significance
of this moment is that it enforces an awareness of isolation:
'J'existe, j'en ai conscience, mais cette conscience me
révèle mon isolement absolu. Elle m'enferme en moi-même.
Elle me situe dans un désert ou dans une prison.'[3] If it were
not also the moment in which we understood the existence
of God—'Je pense, donc Dieu est'[4]—it would be a tragic
moment. As it is, it is only a step away from the problem
faced by Existentialism, the 'forme proprement moderne du
Cogito'.[5] The letters in *Clarissa* become, as Anthony
Kearney has shown, a study of isolation.[6] The characters are
all seen all the time in moments of crisis, moments in which
they are severed from each other, from themselves and from
the future. They are all seen at those moments when their
connections with reality are imperilled, that is when they
are involved in the process of writing and reading. Thus
their crisis is the crisis of the novel itself, a crisis of form.
And therefore it is a crisis for the reader as well. Richardson's
novel is about the kind of situation which in any case it must

---

[1] *The Sense of an Ending*, p. 46
[2] *Etudes sur le temps humain, III, Le Point de Départ*, p. 218
[3] Ibid., p. 218        [4] Ibid., p. 219        [5] Ibid., p. 222
[6] *'Clarissa* and the Epistolary Form', p. 45

be creating for the reader. It is about literature as a process
of estrangement.

## II

This is where the comparison with Fielding is especially
revealing. The differences between them are not superficial,
or merely temperamental. They are generic and help to
define two quite contrary concepts of the novel. The history
that lies behind them is that traced by Auerbach in *Mimesis*,
the history of 'the representation of reality in Western
literature'. At the beginning of the book he speaks of the
two basic types of European realism and finds their origins
respectively in Homer and the Old Testament:

> The two styles, in their opposition, represent basic types: on
> the one hand fully externalised description, uniform illumina-
> tion, uninterrupted connection, free expression, all events in the
> foreground, displaying unmistakable meanings, few elements of
> historical development and of psychological perspective; on the
> other hand, certain parts brought into high relief, others left
> obscure, abruptness, suggestive influence of the unexpressed,
> 'background' quality, multiplicity of meanings and the need for
> interpretation, universal-historical claims, development of the
> concept of the historically becoming, and preoccupation with the
> problematic.[1]

We could say that what is in question is syntax. On the one
hand there is the experience of discontinuity. Sartre speaks
of this as a characteristic of the modern mind. 'The presence
of death at the end of our path', he says, 'has made our
future go up in smoke; our life has "no future"; it is a series
of present moments. What does this mean, if not that the
absurd man is applying his analytical spirit to Time? Where
Bergson saw an indestructible organization, he sees only a

[1] *Mimesis*, p. 19

series of instants'.[1] And this must have an effect on language:
'the discontinuity between the clipped phrases [must]
imitate the discontinuity of time'.[2] Evidently a lot of this
would be as relevant to Richardson as it is to Camus.
And on the other hand the sense of continuity is just as
characteristic of Fielding. His confidence in progression
and consequence is manifest in his sentence construction.
His style (as words like 'hath' and 'doth' suggest) is back-
ward-looking and conservative. 'And', 'but', 'for', 'since':
these are important words in his sentences; they permit
those long free-wheeling statements:

> It will not be wondered at, that a Creature, who had so strict
> a Regard to Decency in her own Person, should be shocked at the
> last Deviation from it in another. She therefore no sooner opened
> the Door, and saw her master standing by the Bed-side in his
> Shirt, with a Candle in his Hand, than she started back in a most
> terrible Fright, and might perhaps have swooned away, had he
> not now recollected his being undrest, and put an End to her
> Terrors, by desiring her to stay without the Door, till he had
> thrown some Cloaths over his Back, and was become incapable
> of shocking the pure Eyes of Mrs. *Deborah Wilkins*, who, tho'
> in the 52d Year of her Age, vowed she had never beheld a Man
> without his Coat. (*Tom Jones*, I, iii)

This last sentence is witty because it *is* a sentence. That is,
its wit depends on establishing real or ironic relationships,
on drawing attention to what has been put in, or left out. It
is amusing to see where it arrives, and thus it is itself a
miniature comic plot. By contrast Richardson worked by
emphasis and interruption. 'What', 'why', 'how', surely',
these exclamatory words dominate his pages:

> But, hang the man, I had almost said—What is he to me?
> What *would* he be—were not this Mr. Sol—O my dear, how
> I hate that man in the light he is proposed to me!

[1] 'Camus's *The Outsider*', *Situations* I, tr. A. Michelson, rep. in *Camus:
A Collection of Critical Essays*, ed. G. Brée, p. 118
[2] Ibid., p. 119

All of them at the same time are afraid of Mr. Lovelace; yet
not afraid to provoke him!—How am I intangled!—to be obliged
to go on corresponding with him for *their* sakes—Heaven forbid,
that their persisted-in violence should so drive me, as to make it
necessary for *my own*!

But surely *they* will yield—Indeed *I* cannot. (I, 14; i, 63)[1]

Significantly the letter is unfinished: 'An interruption
obliges me to conclude myself, in some hurry, as well as
fright, what I must ever be, *Yours more than my own*,
CLARISSA HARLOWE.' (Ibid.)

Statements that Fielding would want to unify, Richardson
keeps disjunct. Sometimes he does this for a special effect,
as when little cousin Dolly is sent to take away Clarissa's
writing materials: 'Madam!—Madam! said the poor
weeping good-natured creature, in broken sentences—
You must—indeed you must—deliver to Betty—or to me
—your pen and ink! (II, 19; i, 407) But the letters all
tend to fall into 'broken sentences', as if the syntax at all
times were under unusual stress. The full stops do not
terminate sentences, they invade them. They are like a
catch in the breath or a mental block:

I have no manner of doubt, that this is a poor device, to get
this man into my company. I would have sent down a verbal
Answer: but Betty refused to carry any message, which should
prohibit his visiting me. So I was obliged either to see him, or
to write to him. I wrote therefore an Answer, of which I shall
send you the rough draft. And now my heart akes for what may
follow from it; for I hear a great hurry below. (I, 59; i, 301)

These are utterances, not sentences. The punctuation is a
threat to syntax, it creates silences. Sartre noted the same
kind of thing in Camus's style. 'The sentence is sharp,
distinct, and self-contained. It is separated by a void from
the following one, just as Descartes's instant is separated
from the one that follows it. The world is destroyed and
reborn from sentence to sentence'.[2] The difference is that

[1] See the note on the text, p. 212 below          [2] Op. cit., p. 119

whereas Camus can still conceive complete sentences, Richardson presents the disintegration of a sentence. Camus creates (or finds in Hemingway) a new form of syntax; Richardson shows how the old form collapses under pressure of the 'Cartesian moment'.

## III

The full stop, then, is no longer a point of arrival: it stands for an empty space, a lapse. And this is what Richardson is concerned with. Whereas Fielding could contemplate without worry the 'Blanks in the grand Lottery of Time', Richardson seems to feel them almost as a threat to being. Or rather, his characters do. It is they who have to feel the weight of hiatus. They are represented as *having* to be narrators and as having to write down their narration. Their vocabulary has to include the signs of silences, the full stop, the dash, a row of dots. In transforming their lives to manuscript they become expert in varieties of notation of what cannot be uttered. Since their lives are intended to be read, their readers have before them the marks, the notations, of a language under stress. The characters need the reader. That is, they reveal themselves in the form of language, indeed in the form of writing. And their anxiety reveals itself as a form of punctuation.

In this way a novel told in letters confronts the reader with the essential nature of his experience of the novel. It makes him attend to the act of reading. Normally the signs on the page disappear in his consciousness of what they signalize. Thus the talk of Birkin and Ursula is represented very much in Richardson's way, in the same exclamatory, elliptical manner:

> 'How hateful—your hateful social orders!' she cried.
> 'Quite! It's a daisy—we'll leave it alone.'

'Do. Let it be a dark horse for once,' she said: 'if anything can be a dark horse to you,' she added satirically.

But what Lawrence wants us to attend to is the situation, the presence of these people:

> They stood aside, forgetful. As if a little stunned, they both were motionless, barely conscious. The little conflict into which they had fallen had torn their consciousness and left them like two impersonal forces, there in contact.[1]

Richardson, however, allows no insight beyond the printed signs. They do not refer to a situation, they *are* the situation. He reminds us that such signs mean what they are. Typography, that is, is a form of mimesis. His novel is not an imitation of life, but rather of writing. We realize that we are not the only readers of these narratives, that the act of reading is assumed to lie within the novel as well, indeed that it is necessary to the continuance of the novel. The novel is in this sense *about* writing and reading. Ian Watt hardly gives enough weight to this when he refers to 'the authority and illusion of print' and to Richardson's attempts to convey typographically 'the impression of a literal transcript of reality'.[2] What he says is true of novels in general, but not of this one. The typography is certainly integral to the meaning, but in another sense. It is intended to keep before the reader the consciousness of *being* a reader. It is in fact a deliberate reminder of the unreality of writing. It indicates how the characters in this book have become literature, even to themselves.

The consequence of this is that those parts of their lives which cannot be shown to the reader seem not to exist at all. No one within the novel knows any more than the reader does about these letter-writers. They create themselves on the pages of their letters. What does not get onto the pages is not only unknown, it is non-existent. Again the reader's

---

[1] *Women in Love*, Ch. xi     [2] *The Rise of the Novel*, p. 197

normal sense that he is confined to 'the words on the page' becomes a direct enactment of an existential problem. The narrators appear to need words in order to possess themselves. At the points where words fail, where syntax collapses, their existence collapses. So it is precisely the reader who best understands, who suffers, in fact, the crucial lesions in experience, the lapses, the moments of vacancy. We have traced these first in the style, but they also invade the whole action of the book. For the action is always on the point of slipping out of sight. The narrative moves up to and away from an event that is not there at all. In the anxious period just before Clarissa elopes with Lovelace, Richardson makes us notice the moments of emptiness:

> I dare say, we shall be all to-pieces. But I don't care for that. It would be hard, if I, who have held it out so sturdily to my Father and Uncles, should not—But he is at the garden door—
>
> *        *
>
> I was mistaken!—How may noises *un-like*, be made *like* to what one fears!—Why flutters the fool so!—
>
> *        *
>
> I will hasten to deposit this. . . . (II, 31; i, 470)

What goes on in these silences? And in what sense can this be a 'present tense recording of the action'?[1] It is written in the present tense, and records the present sense of anxiety. But the present tense looks towards the future; it is full of apprehension. 'She is', says Richardson in his summary of the letter, 'apprehensive of the contest she shall have with him, on her refusing to go off with him, as he will come with a different expectation.' And, as for the action, this is simply not recorded at all; it becomes a row of asterisks, an impenetrable interval.

This is the narrative of the few hours preceding the first climax of the novel, the elopement. But that event also, which it has taken two volumes to prepare for, is missing

---

[1] Ian Watt, *The Rise of the Novel*, p. 192

from the record. Here the gap is even more pronounced
and calamitous. Between the end of Letter xxxi, written in
the ivy summer-house, and the beginning of Letter xxxii,
dated twenty-four hours later from St Albans, there is
nothing, not even a pause, simply a lack of connection. Of
course there would have to be: a letter simply cannot be
simultaneous with the event. But only if we assume that
Richardson wishes the narrative to keep pace with events do
we find letters frustrating. Their significance, if we are
willing to attend to it, is that they represent an almost
schizophrenic state of mind. Some things the mind cannot
accommodate; they must be left as a fracture in experience,
reduced to non-existence. Later, of course, the missing
event is pieced together from Clarissa's accounts and
Lovelace's. But by then it has slipped into the past; it has
become a story and subject to the psychological needs, the
fantasies and desires, of the narrators. But at first it is a
shocking silence, a sense of disorder:

> *O my dearest friend!*
> After what I had resolved upon, as by my former, what shall
> I write? What *can* I? With what consciousness, even by *Letter*,
> do I approach you!—You will soon hear (if already you have
> not heard from the mouth of common fame) that your Clarissa
> Harlowe is gone off with a man! (II, 32; i, 471)

Thus what is written in 'the utmost anguish of mind', as the
summary puts it, offers directly to the reader an experience
of alienation. What cannot be said is felt by the reader also
as a loss of consciousness, a lapse of being. And this is
particularly so at the culmination of the whole novel. The
violation of Clarissa is not *in* the novel at all. Lovelace's
letters leave a gap; in the early hours of Tuesday, June 13th
he is writing:

> And thus, between terror, and the late hour, and what followed,
> she was diverted from the thoughts of getting out of the house
> to Mrs. Leeson's, or anywhere else. (V, 5; iii, 196)

These words lead without a break into his next letter:

## LETTER VI

*Mr*. Lovelace, *To* John Belford, *Esq.*

*Tuesday Morn. June* 13.

AND now, Belford, I can go no farther. The affair is over.
Clarissa lives. And I am

*Your humble Servant,*
R. LOVELACE.

'The whole of this black transaction', as Richardson explains,
is given in Clarissa's letters long after the event. In fact the
accounts of it become more coherent and more circumstantial the further it recedes into the past. What is felt most
immediately, as an actual experience and not a report on it,
is felt above all by the reader. For the direct effect is to
disorganize the texture of the novel. Clarissa's state of mind
is represented as the disintegration of a book:

## PAPER I

(*Torn in two pieces.*)

*My dearest Miss Howe!*
O What dreadful, dreadful things have I to tell you! But yet
I cannot tell you neither. . . . (V, 10; iii, 205)

This is really the point the novel has been leading up to.
Here the constant pressure on syntax becomes unbearable;
the threat to continuity of being, which was latent, is now
critical. The letters are, we see, a medium for people who
seem unable to deal with the present, or to connect the
present with the past or future. They are a medium for those
who have lost the syntax of experience. And they represent
this loss in terms of the rupture of a narrative, terms which
will be particularly significant for a reader.

## IV

We ought to remember, of course, that when Richardson spoke of writing 'to the moment' he was thinking of 'the unfoldings of the story, as well as of the heart'. The story mattered to him. Indeed a twentieth-century reader might think it mattered too much. Fluchère, for instance, finds him quite old-fashioned in this respect. The concern for story, he believes, is fundamentally 'unrealistic'; it 'deliberately isolates a character and his deeds from real life'.[1] There is something archaic in a story's 'forward march'[2] of events through time, and 'in those days, of course, it was chiefly a matter of events that took place not in the consciousness of the characters but in the material world'.[3] It was Sterne, he maintains, who was the more modern: he substituted 'for story, plot and perhaps character as well, the vigil of consciousness, and in so doing opened up unlimited perspectives for the novel of the future'.[4] But, in fact, Richardson does neither the one thing nor the other.

Story, that is, remains equivocal. It neither dominates nor drains away into the inner life. It belongs exclusively neither to past nor to present. Thus Clarissa gives an account of a stormy passage with sister Bella. At first, as she can now admit, her story existed only in her own excited fancy. Her mind was full of the family conference that was to decide her fate: 'And then I ran thro' the whole conference in my imagination, forming speeches for this person and that, *pro* and *con*. till all concluded, as I flattered myself, in an acceptance of my conditions, . . .' (I, 43; i, 223). Now, though, she has to report 'a very different result from the hopeful conference' (i, 224). Yet in spite of the discrepancy between her reverie and the reality, her narration gives equal credit to both. In fact there comes a point

---

[1] *Laurence Sterne: From Tristram to Yorick*, p. 101
[2] Ibid., p. 91    [3] Ibid., p. 92    [4] Ibid., p. 88

when the play of fancy seems indistinguishable from the
reality. 'And now is my Sister coming to declare the issue of
all (as anything stirred): Tears gushing again, my heart
fluttering as a bird against its wires; drying my eyes again
and again to no purpose.' Tense is ambiguous; past, present
and present participle merge. The story flickers between
subjective and objective in the area of the virtual. The
dialogue that follows abandons the perspective of tense
altogether. The words on the page become the script of a
play, still attached to the past ('interrupted she', 'was her
expression') but only loosely: more often the narrative
interjections have the appearance of stage directions:

> Shall I conduct your Ladyship down? [offering to take my
> declined Hand].
> What! not vouchsafe to answer me?
> I turned from her in silence.
> What! turn your back upon me too!—Shall I bring up your
> Mamma to you, Love? [following me, and taking my struggling
> hand] What! not speak yet! Come, my sullen, silent dear, speak
> one word to me—You must say *two* very soon to Mr. Solmes,
> I can tell you that.
> Then [gushing out into tears, which I could not hold in
> longer] they shall be the last words I will ever speak.
>
> (I, 43; i, 225)

Such a scene waits for the reader. Like a dramatic script
it is in a kind of latent present tense; in a sense it does not
exist until it is read or enacted, and then it is taken to be
happening now, in the present. Of course in this sense all
written words wait, outside time, for the reader. They have
the permanence of potentiality; and the reader of a fiction
has the assurance that time is always virtual. Yet most
narratives try to distract attention from this. The reader,
who, *as* reader, knows that the words are always there, to
be read and re-read and thus to assume the aspect of time,
is to be persuaded that they belong to the past, having
existed in time as history. He is to be ready to accept the

fiction of time. This may well put him in possession of a
subtle and rewarding experience. We shall see, for instance,
how Fielding plays with the relationships between the
novel's 'history' and the reader's sense of the present. But
frequently the reader is glad to abandon himself to the past
tense of fiction. When Sartre writes of the 'strange operation'
of reading, the critic lending 'his body to the dead in order
that they may come back to life', yet glad 'when contem-
porary authors do him the favour of dying',[1] he is touching
on one of the motives for our choice of fictional time. We are
worried by a literature of the 'now', a *littérature engagée*.
Yet this is just what letters are. Richardson underlines
this by allowing them to keep manifold aspects of time in
play simultaneously. Their narratives do not retire decently
into the past: they confuse with constant shifts from the
reader's present tense to the narrator's, from the narrator's
past tense to the actor's, and from the narrative preterite
to the present participle of 'stage directions':

> *Pretty Mopsa-eyed soul*, was her expression!—And was it will-
> ing to think it had still a *Brother* and *Sister?* And why don't you
> go on, Clary? [mocking my half-weeping accent] I thought too I
> had a *Father*, and *Mother*, *two Uncles*, and an *Aunt: But I am
> mis—taken, that's all*—Come, Clary, say this, and it will in part
> be true, because you have thrown off their authority, and because
> you respect one vile wretch more than them all. (I, 43; i, 225)

This scene cannot be said to exist only in the reflective
consciousness of the narrator. It has the accent and the feel
of a real presence. Yet we do not lose our sense that it is
being told, and that it is important to the teller. Even more
we are conscious that it is written, that the reader, therefore,
is also important to the teller. Thus a tension is set up
between narrator and story. Neither can digest the other.
Nor can the reader merely absorb the story, or be absorbed
in it. Such writing keeps open the transactions between
literature and reality. But the effect is not comfortable.

[1] *What is Literature?*, pp. 22–3

## V

Writing must be discontinuous with the event. It is an event itself and has to take the place of other events. Fielding gets a good deal of fun out of this obvious fact: 'Mrs. Jarvis and I are just in bed, and the door unlocked; if my master should come—— Ods-bobs! I hear him just coming in at the door. You see I write in the present tense, as Parson Williams says. Well, he is in bed between us...'[1] But Richardson, as we have seen, certainly does not understand the matter of tense in this simple way. A 'present tense' narration is only one among the other fictions of time, an 'as if'. It amounts to no more than playing with possibilities that the letter in fact forbids. Lovelace sharply distinguishes this kind of fiction from reality: 'Thou'lt observe, Belford, that tho' this was written afterwards, yet (as in other places) I write it as it was spoken and happened, as if I had retired to put down every sentence as spoken, I know thou likest this lively *present tense* manner, as it is one of my peculiars' (V, 6; iii, 195). 'As if I had retired': he cannot ignore that moment's delay, which severs the action from the words. Obviously even letters, however entangled with the business of life, do not evade the writer's dilemma.

In fact they aggravate it. Literature is at a remove from events, but letter-writing seeks to displace them. The only action it can tolerate is the act of writing. In this novel the only activity rendered with immediacy is that of letter-writing. The characters exist within the limits of the letters. The book is made up of documents, and the documents are what the book is about.

The characters evidently value letters as a way to meet. Richardson quotes from his own letters when he makes Lovelace speak of correspondence as 'friendship recorded; friendship given under hand and seal' (IV, 11; ii, 431).

[1] *Shamela,* Letter 6

But it is obvious that letters also exercise a fascination of their own. Often they seem to be more important than the people who write them. 'I shall never rest', writes Lovelace, 'till I have discovered in the first place, where the dear creature puts her Letters ... I must, must come at them. This difficulty augments my curiosity' (III, 52; ii, 269). And 'I wish', writes Anna Howe to Clarissa, 'I wish you could come at some of his Letters' (III, 55; ii, 278). No doubt the letters are felt to go beyond speech; they embody some vital quality of the writer, they are almost a physical risk. When Clarissa first discovers that Lovelace has taken her letter she experiences strictly a loss of virtue. 'The man, my dear, has got the Letter! What a strange diligence! I wish he mean me well, that he takes so much pains! ... Now the Letter is out of my power, I have more uneasiness and regret than I had before '(II, 24; i, 434). Each of her letters, as Anthony Kearney well says, is liable to the 'violations' of Lovelace; it 'carries with it something of the pathos of Clarissa herself'.[1]

But for the reader, who is, we recall, conscious of a special significance in their typography, the letters have a particular presence and substantiality. Everything else in the novel is narrated, the letters *are*. In Letter xlii of Volume I (i, 212–222) the action, which is being reported, moves from the imaginary room to the page in front of us. From being the spectators of a scene we become participants in the correspondence. Bella has promised to take a letter from Clarissa to her brother. 'And how do you think Bella employed herself while I was writing?—Why, playing gently upon my harpsichord: and *humming* to it, to show her unconcernedness.' This provides a vivid impression of the background to the letter, which is printed along with it. But by contrast with the thing itself, the document, it has an air of fabrication. The letter cannot be thought to exist in a form other than that which we have in front of us. The

[1] Op. cit., p. 48

narrative, however, is *about* something; its authenticity
depends on its power to evoke something outside itself. It
does not vouch for itself but for that situation from which
we were absent, for the hearsay, the report. Thus, when
Clarissa resumes her narration later that night, she is
interrupted by the delivery of a reply from her brother. Or
so we are told. The belief we give to the telling is different
from our belief in the letter itself.

> *Monday Night*, 11 *o'Clock.*
> I am afraid I shall not be thought worthy—
> Just as I began to fear I should not be thought worthy of
> an answer, Betty rapped at my door, and said, If I was not in
> bed, she had a Letter for me. . . .
> I inclose my Brother's Letter. . . .
> > *To Miss* CLARISSA HARLOWE.
> > [*Inclosed in the preceding.*]
> > Your proposals will be considered by your Father and Mother,
> > and all your Friends, to-morrow morning. What trouble does
> > your shameful forwardness give us all! I wonder you have the
> > courage to write to me, upon whom you are so continually empty-
> > ing your *whole female quiver*. . . .

We have moved from testimony to evidence. The present
tense of this letter belongs to the essential drama of the
novel, the drama conducted on the pages of the letters, the
drama in which as readers we have a role. The document is
the act itself, not a description of one. Our reading, therefore,
is an act also.

Of course, the two *are* equally fictional, or equally actual.
James's letter is enclosed in a narrative, which is itself a
letter. Clarissa's narrative *as* a narrative lacks the kind of
credit given to the enclosed letters. But as a *letter* it too is a
part of the substance of the book. That is, it too involves the
dislodgement of an imagined situation. The situation it
offers is *our* situation, of a document and its readers. So it is
throughout the book: the action is that which has emerged
as a literary act. The event narrated is at a distance, the

act of narrating is immediate, and inseparable from the act of reading. The only realities for the writers are those concerned with telling. And it is clear that the reader is in the same predicament. The words on the page are the scope of his experience, and the fictional perspectives of this novel lead him back constantly to confront that experience. What he reads about is the process in which he is himself involved. That is, if the novel defines an existential dilemma in the literary process it also shows the reader to be profoundly implicated. The meaning of the book is bound up with the role Richardson assigns to his reader.

## VI

The writer *needs* his reader, the letter-writer particularly. Richardson's relationship with his reader will be crucial to the meaning of his work. What this relationship was emerges only too clearly from his own personal letters. They do not suggest that he can allow his correspondents to have a life of their own. He claims, it is true, that he wants to school, to bring on his lady correspondents: 'When I love my correspondents, I write treatises, you know, Madam, rather than letters. What care I for that, if I can but whet, but stimulate ladies, to shew what they are able to do, . . .'[1] But after all we find his playful tone often immature, not to say schoolgirlish:

> I am accused of playing off a sheet full of witticisms (Witticisms, Miss W.! Very reverent indeed!) which you, poor girl, can't tell what to do with. Very well, Miss W. But I did not expect—But no matter—What have I done with my handkerchief? I—I—I did not expect—But no matter, Miss W.[2]

There are indeed in all his letters the accents of a deep imperfection of being. It is evident that for Richardson

[1] *Selected Letters*, p. 184    [2] *Correspondence*, iii, 303

letters made it easy to escape from the responsibility of
personal relationships. He confesses himself shy and awk-
ward in the presence of others, but 'in writing, I own, I was
always an impudent Man'.[1] In writing he can fashion
reality into something that cannot affect him. Glad to be
uninvolved ('For the pen is jealous of company'[2]) he keeps
his privacy intact by creating a kind of pseudo-situation. He
uses the letters, that is, to turn the real world into a fiction,
and to reduce his readers to characters in that fiction. And
in one way this is a measure of his imaginative intensity as a
novelist: 'I am all the while absorbed in the character. It is
not fair to say—I, identically I, am any-where, while I keep
within the character.'[3] But it is disconcerting to find that
his fictional characters are, on the pages of his letters, as
real as his real readers:

> For is not Clementina my child as well as Harriet? A child
> endeared to me by her calamity—But how shall I say it?—She
> was ever, ever, unpersuadable. A *spoiled child*, your Ladiship
> once called her.[4]

Letters like these are a travesty of the novels. 'Tedious
prattling disputations with his female correspondents, upon
the duties of wives and children', Jeffrey called them; 'the
whole so loaded with gross and reciprocal flattery, as to be
ridiculous at the outset, and disgusting in the repetition.'[5]
Their publication, he considered, could 'only tend to lower
a very respectable character, without communicating any
gratification or instruction to others'.[6] This is harsh. There
is evidence enough in the correspondence of Richardson's
insight into the nature of his craft and his endeavour to get
it properly understood. Yet there is no denying that it
presents a parody of living relationships.

In particular he tries to obliterate the reader, or to absorb

---

[1] *Selected Letters*, p. 319      [2] Ibid., p. 66
[3] Ibid., p. 286                    [4] *Selected Letters*, p. 288
[5] *Contributions to the Edinburgh Review*, i, 314
[6] Ibid., i, 313

E

him. And the reader of the novel too, is sucked in by it.
Yet it is surprising it should be so, for the reader is written
into the novel; in a sense he gives it its significance. The
letter-form ensures this. Letters are delivered and received.
They belong to the recipient, the reader. A collection of
letters is a reader's collection. Novels like *Pamela* or
*Evelina*, which do not admit this and so consist of letters
either not sent or not answered, make strange reading.
François Jost calls these the passive, or static type of epistolary novel, and distinguishes them from the active, kinetic
or dynamic type found in *Les Liaisons Dangereuses*.[1] But
*Clarissa* belongs to neither category. As we have seen, it
falls between pure drama and pure narration. Or, *as* narration, it falls into the form of a drama which involves the
reader. It is a fiction which depends on the reader. Without
a spectator it is incomplete; it asks for a witness. Thus
certain characters are important as confidants. Anna Howe
and Belford participate in the correspondence in a different
way from Clarissa or Lovelace. They write replies: they
think of their own affairs chiefly in relation to what they
recognize as the central drama. 'I have been called your
Echo', writes Anna Howe to Clarissa (III, 6; ii, 104). This
is not to say that she has no mind or will of her own: quite
the contrary. But her mind is full of Clarissa's story. She is
*really* a reader; when she writes it is in order to define a
reader's feelings. She has her own life to live, but for the
time being is living it in comparison with Clarissa's more
glowing and dangerous one.

> I verily think, that the different behaviour of our two heroes
> to their heroines, makes out this doctrine [i.e. of the need for
> passion in a lover] to demonstration. . . . I really believe, that,
> could Hickman have kept my attention alive after the Lovelace-
> manner, only that he preserved his morals, I should have married
> the man by this time. (ii, 104)

[1] 'Le Roman Epistolaire et la technique narrative au xviii$^e$ siècle', *Comp.
Lit. Studies*, iii, 1966, p. 406

Similarly Belford's strongest feelings are reactions to what he reads:

> I am inexpressibly concerned at the fate of this matchless Lady! . . . Poor, poor lady! . . . What must have been the poor Lady's distress (watchful as she had been over her honour) when dreadful Certainty took place of cruel Apprehension!—And, yet a man may guess what it must have been, . . .' (V, 7; iii, 196–7)

It is becoming clear that Richardson's attempt to accommodate the reader defeats its own ends. The more the story needs the participation of a reader, the more obvious it becomes that the reader is to be subordinated to the story. Anna Howe and Belford enact an undistinguished role that we have to admit is very similar to our own. The effect of this is in some ways the reverse of what Richardson must have intended. Instead of intensifying it chills the reader's response to the central characters. One might argue that this is an advantage and helps to preserve the sense of aesthetic distance. But in fact it only heightens the sense of frustration felt by the reader. For it offers no example of cool detachment and objectivity. Instead it exacerbates the feelings; it places us on the same footing as those characters who are emotionally involved, yet denied entry into the action. There is for characters and readers the same barrier of words on the page. Both are persuaded that reading is the most intimate kind of participation; both are unable to shake off their destiny as readers, or to refuse the implications of what Richardson wants them to be.

This is so even in the final episodes of the novel when Belford moves onto the scene, and becomes in effect the narrator of Clarissa's last days. For he cannot be said to make his presence felt. He means nothing to Clarissa; at least she remains unaffected by him. She only needs him as a means to perfect her destiny: she turns to him as

> ' . . . the *only* person possessed of materials that will enable him to do my character justice;

'And who has courage, independence, and ability to oblige me;
'To be the protector of my memory, as I may say;
'And to be my *Executor*; and to see some of my dying requests
performed; . . .' (VI, 44; iv, 78)

When he writes of meeting her he effaces himself: he is
there to celebrate:

> I could not help telling her, that every time I saw her, I more
> and more considered her as a beatified spirit; and as one sent
> from Heaven to draw me after her out of the miry gulph in which
> I had been so long immersed. (VI, 96; iv, 214)

What she replied to this we are not told; in fact Belford
seems not to have felt himself in the presence of another
person; he has been worshipping an image. He is really
present on the scene to *read* it for us. Though he appears,
ironically, to have changed places with Lovelace he cannot
be said to be involved with her at all as Lovelace was. In
no sense has he entered her life. Paradoxically, by giving
him proximity to Clarissa, Richardson has heightened our
sense of being separated from what is going on. This is
reinforced by Lovelace's new role. Now he has to be *told*
everything; he is in the reader's position of knowing without
sharing, of being both intimate and excluded: 'forbidden to
attend the dear creature, yet longing to see her, I would
give the world to be admitted once more to her beloved
presence' (VII, 5; iv, 295). Significantly, it is at this point,
when he no longer has access to her, that he believes himself
in love with Clarissa. Yet the love he professes is without
mutuality; it has nothing to do with the demands of a vital
relationship; for Lovelace it is an act of abdication:

> Hence it is, that I admire her more than ever; and that my
> Love for her is less *personal*, as I may say, more *intellectual*, than
> ever I thought it could be to woman.
> Hence also it is, that I am confident (would it please the Fates
> to spare her, and make her mine) I could love her with a purity

that would draw on *my own* FUTURE, as well as ensure *her*
TEMPORAL happiness.—And hence, by necessary consequence,
shall I be the most miserable of all men, if I am deprived of her.
(VI, 108; iv, 262)

Words like these are dependent on the remoteness to which
Belford ministers. As we shall see in the next chapter,
Lovelace has throughout regarded Clarissa as an object; at
this stage he is in a position to regard her as an object of
adoration.

Richardson evidently approves of this; everything in the
book must in the end be made to elevate Clarissa. Everything, that is, must induce the reader to do so. The novel
ends by depicting the kind of response it desires, and
presenting different images of the ideal reader. But it is
disconcerting to see that the ideal is either to become like
Belford, totally eclipsed by the story, or like Lovelace,
redeemed by his evacuation from the story. The reader is
expected to sustain the novel, but he is to abandon himself
in doing so. This is no doubt why the book has such compulsive power. But it also explains why we feel it leads to
alienation. It asks us to recognize the act of reading as a
reflection of the existential crisis generated within the novel
itself. We are to understand that the novel offers to the
reader, as to the characters, only the illusion of a real
situation. Like the actors in the story, we grasp life as a
literary experience. There is no reciprocity in our encounters
with these fictional people. In fact there is no encounter
with people at all, but rather with their written words. This
novel thus presents in an unusually intransigent form the
experience of reading a novel. Not only does it, in its
narrative, expose some of the existential problems of relating
literature to reality, it also faces the reader with questions
about the value of the fictional. It keeps returning him to
the possibility of that split between fantasy and reality that
is so threatening to integrity of being.

Yet the novel itself cannot be said to forfeit such integrity. Sartre describes the kind of imagination that does so:

> It is ... to adopt 'imaginary' feelings and actions for the sake of their imaginary nature. It is not only this or that image that is chosen, but the imaginary state with everything that it implies; it is not only an escape from the content of the real (poverty, frustrated love, failure of one's enterprise, etc.), but from the form of the real itself, its character of *presence*, the sort of response it demands of us, the adaptation of our actions to the object, the inexhaustibility of perception, their independence, the way our feelings have of developing themselves.[1]

This is a representation of a 'morbid' state, a schizophrenic manifestation of the imagination. R. D. Laing, commenting on the passage, relates it to Minkowski's concept of autism. It is not, as this novel makes us realize, remote from the kind of response we make to literature. In labouring to establish the functions and conditions of this new form, the novel, Richardson exposes its kinship to various kinds of fantasy. As we shall see, in the character of Lovelace he depicts a nature which we may call schizoid. And we have observed that his own correspondence reveals in him a dissociation from the real world. In a sense he is the alienated mind embodied in the book. This is the kind of novel he would have to write, a novel of crisis and the severance from reality. But it *is* a novel, and not a personal fantasy. It enacts the processes of alienation, it gives full weight to the existential dilemma inherent in literature, but it does not sanction them. It places alienation, with pathos and irony, within reach of a concept of wholeness and freedom. It depicts the isolated self, but it indicates the possibility of relationship.

This novel contains the refutation of its own thesis. To see how this can be we must go on to consider the role of the reader from another point of view, and to relate it to other aspects of the story.

[1] *The Psychology of Imagination*, quoted in R. D. Laing, *The Divided Self*, p. 85

# CHAPTER 4

# Clarissa *(ii):*
# *A Form of Freedom*

## I

'STANDER-BY', writes Anna Howe, 'is often a better judge of the game than those that play' (I, 12; i, 49). As we have seen, there is reason to doubt this. In this novel there is in any case little to choose between taking part and standing by. Even the principal characters stand aside from their own actions in order to write about them. And the subordinate characters, especially Anna Howe and Belford, are there to read what is written. The medium (the written word and the narrative letter) is its own story: it is opaque, it attests nothing but itself. The letters are *there*, the writers are only inferred from the letters; and readers may make the wrong inferences. So a stander-by (that is, in this novel, a reader) may after all be a rather unreliable judge.

And Richardson knows this. In fact part of his story is that the medium is untrustworthy. Letters can be intercepted, altered, forged, misdirected. Miss Howe's long letter, written soon after Clarissa's escape to Hampstead, falls into Lovelace's hands. We read it as if over his shoulder. The 'indices' in the margin, marking 'the places which call for vengeance upon the vixen writer, or which require animadversion' (V, iv; iii, I), graphically render the letter's miscarriage. The hazards of this kind of dialogue leave their marks on the page.

63

The women of the house where you are— O my dear—
The women of the house—But you never thought highly of
them—So it cannot be very surprising—Nor would you have
☞ *staid so long with them had not the notion of removing to one of*
*your own,* made you less uneasy, and less curious about their
characters, and behaviour. Yet I could *now* wish, that you
had been less reserved among them—But I teaze you—
☞ In short, my dear, you are certainly in a devilish house!—Be
assured, that the woman is one of the vilest of women.—Nor
does she go to you by her right name—Very true!—Her name
is *not* Sinclair—Nor is the Street she lives in, Dover-street—
. . . (IV, 30; iii, 2)

This is followed immediately by what appears to be a reply
from Clarissa—but how can it be? '*My dearest Creature,*
How you have shocked, confounded, surprised, astonished
me, by your dreadful communication! . . . I am too ill at
present, my dear, to think of combating with this dreadful
man; and of flying from this horrid house!—*My bad*
*writing will show you this* . . .' (IV, 30; iii, 13). Lovelace has
forged the letter. But in the end he decides not to send it to
Miss Howe, though he lets Belford have a copy of it. Also he
intercepts a decoy letter to Miss Howe from Clarissa herself: 'I write this, my dear Miss Howe, only for a feint, and
to see if it will go current. I shall write at large very soon, if
not miserably prevented!!! Cl. H.' (IV, 32; iii, 22). On the
other hand her genuine letter to Miss Howe—'O my
dearest friend, the man has at last proved himself to be
a villain!' (IV, 31; iii, 16)— *is* delivered, as is Miss
Howe's reply: 'I congratulate you, my dear, with all my
heart and soul upon [your escape] from the villain. . . .
[Meantime I] am excessively uneasy for a letter I sent you
yesterday by Collins, . . .' (IV, 39; iii, 90). Again we follow
Lovelace's reading of the letter: the square brackets indicate the words he could not make out without breaking the
seal. He is now able to arrange for Clarissa to receive an
altered version of Miss Howe's original letter (IV, 40; iii,

94–8). Finally he intercepts Clarissa's reply to this and sends Miss Howe a forged letter in its place.

Obviously the recipients of these letters are by no means 'standers-by', exempted from the plot. The situation is not likely to give us much confidence in what a reader can find out. It is true that we see more than the participants see of this transaction. But this might only instruct us to be wary of the medium. If Belford and Anna Howe stand for the reader, the reader can see he is not in a very comfortable position.

However, there are occasions on which the reader of the novel *is* put on a different footing from the readers in the novel. One is when he comes to the letter that Lovelace has '*permitted* Miss Howe to write to her lovely friend' (IV, 40; iii, 94). He first sees how Belford is expected to read it: 'If thou art capable of taking in all my *providences*, in this Letter, thou wilt admire my sagacity and contrivance almost as much as I do myself' (iii, 98). But this is not all. Richardson wants the reader not only to remember the original letter (as Belford, who was told to return it, has to do) but to refer back to it (as Belford cannot do). There are thus two ways of indicating how the letter has been tampered with. For Belford, Lovelace makes a copy with 'the additions underscored' (IV, 40); for the reader, Richardson refers in the footnotes to the pages of the novel which contain Miss Howe's genuine letter. So here we have a forged letter with two quite different directions for reading it, thus:

> *My reasons for the contrary opinion; to wit, that he is now resolved to do you all the justice in his power to do you;* are these: That he sees that all his own family (*h*) have warmly engaged themselves in your cause: That the horrid wretch loves you; with such a Love, *however*, as Herod loved his Mariamne: . . .
>
> (*h*) p. 211.

That '(*h*) p. 211.' gives the reader a hold on truth. It makes available a comparison with the authentic letter, the one

he has read already as quoted by Lovelace, with that pointing
finger in the margin:

> . . . 'That therefore, if he can obtain no new advantage over
> you as he goes along, he is resolved to do you all the *poor justice*
> that it is in the power of such a wretch as he, to do you. He
> is the rather induced to do this, as he sees, that all his own
> family have warmly engaged themselves in your cause: and
> ☞ that it is his *highest interest* to be just to you. Then the horrid
> wretch loves you (as well he may) above all women. I have
> no doubt of this; with *such* a love as such a wretch is capable
> ☞ of: With *such* a Love as Herod loved his Mariamne.—He is
> now therefore, very probably, at last, in earnest.' (IV, 40;
> iii, 10)

There is a lot for the reader to attend to here. He is
being asked to see Lovelace's duplicity both as an event in
the story and an event in the book. It complicates the plot;
it also complicates the text. What happens happens to the
words on the page. The book begins to seem to be about
the literary evidence itself, letters rather than people. It is
true that the letters make us ask the questions about
character and motive and behaviour that we ask in our
dealings with other people. Leslie Stephen notes that the
reader is in a position to see the people 'all round', with
'stereoscopic distinctness' and 'by a process resembling
that by which we learn to know people in real life'.[1] But the
letters also introduce complications of their own. They are
actually unreliable evidence, documents about which also
there are questions. They are in fact a kind of drama in
themselves, and the 'action' is one in which *they* are acted
upon, altered, manipulated. In this sense they are a drama
in which the reader necessarily takes a part. Jean-Luc Seylaz
surely misrepresents the effect they make. He claims that
they strike a twentieth-century reader rather as 'une
autobiographie déguisée que comme une véritable roman

[1] *Hours in a Library,* i. 63

par lettres'.[1] He thinks that there is lacking an 'accord réel entre la matière et la forme adoptée'.[2] But the fact is that the 'géometrie sensible', the complexity and simultaneity which he admires in *Les Liaisons Dangereuses*,[3] are already evident in the letters of *Clarissa*. They too, it can be said, 'par leur composition même, et non seulement par leur disposition créent le climat de tension, de lutte qui donne au livre sa tonalité'.[4] Frank Bradbrook maintains that it is the letter form that permits 'the complex interweaving of comments by different groups of people, the sense that the reader has of individuals working at cross-purposes and according to different standards, the sudden dramatic and ironic contrasts'.[5] We may go further. Not only does it permit them, it enacts them. The complexity is actually in the letters, the literature, the fact of the book itself.

This must be partly why Richardson fusses over the reader. He is thinking of the novel as a process and is, therefore, acutely conscious that it involves the process of reading. And this is something he feels he must be able to control. He is here in a dilemma: he needs but can hardly tolerate the reader as an independent contributor to the project. Thus he was always asking his readers to help him: '. . . set your charming imagination at work', he wrote to Hester Mulso, 'and give me a few scenes, as you would have them, that I may try to work them into the story'.[6] On another occasion he plays with the fancy that his readers could enact the story for him:

> . . . That every one of my Correspondents, at his or her own Choice, assume one of the surviving Characters in the Story, write in it; and that out of more than Half an hundred, . . . I shall pick and choose, alter, connect, and accommodate, till I have completed from them, the requested Volume.[7]

[1] *Les Liaisons Dangereuses et la Création Romanesque chez Laclos*, p. 17
[2] Ibid., p. 18   [3] Ibid., pp. 33, 28   [4] Ibid., p. 23
[5] 'Samuel Richardson', *Pelican Guide to English Literature*, iv. 294
[6] *Selected Letters*, p. 187   [7] Ibid., p. 306

But, of course, in the end he does it his own way. In fact his respect for the logic of his stories goes along with a marked disrespect for the reader's expectations: 'I could not . . . help endeavouring to teaze and surprise'.[1] He is not really in any doubt as to how to proceed. In these transactions with the readers he seems to be trying to define the novel by defining the terms on which it is to be read.

> . . . in this Sort of Writing, something, as I have hinted should be left [to the reader] to make out or debate upon. The whole Story abounds with Situations and Circumstances debatable. It is not an unartful Management to interest the Readers so much in the Story, as to make them differ in Opinion as to the Capital Articles, and by Leading one, to espouse one, another, another, Opinion, make them all, if not Authors, Carpers* . . .[2]

Yet it is not merely because he is very conscious of his readers that we take Richardson to be conscious of the responses appropriate to the novel. As a matter of fact, at this point he seems to envisage, and in the correspondence to sanction, a kind of discussion that is quite inappropriate, and really quite damaging to the concept of the novel as a work of art. By 'opinions' he probably means opinions of conduct; the novels become, as Jeffrey said, 'the scriptures of this congregation',[3] a focus for their tireless moral casuistry. Yet Richardson *does* keep reminding his readers that they are talking about novels. 'I must not have every good Lady enter *herself* into the Question, *Should I, Could I have done so, or so?* But say to herself, 'Here is a Character that somewhat differs from my own. Does she support it? Is she uniform? She is in a Situation I never found myself in; how can I tell how I should have acted had I been in hers?'[4] The difficulty, as he realized, was that the publication of the novel over several months, and the principle of writing 'to

---

[1] *Selected Letters*, p. 295
[2] Ibid., p. 296. The asterisk is the editor's indication of a doubtful reading
[3] *Contributions to the Edinburgh Review*, i, 314
[4] *Selected Letters*, p. 251

the moment' encouraged the assumption that they were 'like life', and therefore still subject to change and development, still in process. In fact, of course, this was the effect he wanted. But, paradoxically, he could only really secure it when he had schooled his readers to look beyond their immediate impressions, to take the evidence, not as it came, but in relation to the whole sequence. 'We often cheat ourselves', he explained, 'on the Entrance into a Character, by setting it down in our minds for such or such and when it rises or sinks upon us, are hardly able to reconcile it to our first hasty Impressions. And who is it that is not fond of justifying his first impressions, in compliment to himself? . . .'[1] This is the context in which we should take his comment about 'writing to the moment':

> Ye World is not enough used to this way of writing, to the moment. It knows not that in the minutiae lie often the unfoldings of the Story, as well as of the heart; & judges of an action undecided, as if it were absolutely decided. Nor will it easily part with its first impressions. How few Lady B's who will read it over once for Amusement, and a second time to examine into the unjustness or justness of its several parts, as they contribute to make one Whole![2]

You cannot really understand any episode, he argues in effect, unless you relate it to the completed work: '. . . such is the Disadvantage of this way of writing to the Moment, that I must once more refer your Ladiship to the Conclusion of my Story, when you will have it all before you'.[3] Yet, he adds at once, his aim is still to 'occasion many Debates upon different Parts of my Management'.[4]

This is a strange position to be in. In effect Richardson is telling the reader that he will not get the full force of the actual unless he sees it in the shape of fiction. For the essence of fiction is that it is the *whole* story; each of its parts contributes to a design and the design determines our

[1] *Selected Letters*, pp. 287–8  [2] Ibid., p. 289
[3] Ibid., p. 257  [4] Ibid., loc. cit.

reading of the parts. It is 'an action complete in itself'. But whereas for Aristotle, as Frank Kermode puts it, 'the literary plot was analogous to the plot of the world in that both were eductions from the potency of matter',[1] Richardson has already moved into the modern world in which the notion of a 'completed action' does not conform to actual experience. At least this is what his representation of 'crisis' and of the experiential moment suggests. The concept of a whole action is what we want from fiction. Or, rather, it is a fictional concept. If we value it we have a reason for valuing fiction. But to make it work we have to be sure that the reader is in the right position to possess the whole story. We have already seen that this position may be literally in the margins of the book, defined, that is, by means of the footnotes. We had better look a little more closely at what Richardson does with them.

## II

We have seen how, through the footnotes, the reader has an advantage over Belford. The same sort of thing happens towards the end of the novel when, for the first time, Lovelace loses command of the situation. 'They tell me', he writes to Belford, 'of an odd Letter I wrote to you. I remember I did write. But very little of the contents of what I wrote, do I remember' (VII, 53; iv, 438). He has lost contact with his past: 'I am still, I am still, most miserably absent from myself' (iv, 439). But here the reader has access, through a footnote, to Lovelace's forgotten 'delirious Letter, No. xxxix': 'My brain is all boiling like a caldron over a fiery furnace. What a devil is the matter with me I wonder? I never was so strange in my life' (iv, 378). The footnote is a position of privilege. It may be, as here, a kind of memory, or an anticipation: 'The Reader will see how

[1] *The Sense of an Ending*, p. 138

Miss Howe accounts for this in p. 28' (III, 1; ii, 85).
Either way it represents an entry into the 'virtual' time in
which the whole story takes shape. It helps us to read, that
is, by reminding us that we are reading a book. It does this
even in a literal sense: 'see vol. iii. pp. 293–8', 'see pp. 71–2
of this volume', 'see Letter I of this volume', etc. Reading is
almost a physical act. Actually handling the book, turning
these numbered pages of print, looking for the right page,
all this adds to the meaning of the letters. The footnotes
spell out that aspect of the meaning.

But more importantly they relate the single statement
or event to the tessellation of the whole story. It is unusual,
in fact, to find a note suggesting that a letter may be understood in isolation. When this does happen it seems to
indicate that Richardson wants to make an unambiguous
'authorial' statement about the meaning of the story. An
instance is Lovelace's important letter (II, 50; ii, 35–42)
about the principles on which he is to make trial of Clarissa's
virtue. Richardson evidently endorses his arguments: 'The
particular attention of such of the Fair Sex as are more apt
to read for the sake of amusement, than instruction, is
requested to this Letter of Mr. Lovelace' (ii, 35). But more
often the significance of a letter is left to be deduced from
its context:

> The Reader, perhaps, need not be reminded, that he [ie. Love-
> lace] had taken care from the first (see vol. I, p. 193) to deprive
> her of any protection from Mrs. Howe. See in his next letter,
> p. 19, a repeated account of the same artifices, . . . (III, 2;
> ii, 91)

Of course the reader ought not to need the reminder. There
is nothing in the note that he could not discover for himself
from the book. Yet it does seem that the reader understands the book better by being made conscious of the *way*
he understands it. The notes make him conscious of the act
of reading, and this in turn gives him a greater insight into

the kind of experience provided by reading, by taking possession, that is, of the whole story.

The reference to Lovelace's letter, for instance, makes it very clear that reading means something quite different from 'identifying' with the feelings and predicament of a character. What for Lovelace is a sign of breakdown is an enlargement of understanding for the reader. And at the end of this letter there is a still more striking difference between what the reader knows and what the character knows. Lovelace is writing to Belford about Mrs Sinclair: 'But, it seems, the old wretch is in the way to be rewarded, without my help. A shocking Letter is received of some-body's, in relation to her—Yours, I suppose—Too shock-ing for me, they say, to see at present' (VII, 53; iv, 441). A footnote to this passage explains that he is referring to Belford's letter (VII, 41) about the death of Mrs Sinclair:

> O Lovelace! I have a scene to paint in relation to the wretched Sinclair, that, if I do it justice, will make thee seriously ponder and reflect, or nothing can. I will lead to it in order; and that in my usual hand, that thy compeers may be able to read it as well as thyself. (iv, 379)

The letter is meant to shock its reader into seeing things as they really are. We assume, when we first read it, that in this respect it belongs to the changing relations between Belford and Lovelace. Lovelace must be brought to submit to external reality, to see the naked truth of things, to recognize the real meaning of the world he has built around him. Only later do we find that Lovelace did not actually see the letter. The reader was after all its *only* reader. Though he has already had the sense of reading it through Lovelace's eyes, he now has to understand that that reading never took place. The letter's insights are, so to speak, available in the book but not in the story, to the stander-by but not to the actor.

Later, it is true, Belford asks Lovelace to get hold of the letter, and even anticipates his reactions to it:

> I will suppose, that thou hast just read the Letter thou callest shocking, and which I *intended* to be so. And let me ask, What thou thinkest of it? Dost thou not tremble at the horrors the vilest of women labours with, on the apprehensions of death, and future judgment? (VII, 56; iv, 446)

The reader may well find this too strident. As Lovelace says in reply, 'Fate, I believe in my conscience, spins threads for Tragedies, on purpose for thee to weave with. . . . And, by my soul, *thou dost work it going,* as Lord M. would phrase it' (VII, 57; iv, 450). This cleverly pulls the letter back into the dramatic context just when it is in danger of becoming an aggressively direct approach to the reader. It helps to neutralize the effect made by a footnote to the letter itself: 'Whoever has seen Dean Swift's Lady's Dressing-Room, will think this description of Mr Belford not only more *natural* but more *decent painting,* as well as better justified by the *design,* and by the *use* that may be made of it' (VII, 41; iv, 381). This kind of endorsement defeats its own object. Yet it is important that the letter should be seen to be meant for the reader. We have to be able to compare our own reaction to it with Lovelace's. The letter is really neither in the story nor out of it. It is, in other words, a part of the story made known properly only to someone who has no place within the story.

### III

Yet, as we have seen, the footnotes do give the reader a place in the book, if not in the story. The novel, that is, includes a representation of the stander-by: he is the editor or annotator. And in this role he seems to see himself as confirming the reader's superior understanding of what is going on. If there is any trace of doubt or ambiguity in the evidence the editor tries to remove it. Cousin Dolly suspects that she is being used: 'You will know', she writes to Clarissa, 'better than I what to make of all these matters;

F

for sometimes I think Betty tells me things as if I should not tell you, and yet expects that I will' (II, 30; i, 463). But here the editor comes into his own: he takes up the matter in a footnote:

> It is easy for such of the Readers as have been attentive to Mr. Lovelace's manner of working, to suppose, from this hint of Miss Hervey's, that he had instructed his double-fac'd agent to put his sweetheart Betty upon alarming Miss Hervey, in hopes she would alarm her beloved Cousin (as we see she does) in order to keep her steady to her appointment with him.

The same sort of thing happens when Mrs Sorlings has shown Clarissa a letter from Mrs Greme about Lovelace's feelings towards her. 'What, my dear', writes Clarissa, 'shall I say to this? How shall I take it? Mrs. Greme is a good woman. Mrs. Sorlings is a good woman. And this Letter agrees with the conversation between Mr. Lovelace and me, which I thought, and still think, so agreeable' (II, 60; ii, 72–3). In the next volume we are to read that Lovelace *'makes such declarations to Mrs. Greme of his honour and affection to the Lady, as put her upon writing the Letter to her Sister Sorlings'* (III, 5; ii, 96). But the editor does not want even this temporary misunderstanding: he notes at once that 'This Letter Mrs. Greme (with a good intention) was put upon writing by Mr. Lovelace himself, as will be seen, Vol. III, p. 17'.

It is true that Richardson sometimes seems to want to 'teaze' the reader. When Captain Tomlinson first appears there is no note to warn the reader that he is in collusion with Lovelace. The clues in the text should be obvious, no doubt: 'tho' this incident has not turned out to answer *all I wished from it*' (IV, 15; ii, 443), etc. And, when at last Lovelace reveals who 'Tomlinson' is, he assumes that Belford must have guessed already (IV, 18; ii, 462). Still, Lovelace means to mystify, and the editor for once does not clear the matter up. The reader has only the letters to go on. For the time being he is in Lovelace's hands, just as Belford is. The experience is unsettling. It suggests that the reader can hardly expect to be insulated from his mischievous energy.

Near the end of the novel, however, Lovelace is himself deceived—by Clarissa's 'allegorical' letter: 'I have good news to tell you. I am setting out with all diligence for my Father's house, . . .' (VI, 76; iv, 157). Again the editor has nothing to add, though again there are clues in the text. Lovelace feels 'a Solemnity . . . in the style of her Letter', but attributes this to her loving him still and being 'half-ashamed (dear blushing pretty rogue!) to own her Love' (VI, 76; iv, 159). Obviously this cannot be right; nor, surely, can his reading of the 'subscription': '*Till when, I am,* CLARISSA HARLOWE: as much as to say, *after that,* I shall be, if not *your own fault,* CLARISSA LOVELACE!' (Ibid.) This, as Belford evidently feels, is grotesque. But he too cannot account for the letter 'in any shape': 'You are in ecstasies upon it. You have reason to be so, if it be as you think. Nor would I rob you of your joy: But I must say, that I am amazed at it' (VI, 79; iv, 171). And, as the editor makes no comment, it looks as if this must be the reader's reaction also. He takes his cue from Belford. At least the editor does not on this occasion suggest that he should *not* take his cue from Belford. Lovelace could be trying to trick the reader again: the editor does not contradict Belford: 'Surely, Lovelace, this surprizing Letter cannot be a forgery of thy own, in order to carry on some view, and to impose upon me. Yet by the style of it, it cannot; tho' thou art a perfect Proteus, too.' (Ibid.)

Obviously the editor's silence is significant. Clarissa's real meaning could have been made clear from the start. Instead the letter is deliberately left open to conflicting interpretations. What Belford is saying is that it sounds like, yet shockingly unlike Clarissa. The letter does really seem to have two kinds of meaning. As Morris Golden notes, her father's house is 'the image of death and salvation closest to her earlier wishes for secure support in this world'.[1] Her transcendence of the world takes a lot of its pathos and truth from the suggestion that it is also a mending of what was damaged at the beginning of the novel. She is 'setting out' and also going back, to be 'received', to a 'reconciliation'. Similarly she is still fighting Lovelace off, yet seems to be accepting him: 'So, pray, Sir, don't disturb or interrupt me—I beseech you, don't. You may possibly in time see me at my Father's; at least, if it be not your own fault! (VI, 76; iv, 157). In effect the letter is the ultimate and crucial expression of all Clarissa's confused feelings. It would be ruinous to the whole design to present it merely as a subterfuge. When she later maintains that she was deceiving Lovelace we are prepared to believe that we understand her action better than she does herself. Her own explanation is no more authoritative and final than any other that forms part of the story. Hence it is hard to imagine acceptable terms in which the editor could 'explain' the letter. It has to be ambiguous, but his annotations do not allow for ambiguity. He writes as if he *knows*, as if in all cases there were only one 'right' explanation, and as if the reader had better not be allowed to get hold of the 'wrong' one. But in this instance such an attitude would plainly not do. Is it, then, ever adequate to what happens in the story? It seems to be intended to secure a reliable reading of the book, but does it not really impoverish it? We come here to a crucial question about the whole concept of the work. A lot hinges on what is taken to be the editor's role and his relationship to the reader.

## IV

Clearly the 'editor' is one way of representing the 'implied author'. He is, to use the term Wayne Booth has brought

[1] *Richardson's Characters*, p. 175

into currency, the 'second self' created by the author.[1] He is not Richardson, but 'Richardson', or 'Richardson-as-editor'. The implied author, Booth argues, 'chooses, consciously or unconsciously, what we read; we infer him as an ideal, literary, created version of the real man; he is the sum of his own choices'.[2] And, as we have seen, in this novel he chooses to ally himself very closely with the reader. His role allows him to vacate the story and close it behind him. It permits the concept of the whole story, the completed action. And the editor sustains this concept by his belief that everything can be known for a certainty. He chooses, that is, to reduce the area of the possible, to exclude surmise and potentiality. This is by no means forced on him by the letter form of narrative. He could have avoided commentary altogether or used it to question the narrative. But, having made his choice, he is bound to seem inadequate to the possibilities in the book. He has taken up the position of the reader, and this does suggest the way in which the reader can possess the story as a whole, as a fiction; but now it appears that at some crucial points the way to possess the story is to become involved in it in ways that the editor hardly appreciates.

This might suggest that 'Richardson' is meant to be an 'imperfect narrator'. His limitations as an editor would then look like part of the story and would themselves have to be measured in relation to the total significance of the book. This would be one way of acknowledging what has often been felt, that the novel is bigger than the man. For instance, Arnold Kettle writes that 'though Richardson is sentimental *Clarissa* by and large is not', and thus its success is 'almost fortuitous', it 'was less than fully conscious'.[3] However, I do not think this is actually the effect of the annotations. For Richardson sees clearly what is at issue. It is a matter of 'attention'. He is always using the

---

[1] *The Rhetoric of Fiction*, pp. 71 ff.       [2] Ibid., pp. 74–5
[3] *Introduction to the English Novel*, i, 68

word, and when he introduces the Contents in the 1751 edition, speaks of 'the Attention that is humbly bespoke in favour of a HISTORY of LIFE and MANNERS; and which, as such, is designed for more than a transitory amusement'. Admittedly this suggests a narrowing of the attention to the overtly 'moral' issues. But in the notes he made for a Preface to the novel he gives a different impression: 'Attentive Readers have found, and will find, that the Probability of all Stories told, or of Narrations given, depends upon small Circumstances'.[1] Here he is concerned with the book's authenticity, and in the Postscript he argues for its psychological truth: those who 'have censured the Heroine as too cold in her love, too haughty, and even sometimes too provoking' display a 'want of attention to the Story, to the character of Clarissa, and to her particular situation'.

'Attention' is in fact precisely the word for what is asked of a reader, especially the reader of fiction. It presupposes a special kind of relationship with the object. It is an encounter which is not a meeting. It is full of feeling, but the feeling is not reciprocated. It is neither really passive, nor active. What Wayne Booth has to say about reading is relevant. There is a great deal of difference, he points out, between our response to people in real life and our response to characters in fiction: 'since we are not in a position to profit from or be harmed by a fictional character, our judgment is disinterested, even in a sense irresponsible'.[2] Yet, he continues, our interest in them 'springs in part from our conviction that they are people who matter, people whose fate concerns us not simply because of its meaning or quality, but because we care about them as human beings'. Booth is interested in a particular aspect of the matter, the 'role that moral judgment plays in most of our worthwhile reading'.[3] And this, as we have seen, is an important part

[1] *Hints of Prefaces* for *Clarissa*, p. [4]
[2] *The Rhetoric of Fiction*, p. 130      [3] *The Rhetoric of Fiction*, p. 131

of what Richardson means by 'attention': it is as 'editor' that he is able to control the way we relate our reading to our moral judgments. But, for our present purpose, it is more important to note that, as editor, he also wants us to be clear where we stand as readers. He appears in the footnotes as a man engrossed in the story but unable to alter it, with an intimate knowledge of the characters though he is quite unknown to them. His role is both unobtrusive and crucial: it spells out what is meant by attention; it keeps the reader in mind of his own necessarily reflective attitude, both involved and detached, deeply implicated in the lives of people for whom he himself is non-existent.

There is another way in which 'attention' is crucial to the book's meaning.

' "Falling in love" ', writes Ortega, 'is a phenomenon of attention.'[1] He points to its obsessive nature: it is a 'concentration of consciousness', 'a paralysis of the attention', which he finds analogous to a mystical or hypnotic trance. What he describes is also analogous to the process of reading. The reader also finds that everything outside the book he is reading is obliterated, and this is one of the things that makes a book important: 'What we fix our attention upon has for us *ipso facto* greater reality, a more vigorous existence than what we do not focus upon, an anaemic and almost phantasmic background which lurks on the periphery of our minds'.[2] Though falling in love is really a narrowing of the attention, 'the person in love has the impression that the life of his consciousness is very rich';[3] and, finally, the most important thing is that attention of the kind is not compelled, as in the 'vital obligations' of practical life, but is given voluntarily: 'whoever falls in love does so because he wants to fall in love'.[4] This is like reading. At any rate it is like the kind of reading that Richardson asks for. The kind of attention he expects for the novel is analogous to falling

[1] *On Love . . . Aspects of a Single Theme*, p. 40
[2] Ibid., p. 41  [3] Ibid., p. 44  [4] Ibid., p. 48

in love. And thus the act of reading is itself a contribution to the theme of the novel, to what it has to say about love.

Or, rather, (since Ortega is careful to distinguish between love and falling in love) it involves us in that powerful mechanism of attraction and absorption, of obsessive and heightened attention in which Clarissa and Lovelace are involved. Our reading is a kind of reflection of one phase in the whole experience of love. 'Love is a much broader and more profound operation, one which is more seriously human, but less violent.'[1] At one point it looked as if *Clarissa*, always confronting us with the process of reading, locked onto the literary experience, could not take in this dimension. And in a sense it cannot; this 'more seriously human' enterprise begins where reading ends, and the characters in this novel never cease to be readers. Yet it does find a way to represent an experience of love, the tragic condition of love needed, offered and refused. But it does this, as it must, in terms that are not analogous to reading. In fact it is just this which gives tragic emphasis to the theme. The point beyond which neither reader nor characters can go without ceasing to be what they are, readers, is the point at which its meaning must take on tragic weight.

V

One way to speak of this novel is to argue, as I did in the last chapter, that it enforces the tragic implications of its form. Writing and reading look then like a kind of estrangement, or alienation. And so they are, even though some kinds of reading, as we have found, allow us to be involved in the story whilst remaining detached, and in possession of it as a whole. For even the 'stander-by' cannot help feeling that his reading detaches him from the real world but gives him

---

[1] *On Love* . . ., p. 66

access only to the margins of the fictional one. He 'attends': that is to say he misses nothing, yet is not on the scene. He is absent, both from the actual and the fictional worlds. He is in a state comparable to daydream, or fantasy. What the process of reading in itself cannot offer is a living relationship: it is a relationship (if at all) free of any care for another person, irresponsible (as Wayne Booth noted) and therefore in itself isolating. But at this point we shall have to speak of this novel as tragic in another and profounder way—not because it must exclude the possibility of relationship, but because it affirms the reality of what it must exclude. It has tragic scope because it can envisage the possibility of what it cannot itself make possible. It offers the reader an insight into the kind of experience it cannot give him. It confronts the world of fantasy, the world of Lovelace, and necessarily in some degree the world of the reader, with a world of real encounters, the world of Clarissa, that it cannot itself establish. The terms in which it is conceived are not after all the terms it wishes to endorse. It is about love, which is to do with our ability to engage with reality. But it cannot evade the conditions of fantasy, just as it cannot represent Clarissa's capacity for love except in relation to Lovelace, or 'Love-less', the man for whom love has no meaning.

Lovelace lives a life of fantasy. He is divorced from reality, or would be so if his wealth did not allow him to consider giving substance to his fantasies. Fact is not stubborn for him. He is 'a perfect Proteus', we have seen. He can command not only his own appearance but the appearance of those around him. 'Lady Betty' and 'Cousin Montague' are, like 'Captain Tomlinson', his accomplices. So is 'Capt. Mennell':

> . . . I have changed his name by virtue of my own single authority. Knowest thou not, that I am a great Name-father? Preferments I bestow, both military and civil. I give Estates, and take them away at my pleasure. Quality too I create. And by a still more valuable prerogative, I *degrade* by virtue of my

own imperial will, without any other act of forfeiture than for
my own convenience. What a poor thing is a monarch to me!
(III, 52; ii, 267)

Even Miss Howe he describes as a 'puppet danced upon
my wires at second or third hand' (III, 5; ii, 100). Clarissa's
servant seems to be an obstacle to his will: he 'seems to be
one *used to poverty*, . . . Such a one is above temptation,
unless it could come cloathed in the guise of *truth* and *trust*.
What likelihood of corrupting a man who has no hope, no
ambition?' (Ibid.; ii, 97). But this is never a serious threat
to Lovelace's dream-world. The man is unimportant.

> Let him live. Were I a King, or a Minister of State, an
> Antonio Perez, it were another thing. And yet, on second
> thoughts, am I not a *Rake*, as it is called? And who ever knew
> a Rake stick at any-thing? But thou knowest, Jack, that the
> greatest half of my wickedness is vapour, to shew my invention;
> and to prove that I *could* be mischievous if I would. (Ibid.)

Dorothy Van Ghent rightly insists on the 'mythical re-
sonances' of Lovelace's character: he is clearly intended to be
Satanic, the archfiend, a figure of powerful evil.[1] But
Satanism here is perilously close, as it is with Dryden's
Achitophel, to madness. Lovelace is 'technically mad'.[2]

He also has the power to make the real world conform to
his fantasies. His servant Joseph reports that James
Harlowe is plotting with a Captain Singleton. Lovelace
replies that Joseph should persuade Singleton 'to propose
to James Harlowe (who so much thirsts for revenge upon
me) to assist him with his whole ship's crew, upon occasion,
to carry off his Sister to Leith, where both have houses, or
elsewhere' (III, 18; ii, 151). This sounds wildly unrealistic,
but we now recall that Miss Howe has already reported to
Clarissa as a fact that James 'has taken a resolution to find
you out, way-lay you, and carry you off. A friend of his, a
captain of a ship, undertakes to get you on ship-board; and

---

[1] *The English Novel*, pp. 51–2          [2] *Richardson's Characters*, p. 20

to sail away with you, either to Hull or Leith, in the way to one of your Brother's houses' (III, 10; ii, 115). Later Lovelace toys with the similar, if even more outrageous, scheme of trapping Miss Howe and her mother on a boat to the Isle of Wight.

> Well, then we will imagine them on board. I will be there in disguise. . . .
>
> 'Tis plaguy hard, if we cannot *find*, or *make*, a storm . . . And then, securing the footman, and the women being separated, one of us, according to lots that may be cast, shall overcome, either by persuasion or force, the maid-servant . . . Now I know thou wilt make difficulties, as it is thy way; while it is mine to conquer them. (IV, 9; ii, 420)

However remote this is from reality, it is not remote from the schemes that Lovelace has made into reality. He has power, it seems, over the very nature of things. He appears to be free to make up his own world on his own terms.

Yet in many ways he has neither freedom nor power. For instance, as Christopher Hill points out, though his wealth and connections seem to make him free of social and moral sanctions, in economic terms this 'freedom' is illusory: it cannot be maintained without reference to the system, 'the property-marriage system' which is the source of his wealth.[1] He is not a free agent. Still less is he free in his own nature. Gillian Beer has noted how the reader progresses from elation at Lovelace's own sense of freedom to the recognition that his 'relentless gaiety is . . . a psychopathic symptom'. The sequence is expected to correspond to our 'gradual disillusionment' with Satan in *Paradise Lost*. But also, she claims, it enables us to see Lovelace in existential terms. As she says, his dread of acting out of character can be described in R. D. Laing's words; it is a form of 'ontological insecurity'.[2] Lovelace is in a position not of power but

---

[1] 'Clarissa Harlowe and Her Times', *Essays in Criticism*, V, 1955, reprinted in Spector, ed., *Essays on the Eighteenth Century Novel*, p. 48

[2] 'Richardson, Milton and the Status of Evil', *RES*, xix, 75, August 1968, pp. 269, 270 and 267

of fear. Far from commanding reality, he is hardly able
to tolerate it. 'In phantasy', Laing writes, 'the self can be
anyone, anywhere, do anything.' But 'the more this phan-
tastic omnipotence and freedom are indulged, the more
weak, helpless and fettered it becomes in actuality'.[1] He is
describing the schizoid condition in which 'although the
self has an attitude of freedom and omnipotence, its refusal
to commit itself to "the objective element" renders it
impotent: it has no freedom *in* "reality" '.[2] Lovelace is
'unreal' in these terms. Above all he is incapable of sustaining a vital relationship. This, says Laing, is what happens
when 'phantasy and reality are kept apart. The self avoids
being related directly to real persons but relates itself to
itself and to the objects which it itself posits. *The self can
relate itself with immediacy to an object which is an object of its
own imagination or memory but not to a real person.*'[3]

This is how we have to understand the relationship
between Clarissa and Lovelace. She is a real person and
therefore an obstacle, an anomaly in his world. Her 'virtue',
her resistance to his will, these are aspects of the 'real' which
he must either subdue or feel always as a threat to his own
being. He cannot come to terms with the real, he can only
try to make it submit to the unreal. ' "Nor is *one* effort, *one*
trial, to be sufficient. Why? Because a woman's heart may
be at one time *adamant*, at another *wax*"—As I have often
experienced' (II, 50; ii, 41). As long as she resists, it is
possible for him to imagine that she must submit. The
'trial' will never prove that she cannot be subdued to his
image of her. It must continue until one of them is destroyed.
It is in fact the only way Lovelace can deal with Clarissa. It
allows him to keep intact the 'freedom' of his fantasy life:

> And now imagine (the Charmer overcome) thou seest me
> sitting supinely cross-kneed, reclining on my soffa, the god of
> Love dancing in my eyes, and rejoicing in every mantling feature;
> the sweet rogue, late such a proud rogue, wholly in my power,

[1] *The Divided Self*, p. 84        [2] Ibid., p. 89        [3] Ibid., p. 86

moving up slowly to me, at my beck, with heaving sighs, half-
pronounced upbraidings from murmuring lips, her finger in her
eye, and quickening her pace at my *Come hither, Dearest!* . . .

If I could bring my Charmer to this, would it not be the
Eligible of Eligibles?—Is it not worth trying for?—As I said,
I can marry her when I will. She *can* be nobody's but mine,
neither for shame nor by choice, nor yet by address . . .
(IV, v; ii, 251)

Actually Lovelace has to fight against the possibility of
loving Clarissa. She is perilously real: 'These sly women,
how, when a man thinks himself near the mark, do they
*tempest* him!' (IV, 25; ii, 498). 'To be loved', writes R. D.
Laing of the schizoid individual, 'threatens his self; but his
love is equally dangerous to anyone else.'[1] Love is feared as
an invasion of the self; it is as destructive as hate. There is a
point at which Lovelace begins to see that his libertinism
has led only to the fear of love and the inability to be anything but destructive both of himself and others. He is
trapped in a paralysing conflict with himself. He must
continue to be what he hates to be; he must continue to
destroy what he loves. He sees himself as 'the devil', a being
not of boundless invention and resource, but isolated,
hateful to himself, harmful in spite of himself.

By my faith, Jack, as I sit gazing upon her, my whole soul in
my eyes, contemplating her perfections, and thinking when I
have seen her easy and serene, what would be her thoughts, did
*she* know my heart as well as *I* know it; when I behold her
disturbed and jealous, and think of the *justness* of her apprehensions, and that she cannot fear so much, as there is *room* for her
to fear; my heart often misgives me.

And must, think I, O creature so divinely excellent, and so
beloved of my soul, those arms, those incircling arms, that would
make a monarch happy, be used to repel brutal force; all their
strength unavailingly perhaps, exerted to repel it, and to defend
a person so delicately framed? Can violence enter into the heart
of a wretch, who might entitle himself to all thy willing, yet

[1] *The Divided Self*, p. 93

virtuous Love, and make the blessings I aspire after, her *duty* to confer?—Begone, villain-purposes! Sink ye all to the hell that could only inspire ye! And I am then ready to throw myself at her feet, to confess my villainous designs, to avow my repentance, and put it out of my power to act unworthily by such an excellence.

How then comes it, that all these compassionate, and, as some would call them, *honest* Sensibilities go off?—Why, Miss Howe will tell thee: She says, I am the *devil*.—By my conscience, I think he has at present a great share in me. (IV, 3; ii, 399)


## VI


The characterization of Lovelace is of a piece with the whole effect produced by the novel. His story is the end of a process in which the reader too has been involved. His isolation and despair are what our experience of the novel has been preparing us for. But he is not, after all, the protagonist. The novel is meant to be 'The History of a Young Lady'. It is about Clarissa, about her resistance to Lovelace and all that he represents. It is expected to show the moral impossibility of either compromising with Lovelace or changing his nature. It really *is* about the dangerous folly of thinking that 'a Reformed Rake makes the best Husband'. The arguments against Clarissa's marrying Lovelace, Richardson maintains, 'must continue in Force, till the eternal Difference of Vice and Virtue shall coalesce, and make one putrid Mass, a Chaos in the Moral and Intellectual World'.[1] The book is about the struggle that must be unremitting, the struggle against non-being, against moral and intellectual (and, as we may now see, existential) chaos. 'As I understand Vice', Blake writes, 'it is a Negative . . . Accident is the omission of act in self and the hindering of act in another; This is Vice, but all Act is Virtue.'[2]

[1] *Hints of Prefaces*, p. [14]
[2] Annotations to Lavater's *Aphorisms, Poetry and Prose of William Blake*, p. 735

What Clarissa has to cope with is constant pressure from the 'negative'; she has to fight hard to keep a hold on reality, and to escape from the orbit of Lovelace's self-defeating fantasies. As William Sale puts it, she is 'a free spirit, struggling desperately to preserve her integrity and her independence of mind and soul'.[1] Like Isabel Archer, he says, she needs 'a chance to live life more completely in conformity with an ideal of conduct'; and she too has her Osmond.[2] The parallel is even closer than Sale suggests. Lovelace, I have been arguing, does not in reality inhabit 'a world of larger freedoms, of wider spaces'.[3] He *is* another Osmond, a connoisseur and collector, unable to endure a loving relationship. 'Whatever is Negative is Vice': those who do not know this, Blake says, 'suppose that Woman's Love is Sin; in consequence all the Loves & Graces with them are Sins'. Clarissa's struggle for the real, for 'virtue', is above all a struggle to believe in love.

In effect Clarissa has to resist the whole drift and design of the book. In particular she cannot accept the alienation which seems to be involved in reading and writing. It is true that she cultivates letter-writing. 'And indeed, my dear,' she writes to Miss Howe, 'I know not how to *forbear* writing. . . . And I must write on, altho' I were not to send it to any body. You have often heard me own the advantages I have found from writing down everything of moment that befals me . . .' (III, 13; ii, 128). But characteristically she is thinking of writing as a kind of self-discipline and an increase in self-knowledge:

> . . . when I set down what I *will* do, or what I *have* done, on this or that occasion; the resolution or action is before me either to be adhered to, withdrawn, or amended; and I have entered into *compact* with myself, as I may say; having given it under my own hand to *improve*, rather than to go *backward*, as I live longer. (Ibid.)

[1] 'From *Pamela* to *Clarissa*', in *The Age of Johnson*, ed. Hilles, p. 134
[2] Ibid., p. 137      [3] Ibid., p. 135

Letter-writing of this kind is a severe rule of conduct. By contrast Lovelace's attitude looks relaxed and even specious: 'It was writing from the heart', he had been telling Clarissa, '(without the fetters prescribed by method or study) as the very word *Cor-respondence* implied. Not the heart only; the *soul* was in it. Nothing of body, when friend writes to friend; the mind impelling sovereignly the vassal-fingers' (IV, 11; ii, 431). This, of course, comes very close to what Richardson wrote about letter-writing, and suggests a similar wish to indulge the feelings without risk to one's essential privacy. But Lovelace's words are actually subtly altered from Richardson's, for whom correspondence is really 'more pure, yet more ardent, and less broken in upon, than personal conversation can be even amongst the most pure, because of the deliberation it allows, from the very preparation to, and action of writing'. Also, far from having 'nothing of body', it 'makes distance, presence; and brings back to sweet remembrance all the delights of presence; which makes even presence but body, while absence becomes the soul'.[1] Richardson is talking of a heightened awareness of oneself and one's correspondent; what Lovelace describes is a screen of words and a way to conceal oneself, a form of philandering. He says in fact that he has been trying to justify to Clarissa '*my* secrecy and *uncommunicativeness* by her *own*' (IV, 11; ii, 431). Words, especially written words, can be a way of not speaking. The novel as a whole is made up of words which isolate the characters from each other, from themselves and from the real world. And it is Clarissa who can see that these words are untrustworthy:

> I have not the better opinion of Mr. Lovelace for his extrava-
> gant volubility. He is too full of professions. He says too many
> fine things *of* me, and *to* me. True respect, true value, I think,
> lies not in words: Words *cannot* express it: The silent awe, the
> humble, the doubting eye, and even the hesitating voice, better

[1] *Selected Letters*, p. 65

shew it by much, than, as our beloved Shakespeare says,

> ——*The rattling tongue*
> *Of saucy and audacious eloquence.* (II, 38; i, 509)

The compulsive verbalizing which keeps people apart is the substance of this novel. Hazlitt notes that it has the 'truth of reflection' rather than 'the truth of nature'. 'Richardson's nature is always the nature of sentiment and reflection, not of impulse or situation.' And so it must be whilst the characters exist primarily in the words of their letters. 'They regularly sit down to write letters: and if the business of life consisted in letter-writing, and was carried on by the post (like a Spanish game at chess), human nature would be what Richardson represents it'.[1] But in these letters we do sometimes hear of unruly impulse, of feelings that cannot be talked away or rationalized. And it is the eyes, communicating with disturbing immediacy and in unguarded encounters, that tell a story which cannot get onto the pages of a letter or a book.

> Our likings and dislikings, as I have often thought, are seldom governed by prudence, or with a view to happiness. The eye, my dear, the wicked eye—has such a strict alliance with the heart —And both have such enmity to the understanding!

So writes Miss Howe (III, 10; ii, 116–17); and later Clarissa repents that her 'foolish eye' had been 'too much attached'. 'Guard your eye; 'Twill ever be in a combination against your judgment' (III, 54; ii, 277). In the first days after Clarissa has eloped with Lovelace they are both highly conscious of how much can be said without speaking. Each is sharply aware of the other's presence, he self-defensively and she with unremitting watchfulness: Clarissa tells Miss Howe, 'we are both great watchers of each other's eyes; and indeed seem to be more than half afraid of each other' (III, 3; ii, 93). Lovelace knows that

---

[1] *Lectures on the English Comic Writers, Complete Works*, vi, 119

G

the eyes give a lot away. He writes to Belford about Belton's mistress, Thomasine: 'To say the truth, I always suspected her *Eye*: The *Eye*, thou knowest, is the *Casement*, at which the *Heart* generally looks out. Many a woman who will not shew herself at the *Door*, has tipt the sly, the intelligible *wink* from the *Windows* (VI, 2; iii, 497). And when he has to prepare 'Lady Betty' and 'Cousin Charlotte' to meet Clarissa he is worried most by their eyes: 'Curse those eyes! —Those glancings will never do. A down-cast bashful turn, if you can command it—. . . Be sure forget not to look down, or aside, when looked at. When eyes meet eyes, be yours the retreating ones. . . . Have I not told you, that my Beloved is a great observer of the eyes? She once quoted upon me a text, which shewed me how she came by her knowlege—Dorcas's were found guilty of treason the first moment she saw her' (V, 4; iii, 186–7). (The 'text' is quoted in a footnote: 'Ecclus, xxvi. *The whoredom of a woman may be known in her haughty looks and eye-lids. Watch over an impudent eye, and marvel not if it trespass against thee.*') As Lovelace says, Clarissa has already begun to suspect Dorcas, the 'maid-servant' provided by Mrs Sinclair, —'she has a strange sly Eye' (III, 33; ii, 193). 'I should have been apt to think', writes Clarissa, 'that the young Ladies and Mr. Lovelace were of longer acquaintance than of yesterday. For he, by stealth, as it were, cast glances sometimes at them, which they returned; and, on my ocular notice, their eyes fell, as I may say, under my eye, as if they could not stand its examination' (III, 35; ii, 202). 'A worthy heart', she says to Captain Tomlinson, 'need not fear an examination—need not fear being looked into' (IV, 45; iii, 126).

Clarissa herself is not afraid to let her feelings show in her eyes. Belford is struck by this: 'What a piercing, yet gentle eye; every glance, I thought, mingled with Love and Fear of you! What a sweet smile darting through the cloud that overspread her fair face; demonstrating, that she had more apprehensions and grief at her heart, than she cared to express!' (III, 47; ii, 243). Lovelace thinks otherwise: 'Well did I note her Eye, and plainly did I see, that it was all but just civil disgust to me and to the company I had brought her into' (III, 49; ii, 250). Yet he too knows that she is someone who will reveal herself through her eyes: 'her Eye never knew what it was to contradict her Heart' (ibid.). On the other hand Lovelace hardly dare let his real nature show in his eyes. Only once does this happen. This is at the crisis of the book, just before Clarissa is violated. That event is what the book cannot contain, as we have seen. Yet Clarissa *can* describe the momentary revelation of Lovelace's mad violence, the moment in which he speaks the real meaning of his volubility.

> He terrified me with his looks, and with his violent emotions, as he gazed upon me . . . Never saw I his abominable eyes look, as then they looked—Triumph in them!—Fierce and wild; and more disagreeable than the womens at the vile house appeared to me when I first saw them: And at times, such a leering, mischief-boding cast! (V, 63; iii, 370)

A moment later Lovelace taunts her: 'You are *an observer of eyes*, my dear, said the villain: perhaps in secret insult' (ibid.; iii, 371). This is the way Clarissa is violated. It is the violation also of the language that she believes in against all the weight of the book, the silent language of feeling and of reality.

This is a novel, we have found, in which the actual process of writing, the text itself, is the action. It is not a description or a narration of the action, though it contains many such descriptions. Clarissa, Lovelace, Belford and Anna Howe have stories to tell; but it is the telling that constitutes the novel, not what is told. The words in this novel are the acts. Thus the reader of the novel is himself collaborating in the action, or at least, since he is a 'stander-by' and outside the action, he is aware that what he reads is what the characters read, what they do is what he is doing. Yet, after all, we see that some scenes are described of which this cannot be said. They are essentially wordless, they are not on the page, they contradict the whole effect of the book. They record experiences unlike the others in the novel, in that they are not available to the reader *as* reader. He must see in them a reminder of the kind of experience that he cannot get from reading. That is, they are resistant to the sense of alienation inherent in the whole process of the novel. And they go beyond even the state of attentiveness in which the reader comes closest to the condition of love. However diligent as a correspondent, Clarissa is the agent of this kind of experience in the novel. She stands for something which the book cannot make available: she stands for freedom. And that is why, finally, she chooses to die. 'My will is unviolated. . . . I have, thro' Grace, triumphed over the deepest machinations. I have escaped from him. I have renounced him. The man whom once I could have loved, I have been enabled to despise: And shall not *Charity* complete my triumph?' (VI, 83; iv, 186).

But at this point Clarissa is beginning to recede from the novel. She soon becomes someone who speaks through her *actions*, only linked to the procedures of the novel through Belford's narrative. Thus he describes the 'devices' on Clarissa's coffin:

> The principal device, neatly etched, on a plate of white metal, is a crowned Serpent, with its tail in its mouth, forming a ring, the emblem of Eternity: and in the circle made by it is this inscription:
>
> ### CLARISSA HARLOWE
> #### APRIL X.
> [Then the year]
> Ætat. xix.
>
> For ornaments: At top, an Hour-glass winged. At bottom, an Urn. . . . (VI, 106; iv, 257)

She is getting beyond language because she is getting
beyond self. At the end her words again appear in the fabric
of the novel, but only when she is supposed to be released
from them. She writes just before her death to awaken
Lovelace from his 'sensual dream'. But the interval between
the writing and reading of this letter is the gap between
life and death:

> My fate is *now*, at your perusal of this, accomplished. My doom
> is unalterably fixed: And I am either a miserable or happy Being
> to all Eternity. If *happy*, I owe it solely to the Divine mercy; if
> *miserable*, to your undeserved cruelty. . . . Hear me therefore,
> O Lovelace! as one speaking from the dead—Lose no time—
> Set about your repentance instantly— . . . (VII, 52; iv, 435).

This is a letter from the living in the voice of the dead. It
speaks to its readers, that is both to Lovelace and to the
reader of the novel, of a mode of existence they cannot
share without ceasing to *be* readers. It is the ultimate
expression of what cannot be expressed, at least by this
novel. Clarissa's function is to show how the novel must
surpass itself, and how the reader must be willing to become
more than a reader.

# CHAPTER 5

# Tom Jones *(i): Plot as Irony*

## I

THOSE who admire the plot of Tom Jones often find themselves in some embarrassment. To become engrossed in what Professor Kermode calls 'the Swiss precision of the plotting'[1] seems only to increase the difficulty of gauging the novel's imaginative scope. In this sense we must agree that, as Arnold Kettle says, 'in *Tom Jones* there is too much plot'.[2] Fielding's smooth stage-managing of the action may well be thought to trivialize the book. This, indeed, is what Andrew Wright in effect concedes when he maintains that Fielding's art is serious because it is play, 'a special kind of entertainment'.[3] His reading of the plot supports the view that we should 'take *Tom Jones* on an ornamental level', that Fielding provides 'a kind of ideal delight'.[4] But, granted that comedy depends on our feeling able to reshape life, and that the delight we take in this is properly a function of art's 'seriousness', yet it may seem that this reading of *Tom Jones* gives away too much. After all, any achieved work of art takes on the status of play. That is what art is, in relation to life. And it may be that the works we recognize as 'playful' (the Savoy operas for instance) are just those in which play forfeits its seriousness. So, whilst appreciating the ease with which Fielding turns everything into delight, we have still to explain how he can,

[1] *Tom Jones* (Signet Classics), p. 859
[2] *An Introduction to the English Novel*, i, 77
[3] *Henry Fielding, Mask and Feast*, p. 22      [4] Ibid., pp. 72, 30

as James thought, 'somehow really enlarge, make everyone and everything important'.[1] We know that Fielding's presence as narrator contributes to this impression. Can we say that the plot of the novel confirms it?

It may be thought that to do so we should need to be more convinced that the plot was sensitive to the inner experience of the characters. We are not usually satisfied with plot which does not emanate from some 'inwardness', some subtlety in attending to the growth of consciousness. Forster's distinction between plot and story will help to show why this is so. Story is to be considered 'a very low form' of art because it offers a sequence which has no meaning apart from that given by the sense of time. The significance of a train of events, the sense that it is 'caused', arises when we discover in it the signs of personal will, of motives and desires and of the adjustments they call for. This is the kind of causality Forster illustrates: 'The king died, and then the queen died of grief.'[2] Causality without these signs may be as trivial and meaningless as story. Consider 'The king died, and then the queen dyed all the curtains black.' This too is a plot: it answers the question 'why?' But it does not take that question seriously. And it looks as if the plot of *Tom Jones* is unserious in this way. That is why there is something self-defeating about the attempts to analyse it: Fielding has answered the questions of the plot facetiously. Yet I do not think we are justified in deducing from this, as Ian Watt does, 'a principle of considerable significance for the novel form in general: namely, that the importance of the plot is in inverse proportion to that of character'.[3] In fact Fielding makes it quite clear that he has been deliberately unserious about the plot. It is not typical; it has been designed specifically to serve his own special and rather subtle purpose.

There is no doubt that he means to draw attention to the

[1] *The Art of the Novel*, p. 68     [2] *Aspects of the Novel*, p. 93
[3] *The Rise of the Novel*, p. 279

artificiality of the plot. Why else, towards the close of the novel, recommend us to turn back 'to the Scene at *Upton* in the Ninth Book' and 'to admire the many strange Accidents which unfortunately prevented any Interview between *Partridge* and Mrs. *Waters*' (XVIII, ii)? 'Fielding', says Frank Kermode, 'cannot forbear to draw attention to his cleverness.'[1] But is this likely? Fielding expected his readers to know what sort of writer would do this. He had already presented several such on the stage in his 'rehearsal' plays. Trapwit is a good example. He is the vain author of an incoherent and unfunny comedy ('It is written, Sir, in the exact and true spirit of Molière', *Pasquin*, I, i); and he too is particularly proud of the plot.

> Now, Mr. Fustian, the plot, which has hitherto been only carried on by hints, and open'd itself like the infant spring by small and imperceptible degrees to the audience, will display itself, like a ripe matron, in its full summer's bloom; and cannot, I think, fail with its attractive charms, like a loadstone, to catch the admiration of every one like a trap, and raise an applause like thunder, till it makes the whole house like a hurricane. (*Pasquin*, III, i)

Fielding means us to see that in *Tom Jones* the sequences are those of farce and that the real skill consists in using them in a certain way, to get at some truth about human nature. The plot not only does not develop character, it actually subdues character to the demands of comic action. It will have to be in the shape of this action that we discern the shape of human behaviour. And Fielding wants to make sure that we get the right impression of that shape.

We would do well, then, not to take Fielding's self-congratulation at face value. In reminding us of Book IX he intends us to be more subtle about it than he himself claims to be. We find there, of course, 'a plot-node of extraordinary complexity';[2] but may too easily assume, as Ker-

[1] *Tom Jones* (Signet Classics), p. 857          [2] Ibid , p. 857

mode does, that this is exactly what robs this and subsequent actions of 'the full sense of actual life—real, unpredictable, not subject to mechanical patterning'.[1] Actually the succeeding events *are* unpredictable. We could not possibly foresee from Book IX that Fitzpatrick and Mrs Waters would go off together as 'husband and wife', that Tom would be attacked by Fitzpatrick (though for his supposed affair with Mrs Fitzpatrick, not his actual one with Mrs Waters), or that this would involve him again with Mrs Waters, or in what ways. When we look back on the completed sequence, it is true, we see it differently: the unpredictable suddenly appears to have hardened into the arbitrary. After all, we think, it *was* only a trick of the plotting. But, really, the plot faces two ways. From one side it looks like a forced solution, from the other an open question. In one way it looks arbitrary and contrived, in another it not only makes the reader guess but *keeps* him guessing at what has happened. The latter aspect of the plot is sustained by what Eleanor Hutchens calls 'substantial irony': 'a curious and subtle means used by Fielding to add irony to a given detail of plotting is to leave the reader to plot a sequence for himself'.[2] The reader has not, in fact, been told everything and is sometimes as much in the dark as the characters themselves. But irony of this kind is only contributory to the ironic *shift* by means of which the whole direction of the novel is reversed, and the plot has to sustain two contradictory conclusions simultaneously.

It is left to the reader to make this irony work. Fielding suggests as much by placing the reader in a dilemma. He draws him into the middle of the action, which then looks free-ranging, unpredictable, open-ended. If the plot is to behave like life, the reader must be unable to see his way before him. But he can only play this game once. On re-reading the novel he knows in advance the answer to all riddles, the outcome of all confusions. The plot thus poses

[1] *Tom Jones* (Signet Classics), p. 859    [2] *Irony in* Tom Jones, p. 41

questions about the way it should be read. Is it impossible
to read the book more than once? Or is it necessary to read
the book at least twice in order to understand it? On second
reading do we reject the first, or are we in some way expected
to keep them both in mind at once? This last is, I think, the
only possibility Fielding leaves open for us, and it is this
dual response which secures the ironic structure of the plot.

## II

I think we can see why this must be so if we examine more
closely the two 'faces' of the plot, and consider first what the
book looks like when we can take the action as a diagram, or
'architecturally', as Dorothy Van Ghent does. She writes of
it as a 'Palladian palace perhaps; . . . simply, spaciously,
generously, firmly grounded in Nature, . . . The structure
is all out in the light of intelligibility.' This, she considers,
diminishes its scope: 'Since Fielding's time, the world has
found itself not quite so intelligible . . . there was much in
the way of doubt and darkness to which Fielding was insen-
sitive.'[1] Ian Watt offers a similar reading: 'it reflects the
general literary strategy of neo-classicism . . . (it makes)
visible in the human scene the operations of universal order.'
Its function, he claims, is to reveal the important fact 'that
all human particles are subject to an invisible force which
exists in the universe whether they are there to show it or
not'. The plot must act like a magnet 'that pulls every
individual particle out of the random order brought about
by temporal accident and human imperfection'.[2] Read in
this way it will appear as a paradigm of the Deistic world
picture:

> All Nature is but Art, unknown to thee;
> All Chance, Direction, which thou canst not see
>
> (*An Essay on Man*, i, 289–290)

Is this likely to be Fielding's meaning? It is true that in

[1] *The English Novel*, pp. 80–1      [2] *The Rise of the Novel*, p. 271

*The Champion* he asserts (against the Deists in fact) his belief in 'this vast regular Frame of the Universe, and all the artful and cunning Machines therein', and denies that they could be 'the Effects of Chance, of an irregular Dance of Atoms'. But he is still more concerned to deny that the Deity is 'a lazy, unactive Being, regardless of the Affairs of this World, that the Soul of Man, when his Body dieth, lives no more, but returns to common Matter with that of the Brute Creation' (Jan. 22, 1739–40). As James A. Work has shown,[1] the concept of universal order was nothing for Fielding if it was not the evidence of God's providence and a support for personal faith. In fact Fielding's essay on Bolingbroke brings out specifically the moral and intellectual impropriety of reducing the Divine order to the status of a work of art. Bolingbroke, Fielding reasons, must be making game of eternal verities in considering 'the Supreme Being in the light of a dramatic poet, and that part of his works which we inhabit as a drama'. It is the impiety that is offensive of course, the 'ludicrous treatment of the Being so universally . . . acknowledged to be the cause of all things'. But involved in this is the mistrust of those artists who 'aggrandize their profession with such kind of similies' (*Works*, viii, 499–500). Fielding's own procedure, if Ian Watt were right, would be uncomfortably close to this, and it may be that, once more, we should not take him literally when he claims to be in this position.

The beginning of Book X is an occasion when he does so:

> First, then, we warn thee not too hastily to condemn any of the Incidents in this our History, as impertinent and foreign to our main Design, because thou dost not immediately conceive in what Manner such Incident may conduce to that Design. This Work may, indeed, be considered as a great Creation of our own; and for a little Reptile of a Critic to presume to find Fault with any of its Parts, without knowing the Manner in which the

[1] 'Henry Fielding, Christian Censor', in *The Age of Johnson*, ed. F. W. Hilles, pp. 140–2

> Whole is connected, and before he comes to the final Catastrophe,
> is a most presumptuous Absurdity. (X, i)

This is equivocal. It may be taken to indicate that this is the
structural centre of the novel, the peripeteia. It occurs at the
height of the book's confusion and may be necessary to
reassure the reader that the author is still in control. Yet it
would be naïve of Fielding to think that this was the way
to do so, especially as he adopts a tone that suggests otherwise. He sounds touchy and self-defensive and tries to
browbeat the reader. To claim that the work is 'a great
Creation of our own' is arrogant in the way that the essay
on Bolingbroke indicated, and the arrogance is blatant in
the reference to 'a little Reptile of a Critic'. Fielding clearly
wants to discredit the narrator and, in the process, to make
fun again of the pretensions of the plot. He makes a similar
point in a different way in the introduction to Book XVII.
Now he is asserting that affairs have got beyond his control.

> ... to bring our Favourites out of their present Anguish and
> Distress, and to land them at last on the Shore of Happiness,
> seems a much harder Task; a Task indeed so hard that we do
> not undertake to execute it. In Regard to *Sophia*, it is more than
> probable, that we shall somewhere or other provide a good
> Husband for her in the End, either *Blifil*, or my Lord, or Some-
> body else; but as to poor *Jones*, ... we almost despair of bringing
> him to any Good. (XVII, i)

He cannot invoke supernatural assistance: 'to natural Means
alone we are confined; let us try therefore what by these
Means may be done for poor *Jones*' (XVII, i). But this again
is a kind of boast. At any rate it draws attention to the hard
work and (paradoxically) the artifice necessary to reach a
'natural' outcome. It is another way of claiming that the
design is intact. His pride in his own skill is obtrusive here
as elsewhere. But this can hardly mean that Fielding had the
kind of vanity which is the mark of the bad writer, unsure
of his own powers.

We must conclude, I think, that to pose as a bad writer will help Fielding to avoid slipping into shallow rationalism. If he poses as the invisible Divine presence behind events, it is with a full sense of the kind of error this would be. What in one sense is an ironic parody of a form is, in a more profound way, an ironic repudiation of spiritual arrogance. In the same way the plot is less an assertion of Augustan rationality than a recognition of the confusion the rationalist can hardly tolerate. It is in fact a vehicle for what is self-contradictory, what is emotionally as well as intellectually confusing in human experience.

## III

This is an aspect of the plot that Eleanor Hutchens admirably describes:

> Substantial irony is an integral part of the fabric of *Tom Jones*. Just as the straightforward plot moves from misfortune to prosperity along a tightly linked causal chain but brings the hero full circle back to the place of beginning, so the concomitant irony of plot turns things back upon themselves transformed. This larger structure is repeated in multitudinous smaller ironies of plot, character, and logic. . . . The reversal of truth and expectation accompanies plot and theme as a sort of ironic *doppelgänger*.[1]

Her main concern is to identify the specific episodes ('ironies of the plot . . . so numerous as to defy complete cataloguing'[2]) which add an ironic dimension to the whole narrative. But what she calls the 'concomitant irony of plot' can be taken to refer to a reversal of meaning in the plot as a whole, and it is in this way that it produces the effect we noted, of seeming to face two ways at once. The 'causal chain' that 'Fielding-as-narrator' boasts about seems to strengthen the possibility of a comprehensible order in human experience. But the plot also moves through a causal

[1] *Irony in* Tom Jones, p. 67    [2] Ibid., p. 39

sequence of a different kind, a sequence of coincidences, chance meetings and meetings missed, good luck and bad, unplanned and unforeseen events. From this point of view it is easier to see that Fielding is dealing with the unpredictable, not in character or motive—his theory of 'conservation of character' leads in quite a different direction—but, to use his own term, in the 'history', the shape of events. The meaning of history, as Philip Stevick has shown,[1] interested Fielding profoundly, and the plot of *Tom Jones*, set against actual historical events, helps to define that meaning.

The episode of Sophia's little bird (IV, iii), which Eleanor Hutchens cites as an example of irony of substance,[2] is even more interesting as a model of this ironic meaning in the action as a whole. The causal links are firm: the bird is a present from Tom, therefore Sophia cherishes it, therefore Blifil lets it escape, therefore Tom tries to catch it and fails, therefore Sophia raises the alarm, therefore Allworthy and the rest come and eventually pass judgment on the two boys. The sequence does, it is true, depend on character and motive; but, like the plot as a whole, it finds these less interesting than their consequences in the actions and opinions of others. The episode is trimmed to the requirements of parable: it moves from personal predicament to moral judgment. In this way the episode suggests how the whole plot will be designed to exercise and refine the faculty of judgment, an aspect of the book I wish to examine in the next chapter. At this stage, however, it is more to the point to note that the action in this episode can be traced through another kind of sequence. It springs from a paradoxical situation: the affection of Tom and Sophia is expressed in the captivity, Blifil's malicious envy in the releasing of the bird. There is truth to feeling in that situation; it is carefully staged, no doubt, but does not seem forced. Yet the subsequent action is quite fortuitous. Tom's actions could not

[1] 'Fielding and the Meaning of History', *PMLA*, Vol. LXXIX, p. 561
[2] *Irony in* Tom Jones, p. 61

have been predicted, for we had not even been told that he was near at hand; the branch need not have broken; there was no reason to expect that the bird would be caught and carried away by 'a nasty Hawk'. The events no longer seem to explain each other. What seemed to have an almost mathematical logic now defies rationalization. Actions cannot be foreseen, nor can their consequences be calculated: Blifil's malice, for instance, is better served by chance than by design. And intention, will, desire, all are overruled by Fortune.

This is one essential meaning of the plot. It is designed to tolerate the random decisions of Fortune. If Fielding has an arbitrary way with the plot this is not in order to square it with some concept of Reason or Nature, the 'one clear, unchang'd and universal light', but to reflect our actual experience. 'I am not writing a System, but a History,' he reminds his readers, 'and I am not obliged to reconcile every Matter to the received Notions concerning Truth and Nature' (XII, viii). And in *The Champion* he argues that the historian especially should be prepared to allow for the effects of chance. 'I have often thought it a Blemish in the works of *Tacitus*, that he ascribes so little to the Interposition of this invincible Being; but, on the contrary, makes the Event of almost every Scheme to depend on a wise Design, and proper Measures taken to accomplish it.' (Dec. 6, 1739.) He goes so far as to assert that wisdom is 'of very little Consequence in the Affairs of this World: Human Life appears to me to resemble the Game of *Hazard*, much more than that of *Chess*; in which latter, among good Players, one false Step must infallibly lose the Game; whereas, in the former, the worst that can happen is to have the odds against you, which are never more than two to one' (ibid.). No doubt this extreme position is offered with due irony. Fielding briskly corrects it in the opening chapter of *Amelia*: men accuse Fortune 'with no less absurdity in life, than a bad player complains of ill luck at the game of chess'. Also, as

Irvin Ehrenpreis observes, Fielding can see a way to resist
Fortune: he 'opposes Christian providence to pagan Fortune. Since it operates by chance, fortune may indeed
advance vice and obstruct virtue. . . . But steady prudent
goodness will attract the blessing of the Lord, and wisdom
is justified of her children.'[1] Yet this is not to argue that
Fielding rejects the role of Fortune, or does not feel its force.
On the contrary, he implies that Fortune is the term we
must use to describe the human condition, the element in
which human qualities are formed and human virtues and
vices operate. This is in fact the source of his moral confidence. *Amelia*, as George Sherburn points out, is intended
to cure the hero of 'psychological flaccidity' and of thinking
that in an often irrational world 'moral energy is futile'.[2]
And *Tom Jones* celebrates 'that solid inward Comfort of
Mind, which is the sure Companion of Innocence and
Virtue' (Dedication), and which will not be at the mercy of
Fortune. A 'sanguine' temper, says Fielding, 'puts us, in
a Manner, out of the Reach of Fortune, and makes us happy
without her Assistance' (XIII, vi).

There are, then, qualities of mind which rise above Fortune; but Fortune is the medium in which they operate.
And, above all, Fortune is the medium of comedy. This,
certainly, is what more than anything makes it tolerable.
But, particularly because it is the source for comic complication, we shall want to see how it opposes the idea of a
benevolently ordered world. Since comedy does in the end
fulfil our expectations, it may after all persuade us that
Fielding is tampering with events and trying to make the
plot act 'as a kind of magnet'. But in fact Fielding creates
his comedy out of the way his characters try to dominate
Fortune and fail. They try to make things turn out as they
want them to, but neither the narrator nor the reader can

[1] *Fielding:* Tom Jones, p. 51
[2] 'Fielding's Social Outlook', *Eighteenth-Century English Literature*, ed.
J. L. Clifford, p. 263

be persuaded that the desired conclusion has been reached by trying. It is itself a gift of Fortune. The beauty of the comedy is not that it establishes a coherent universe, but that for the time being it allows the reader to believe in *good* Fortune.[1]

The basis of the comic action is the 'pursuit motif' which Dorothy Van Ghent has identified with such clarity.[2] It is implicit in the story of Sophia's little bird, and later comes to dominate events. Sophia follows Tom, Squire Western chases Sophia, Tom later pursues Sophia, Fitzpatrick pursues his wife, Allworthy and Blifil follow the Westerns to town, where Blifil will pursue Sophia. In the Upton scenes the theme comes to a climax, in an intricate comic entanglement. And Fielding turns to 'epic' simile to underline what is happening. 'Now the little trembling Hare, whom the Dread of all her numerous Enemies, and chiefly of that cunning, cruel, carnivorous Animal Man, had confined all the Day to her Lurking-place, sports wantonly o'er the Lawns; . . .' (X, ii). The simile of the hunt is used again in Book X, Chapter vi to describe Fitzpatrick's pursuit of his wife: 'Now it happens to this Sort of Men, as to bad Hounds, who never hit off a Fault themselves . . .' And Fielding makes sure that we notice what he is doing: 'Much kinder was she [Fortune] to me, when she suggested that Simile of the Hounds, just before inserted, since the poor Wife may, on these Occasions, be so justly compared to a hunted Hare.' Immediately afterwards, 'as if this had been a real Chace', Squire Western arrives 'hallowing as Hunters do when the Hounds are at a Fault'. Later, Mrs Fitzpatrick uses the image to describe her own situation: she 'wisely considered, that the Virtue of a young Lady is, in the World, in the same Situation with a poor Hare, which is certain, whenever it ventures abroad, to meet its Enemies: For it can hardly meet any other.' (XI, x.) These images bring out

---

[1] Cf. R. S. Crane, 'The Concept of Plot and the Plot of *Tom Jones*', *Critics and Criticism*, pp. 637–8    [2] *The English Novel*, p. 72

H

an element of crudity in the motif: 'we have got the Dog Fox, I warrant the Bitch is not far off' (X, vii). The chases are anything but rational; they are headlong, indiscreet, urged on by primitive instinct. Thus, when Western is easily diverted from one pursuit to another, from the chase of his daughter to the chase of a hare, Fielding quotes the story of the cat who was changed into a woman yet 'leapt from the Bed of her Husband' to chase a mouse. 'What are we to understand by this?' he asks. 'The Truth is, as the sagacious Sir *Roger L'Estrange* observes, in his deep Reflections, that "if we shut Nature out at the Door, she will come in at the Window; and that Puss, tho' a Madam, will be a Mouser still" ' (XII, ii). Dorothy Van Ghent, who notes that 'instinctive drives must . . . be emphasized as an important constituent of "human nature" ', does not in fact observe that Fielding explicitly links them in this way with the theme of pursuit. Her idea is that the book is based on 'a conflict between natural, instinctive feeling, and those appearances with which people disguise, deny, or inhibit natural feeling.'[1] This is not convincing. It seems better to follow Fielding's hints that the action, a series of rash pursuits, shows human behaviour to be irrational, governed chiefly by instinct not reflection, and therefore particularly exposed to Fortune.

These factors in human behaviour are above all what bring about the loosening of the causal chain and frustrate the intentions of the characters. In Book XII, Chapter viii, Fielding acknowledges that it must seem 'hard', indeed 'very absurd and monstrous' that Tom should offend Sophia, not by his actual unfaithfulness but by his supposed 'indelicacy' in cheapening her name. Some, he thinks, will regard 'what happened to *Jones* at *Upton* as a just Punishment for his Wickedness, with regard to Women, of which it was indeed the immediate Consequence'; and others, 'silly and bad Persons', will argue from it that 'the characters of men are

[1] *The English Novel*, p. 68

rather owing to Accident than to Virtue'; but the author himself admits no more than that it confirms the book's 'great, useful and uncommon Doctrine', which, however, 'we must not fill up our Pages by frequently repeating.' He proceeds to show the absurdity of trying to adjust our behaviour to a system of cause and effect. Tom becomes totally unlike himself, no longer a creature of appetite but a romantic lover, as Partridge tells him: 'Certainly, Sir, if ever Man deserved a young Lady, you deserve young Madam *Western*; for what a vast Quantity of Love must a Man have, to be able to live upon it without any other Food, as you do' (XII, xiii). Yet this does not make Tom immune from Fortune; when he reaches Mrs Fitzpatrick's house in London he misses Sophia by ten minutes. 'In short, these kind of hair-breadth Missings of Happiness, look like the Insults of Fortune, who may be considered as thus playing Tricks with us, and wantonly diverting herself at our Expence' (XIII, ii). In the end his romantic persistence leads him to the most discreditable episode of the book: after hanging round Mrs Fitzpatrick's door all day he finally enters her drawing room to meet Lady Bellaston.

Similarly, the dénouement, the solving of all the riddles, is brought about by chance, indeed by mistake. Tom can do nothing to help himself. In the end it is Mrs Waters who is able to explain matters. But she herself is at first ignorant who Tom is. She only discovers that Jones is Bridget Allworthy's child when she is visited by the lawyer Dowling. He in turn has been sent by Blifil to say that she 'should be assisted with any Money [she] wanted to carry on the Prosecution' against Jones. It is his malice, apparently so obstructive, which in spite of his intentions, leads to the ending we desire. Our expectations are realized only by being twice contradicted.

## IV

It is now possible to see why the reading of the plot should be able to sustain a large irony. We shall be tempted into a choice of readings. But, if we think ourselves objective, surveying a complete design which has been distanced by its past tense and assimilated into 'history', we may well find in it a degree of order that Fielding hardly intended. If, on the other hand, Fielding is trying in many ways to undermine our sense of objectivity and privilege, we must find ourselves drawn into the confusion and hazard of the action, aware now of 'history' as a process in which we are involved, moving toward effects we cannot predict: we are not allowed to understand more of the course of events than the characters do. Yet, as we have seen, this kind of involvement is only possible on the first reading. Fielding has written into the narrative an assumption that must be contradicted by subsequent readings. Indeed, one cannot read even once through the book without finding that many passages have come to take on an altered meaning.

Irvin Ehrenpreis sees this as confirming that, like *Oedipus Rex*, the book is essentially a sustained dramatic irony. Behind the many moments of 'discovery', of 'sudden understanding', which he regards as really the action of the book there is, he says, 'the supreme recognition scene disclosing the true parentage of Tom Jones. The opening books of the novel are permeated with ironies that depend on his being Bridget Allworthy's proper heir.' What we admire, what Coleridge must have been praising, is 'the cheerful ease with which Fielding suspends his highest revelation till the end, the outrageous clues with which he dares assault our blindness in the meantime.'[1] This seems to me an important truth about the novel. But it seems also to imply other more complex truths which Mr Ehrenpreis does

[1] *Fielding:* Tom Jones, pp. 23–4

not consider. Apparently Fielding can, even on a second reading, be supposed to be 'suspending' the final revelation; we can be held to retain our 'blindness' in spite of what we have discovered. That is, we have a sense of duality not only in the book itself, but in our own response to it. We recognize our 'blindness' just because we no longer suffer from it. We know and do not know simultaneously: we are both outside and inside the pattern of events. Like Eliot's Tiresias we 'have foresuffered all', yet are still capable of being surprised. If the book has a core of dramatic irony, if is one in which the reader knows himself to be caught, or ot which he knows himself to be the source. He is the observer of his own ironic mistakes. Our responses to the book are, we may say, part of the reason for Fielding's laughter, a laughter in which we share. We are, in short, never quite ignorant nor yet entirely omniscient. In this way the book leads us to one of the most rewarding experiences of comedy: it simultaneously confuses and enlightens, it produces both question and answer, doubt and reassurance.[1] This is a far cry from the imitation of Universal Reason; yet it offers a way out of the confusion of human experience. The book suggests the power of control in the very act of undermining that power; or, from another point of view, can play with the possibilities of confusion because the sense of control is never lost. It can accept the reality of fortune because it has achieved the wisdom that an acceptance of fortune gives.

Chapters vii, viii and ix of Book V are a notable example of this procedure. Allworthy is ill and is not expected to live. This is the situation as the other characters understand it, and Fielding says nothing that would allow us to understand more of it. Our only advantage over them is in our emotional

---

[1] Cf. Ehrenpreis, op. cit., p. 66: 'such surprises combine puzzlement with relief'; and p. 65: 'The same agent seems repeatedly to save us from perils to which he alone has exposed us; we are continually being lost and found by the same guide.'

detachment, as, for instance, when we see them betray their dissatisfaction at Allworthy's legacies. When the attorney from Salisbury arrives we know no more than they do who he is or what news he brings. (In fact we know less than Blifil; like the other characters we also are his dupes.) Fielding gives no sign that there is anything more in the situation; indeed, by depicting at some length the disappointed greed of Allworthy's dependants he implies that the scene can only carry this limited and obvious irony. Yet when we have read the rest of the novel we know that there is much more to be seen. For instance, we know already that Allworthy's illness will not be fatal; this, in fact is what keeps the scene within the limits of comic decorum. This is what enables R. S. Crane to say that as the novel progresses things become both more and more, and less and less serious, that it offers a 'comic analogue of fear'.[1] Also we know, what Fielding apparently thought we should not know, that the attorney is the lawyer Dowling and that he brings Bridget Allworthy's own dying words, 'Tell my Brother, Mr. *Jones* is his Nephew—He is my Son.—Bless him', words that are not recorded in the novel until Book XVIII, Chapter viii. Thus the scene at Allworthy's deathbed is superimposed on the silent, unacknowledged presence of that other death-bed. Fielding deliberately chose *not* to present this as a dramatic irony. The scene as he renders it takes all its significance from information he has denied us, from knowledge we import into the scene, as it were without his consent. The words that are not spoken reverberate thus throughout the novel. But, as they have *not* been spoken, their sound is produced in one part of the reader's mind whilst he is deaf to it with the other. In fact, as Ehrenpreis shows, what is at the centre of his attention is the *fact* of their not being spoken, the audacity with which Fielding so nearly gives away the riddle of the book. We admire his

[1] 'The Concept of Plot and the Plot of *Tom Jones*', *Critics and Criticism*, pp. 635–6

skill in keeping it dark, but could not do so if we did not at the same time know what it was.

In another way, however, our dual vision of things actually seems to undermine our confidence in the narrator. Since we are left to supply information necessary to the full understanding of a scene, we fancy ourselves better informed than the narrator himself. Often enough, indeed, the narrator professes his inadequacy: 'the Fact is true; and, perhaps, may be sufficiently accounted for by suggesting . . .' (V, x). But this, as Eleanor Hutchens shows,[1] is an ironic trick designed to make us attend in exactly the way the author desires. There is, however, a much more pervasive sense that the narrator cannot (or does not) reveal many things that the reader nevertheless is aware of. Of course the reader is aware of them only because he at last appreciates the design the author has had in mind from the beginning. But since the author does not actually write such things into the text of the novel, since he leaves the reader to supply them silently, he gives the impression that in some important ways the novel has written itself.

In the scenes we have been discussing, Fielding observes that Blifil is offended at Tom's riotous behaviour so soon after Allworthy's illness and Bridget's death. There is no mistaking Blifil's real feelings and motives; '. . . Mr. *Blifil* was highly offended at a Behaviour which was so inconsistent with the sober and prudent Reserve of his own Temper.' Yet, however little sympathy we feel for Blifil, we sense that there is some justice in his attitude: 'He bore it too with the greater Impatience, as it appeared to him very indecent at this Season; "When", as he said, "the House was a House of Mourning, on the Account of his dear Mother." ' Jones's ready sympathy and remorse reflect our own response: 'he offered to shake Mr. *Blifil* by the Hand, and begged his Pardon, saying "His excessive Joy for Mr. *Allworthy*'s Recovery had driven every other

[1] *Irony in* Tom Jones, p. 56

Thought out of his Mind." ' Yet, after all, this does not shake our conviction that Bliful is hateful: he soon reverts to the behaviour we expect of him: 'Blifil scornfully rejected his Hand; and, with much Indignation, answered, "It was little to be wondered at, if tragical Spectacles made no Impression on the Blind; but, for his Part, he had the Misfortune to know who his Parents were, and consequently must be affected with their Loss" ' (V, ix). These are the terms in which the narrator has constructed the episode. This must be our reading of it as it stands. Yet that is not the way in which we do read it. When Blifil speaks of his mother's death we know that he knows that she is also Tom's mother. Tom's generous sympathy, then, far from helping to justify Blifil, actually heightens our sense of outrage. And Blifil's response, no longer just a gratuitous and insulting sneer at Tom's illegitimacy, becomes a piercing revelation of his utter inhumanity. Not only can he allow Tom to remain ignorant that his mother has just died, he can actually, with staggering impudence, make his words a concealed taunt. He finds it possible to use his knowledge for a cruel secret game: 'he had the Misfortune to know who his Parents were, and consequently must be affected with their Loss.'

There are, then, areas of meaning which the narrator does not even mention. But his reticence does not prevent us becoming conscious of them. Thus the book begins to escape from the narrow designs imposed on it, from the conscious intention of the narrator. After all it does seem to acquire something of the 'full sense of actual life'. Fielding is not always obtrusive; in fact, it is at this deep level, where the authenticity of the book is most in question, that he is least in evidence. We noted that in those instances where he pushed himself forward he was wanting the reader to look elsewhere for the real intention. But though the text is centred on the unpredictable, on the random behaviour of Fortune, the full scope of the novel is to be

measured in the dual meaning of the plot. The author leaves
the book to itself, or rather, to the reader. In other words,
Fielding has been able, by means of the plot, to create a
reader wise enough to create the book he reads.

CHAPTER 6

# Tom Jones *(ii)*:
## *The 'Pursuit of True Judgment'*

### I

THE PLOT of *Tom Jones*, then, may be best understood
in terms of the way it is read. Its structure is the
structure of successive responses to the novel. It
exists in the reader's attention rather than in the written
sequences. This means that its effect is epistemological
rather than moral. It helps us to see how we acquire our
knowledge of human experience; it is a clarification of the
processes of understanding. It presents life as a fortuitous
sequence of events, as the play of Fortune, and traces the
ways in which we come to see these events as a pattern. This
certainly does not in any direct way establish a moral sense
in the novel. Take, for instance, Tom's affair with Molly
Seagrim. His remorse, prompting him to make amends to
her, leads him to find her in bed with Square and then to
discover that she had been first seduced by Will Barnes. His
generous impulse leads to the knowledge that will release
him: '*Jones* was become perfectly easy by Possession of this
Secret with regard to *Molly*' (V, vi). But this is luck, not
morality. His remorse pays dividends, but not because it *is*
remorse. To centre the plot on Fortune is to lift the moral
burden from the behaviour of the characters, with the
unexpected effect at times of sharpening their conscience.
At the point when Tom is least to blame he reproaches
himself most bitterly. Hearing of his supposed incest he

first exclaims against Fortune and then blames himself:
' "Fortune will never have done with me, 'till she hath
driven me to Distraction. But why do I blame Fortune? I am
myself the Cause of all my Misery. All the dreadful Mischiefs which have befallen me, are the Consequences only of
my own Folly and Vice" ' (XVIII, ii). This is absurd. Yet
there is a truth in it: he *is* responsible in an essential way.
But this moral discovery cannot be made through the plot
as such.

It is natural to assume that what the plot cannot do will
have to be done by the author's explicit comments. Thus
Ian Watt holds that Fielding's technique was 'deficient at
least in the sense that it was unable to convey this larger
moral significance through character and action alone' that
*Tom Jones* 'is only part novel'.[1] This kind of distinction
between 'showing' and 'telling' has, at least since the
publication of *The Rhetoric of Fiction*, come to seem much less
secure. But it is as well to note that in Fielding's time it
would have been widely accepted. It was in fact confirmed
by just that epic theory that Fielding appealed to. Le Bossu
himself, the approved interpreter of Aristotle,[2] takes up the
assertion that the poet who speaks in his own person is no
imitator: he should seek for 'une manière de rendre la
Narration agissante'.[3] The orator, but not the poet, may
enter into a direct relation with his audience. What makes
the narrative convincing in an epic poem is the 'rapport que
le Poète met entre ses Auditeurs et ses Personnages'.[4] Thus,
as Shaftesbury notes in his 'Advice to an Author', the
advantages of the Platonic Dialogue are that 'the author is
annihilated, and the reader, being no way applied to, stands
for nobody. . . . You are not only left to judge coolly and
with indifference of the sense delivered, but of the character,

---

[1] *The Rise of the Novel*, p. 287
[2] See Ethel M. Thornbury, *Henry Fielding's Theory of the Comic Prose
Epic*, pp. 56 ff.
[3] *Traité du Poëme Epique*, p. 239      [4] Ibid., p. 207

genius, elocution, and manner of the persons who deliver it.' But this unhappily is not the way of the modern writer: 'he suits himself on every occasion to the fancy of his reader, whom, as the fashion is nowadays, he constantly caresses and cajoles.' This is 'the coquetry of a modern author . . . to draw attention from the subject, towards himself.'[1]

In this light Fielding's narrative looks like a planned flouting of decorum; he aligns himself with the vain, egotistical 'modern' author, in the manner of Swift, but with a more subtle ironic intention. Swift apes the bad writer in order to demolish him; Fielding chooses 'bad' art in order to unseat the bad reader. Whilst appearing to ingratiate himself in the 'modern' manner, he is actually trying to school the reader, to induce him to attend more closely and to judge well. Fielding is very far from being defeated by his medium. Rather he employs his narrative method with calculated effect, as a means to draw the reader into the action of the book and so clarify its meaning. His method is, in fact, as William J. Farrell has shown, the proper method for a 'history'.[2] We have seen how Fielding presents the shape of history as a dilemma for the reader; it is important to recognize that conventionally the historian's mode of address also expects the reader's participation. 'The narrator-to-audience observations,' writes Mr Farrell, 'invariably bring into the work a fairly well-defined character called "the reader".'[3] In Fielding's novels, of course, the device is used not to authenticate 'historical' truth but to enforce 'the believability of [the] narrator through whom the reader sees the entire action'.[4] Certainly the rhetorical basis of the novels needs this kind of support; in so far as Fielding successfully projects the persona of his narrator we shall be prepared to accept that 'telling' is after all a kind of 'showing'. But an equally important use for the device is to

---

[1] *Characteristics*, i, 131
[2] 'Fielding's Familiar Style', *ELH*, Vol. 34, No. 1, March 1967, p. 65
[3] Ibid., p. 73        [4] Ibid., p. 76

make the reader's role clear. The reader has his responsibility also: he must try to judge well. To encourage him to
do so is itself a part of the subject of the book. That is, the
book is *about* judgment, and the understanding necessary
for good judgment. This is where the moral sense is
located, in the analysis and evaluation of diverse judgments.
It is epistemological in this way also. It focuses attention,
not only on events, but on the mind which perceives and
judges them. Fielding is quite aware that his fiction has the
same aims as Locke's *Essay*. In one of the *Champion* papers
he quotes from Locke's opening chapter: '*The Understanding, like the Eye* (says Mr. *Lock*), *whilst it makes us see
and perceive all other things, takes no Notice of itself; and it
requires Art and Pains to set it at a Distance and make it its
own Object*' (March 1, 1739–40). But, Fielding continues,
the analogy is not perfect, 'for the Eye can contemplate
itself in a Glass, but no *Narcissus* hath hitherto discovered
any Mirrour for the Understanding,' and self-knowledge
may too easily slide into 'self love'. To provide such a
mirror, to guard against such error is the purpose of *Tom
Jones*. To effect it Fielding must establish his relationship
with the reader.

## II

In his first chapter he shows what this is to be. 'On the
image which Fielding produces just here,' says Andrew
Wright of the offered 'bill of fare', 'the meaning of the novel
depends.'[1] This is true, but not, I think, in the way he
explains it, as an invitation 'to take *Tom Jones* in a festive
spirit'. We know Fielding's opinion of innkeepers and are
hardly surprised that when he poses as one his invitation
lacks cordiality.[2] Like 'one who keeps a public Ordinary,
at which all Persons are welcome for their Money', he is

---

[1] *Henry Fielding, Mask and Feast*, p. 32

quite prepared to find that the critical reader will be ill-mannered. 'Men who pay for what they eat, will insist on gratifying their Palates, however nice and even whimsical these may prove; and if every Thing is not agreeable to their Taste, will challenge a Right to censure, to abuse, and to d——n their Dinner without Controul' (I, i). This is why he publishes his bill of fare: prospective customers may decide either to stay or 'depart to some other Ordinary better accommodated to their Taste'. This is explicitly not an 'eleemosynary Treat'.[1] Fielding thus establishes mutual rights of criticism: if my reader is to be allowed freedom of censure, I must be permitted to make fun of him; in this way we may come to respect each other. Empson, taking his cue from Fielding's work as magistrate rather than his role in the book, puts the matter admirably:

> . . . the unusual thing about Fielding as a novelist is that he is always ready to consider what he would do if one of his characters came before him when he was on the bench. . . . As to the reader of a novel, Fielding cannot be bothered with him unless he too is fit to sit on a magistrate's bench, prepared, in literature as in life, to handle and judge any situation. That is why the reader gets teased so frankly.[2]

Actually Fielding's way of envisaging this relationship has less to do with inns and law-courts than with the theatre, and especially with the audience. The usual analogy between the world and the stage is not enough for him: 'None, as I remember, have at all considered the Audience at this

---

[1] Perhaps Fielding is echoing Burton: '——*ut palata, sic judicia*, our censures are as various as our palats. . . Our writings are as so many Dishes, our Readers Guests. . . . What shall I doe in this case? As a Dutch host, if you come to an Inne in *Germany*, & dislike your fare, diet, lodging, &c. replies in a surly tone, *aliud tibi quæras diversorium*, if you like not this, get you to another Inne: I resolue, if you like not my writing, goe read something else.' *The Anatomy of Melancholy*, pp. 9–10

[2] '*Tom Jones*', *The Kenyon Review*, xx (1958), p. 249

great Drama' (VII, i). He imagines the reactions of the
world's upper-gallery, pit and boxes to the scene in which
Black George steals Tom's £500. Some are abusive, some
offended, some tolerant and others 'refused to give their
Opinion 'till they had heard that of the best Judges. . . . As
for the Boxes, . . . most of them were attending to something else' (VII, i). He is interested more in the audience
than the play, as we see also from several other passages in
the novel. Partridge, for instance, is seen in the gallery at
a performance of *Hamlet*. '*Jones* . . . expected to enjoy much
Entertainment in the Criticisms of *Partridge*' (XVI, 5). On
another occasion Fielding inserts the story of the murderer
of Mr Derby, one Fisher, who also went to see *Hamlet*, 'and
with an unaltered Countenance heard one of the Ladies,
who little suspected how near she was to the Person, cry out,
"Good God! if the Man that murdered Mr. *Derby* was now
present!" Manifesting in this a more seared and callous
Conscience than even *Nero* himself' (VIII, i).

This manœuvre, in which the audience becomes the
centre of interest, exposed to the author's criticism as he
was to theirs, is brilliantly illustrated by Hogarth's etching
'The Laughing Audience'. The ten laughing people are
rendered with a touch both subtle and vigorous, both sym-
pathetic and caustic. There is an infectious gaiety in their
laughter and at the same time a delicate observation of their
different temperaments. We feel a harshness in the drawing
and yet a pleasure in the simplicity and naturalness depicted.
The one 'critic' among them, who is not watching the stage
and sits in contemptuous isolation, is made to seem absurdly
out of place. In the boxes and unobserved by anyone in the
picture there is a scene of foppish affectation and gallantry,
theatrical in appearance and more amusing, Hogarth
implies, than anything the audience could be laughing at.
Who is laughing at whom? This brilliant and complex
design, cutting across the usual distinctions between subject
and object, observer and observed, is an exact parallel to

Fielding's procedure in *Tom Jones*. For he is not, as Andrew
Wright suggests, drawing attention primarily to the artificiality of life, trying to make us see it as a play. On the
contrary, as Partridge's naïveté reminds us, the best acting is
that which most resembles life. And the consummate
'actor' who appears in the very next chapter is Blifil, the
hypocrite. No, if Fielding is watchful of his readers, interested in the way they take his story, this is because their
judgment is in the long run part of that story.

But Fielding is not content merely to observe his audience; he wants to teach them. He looks for intelligent
readers. We have already seen his attitude to the ill-natured
critic. It remains constant throughout the book: 'I must
desire all those Critics to mind their own business . . .' (I,
ii); 'a little Reptile of a Critic' (X, i); 'if we judge according
to the Sentiments of some Critics, and of some Christians,
no Author will be saved in this World, and no Man in the
next' (XI, i). Why does Fielding adopt this petulant tone?
It looks as if he is trying to keep up the role of the bad
writer to whom all critics are a nuisance. But there is a better
use for it. The critic's 'hungry Appetite for Censure' (XVI,
i) is an extreme example of 'judgment' in the wrong sense,
'in which it is frequently used as equivalent to Condemnation' (XI, i). This applies in life as well as literature: the
critic is a type of the 'common Slanderer, . . . a Person who
prys into the Characters of others, with no other Design
but to discover their Faults, and to publish them to the
World' (XI, i). He means to remind us of Blifil of course;
but the remarks are actually referred to our own response
as readers. He is expecting the reader to know how to judge
with generosity, in T. S. Eliot's words to 'compose his
differences with as many of his fellows as possible, in the
common pursuit of true judgment'.[1] 'All Beauty of Character, as well as of Countenance, and indeed of every Thing
human, is to be tried in this Manner' (XI, i). This sounds

[1] T. S. Eliot, 'The Function of Criticism', *Selected Essays*, p. 25

very generalized; but we have seen how it grows out of an imagined situation, out of what Wayne Booth calls 'the "plot" of our relationship with Fielding-as-narrator'.[1] To make us serve his purpose Fielding appropriates us to the world of his fiction.

# III

He also reverses the process and contrives in many ways to suggest that his fictional world is available to us in reality. We could follow Tom's route and, in that case, Fielding would recommend us to stay at the Bell, Gloucester, 'an excellent House indeed' (VIII, viii). And we may, says Fielding, 'have the Pleasure of riding in the very Coach, and being driven by the very Coachman, that is recorded in this History' (X, vi). He always writes as if we were present at the events narrated: 'the reader will, I believe, bear Witness for him' (II, iv); 'I question not but the Surprize of the Reader will be here equal to that of *Jones*' (V, v); 'Reader, if thou hast any good Wishes towards me, I will fully repay them, by wishing thee to be possessed of this Sanguine Disposition of Mind (i.e. like Tom's), . . . which puts us, in a Manner, out of the Reach of Fortune' (XIII, vi.) We are not insulated. We are not only to watch, it seems, but to be subjected to the same hazards as the characters themselves. Fielding does not set us apart from them; indeed *they* are often made to seem more like audience than actors. Some, like Square and Thwackum, are created just to be observers, to offer opinions. And the design of the story gives equal weight to action and to the discussion it provokes. A transparent example of this is in Book IV, Chapter iv when the episode of Sophia's little bird is debated by Square, Thwackum, Western, Allworthy and a 'Gentleman of the Law, who was present'. But hardly anything happens

[1] *The Rhetoric of Fiction*, p. 216

in the novel that does not create its ripples of comment, discussion and conflicting judgments. The reader and even the narrator are, in these situations, on an equal footing with the actors. In other words the story, as distinct from the plot, is really a system of stories within stories, like the house that Jack built. Thus the tale told by the Man of the Hill, often thought to be digressive and disruptive, is actually firmly embedded in the whole design. And, as if to emphasize this, Fielding arranges it in symmetry with the parallel story told by Mrs Fitzpatrick to Sophia.

Reactions to an event are themselves events. In the same way some of the most important acts in the novel are acts of judgment. We discover and express ourselves in judging others; our moral existence consists in our ability to form moral judgments. Hence the importance of that chapter (VII, i) in which we have seen 'the great audience's' reactions to Black George's theft. For Fielding there goes further than Hogarth, who merely shows the audience its own image. He uses the analogy to discover something about the nature of moral judgments. This audience's opinions are worthless. Theirs is the judgment of the 'mob' (i.e. 'persons without Virtue, or Sense, in all Stations, I, ix). They judge superficially and casually, that is on the isolated scene enacted before them. This is why we must go 'behind the Scenes of this great Theatre of Nature' where we shall learn the true character of a man. 'A single bad Act no more constitutes a Villain in Life, than a single bad Part on the Stage.' This is often taken to mean that we may overlook faults where virtues predominate. But this is certainly not what Fielding intends:

> Indeed, nothing can be of more moral Use than the Imperfections which are seen in Examples of this Kind; since such form a Kind of Surprize, more apt to affect and dwell upon our Minds, than the Faults of very vicious and wicked Persons . . . when we find such Vices attended with their evil Consequence to our favourite Characters, we are not only taught to shun them for our

own Sake, but to hate them for the Mischiefs they have already brought on those we love (**X**, i).

So Tom has in the end to face himself. Sophia insists on this, and her insistence has more moral rigour than Allworthy's balancing of 'his Faults with his Perfections' (IV, xi). ' "I think, Mr. *Jones*," said she, "I may almost depend on your own Justice, and leave it to yourself to pass Sentence on your own Conduct" ' (XVIII, xii). One must be harsh with oneself, charitable and compassionate to others. Faults will not go undetected but 'will raise our Compassion rather than our Abhorrence' (X, i); and, Fielding concludes, having been permitted to look behind the scenes 'the man of Candour and of true Understanding is never hasty to condemn. . . . The worst of Men generally have the Words *Rogue* and *Villain* in their Mouths' (VII, i).

## IV

The book, then, is not concerned with judgments made in detachment and isolation. Shaftesbury's ideal reader, judging 'coolly and with indifference', will, Fielding implies, only be sinking deeper into his own illusions. For if our judgments are an expression of our own moral identity, they are also an expression of community, of our attitude to others. Any flaw in this feeling for others will imply a flaw in our own being. This is, of course, nominally Shaftesbury's argument also: 'That to have the natural, kindly, or generous affections strong and powerful towards the good of the public, is to have the chief means and power of self-enjoyment, . . . to want them is certain misery and ill'.[1] Thus Shaftesbury bids 'self-love and social be the same'. What he does not allow for is the difficulty, the stress of living up to these principles. Fielding has to test Shaftesbury's ideals in the thick of life. He puts the matter with a quite different

[1] *Characteristics*, i, 292

emphasis: '[Tom] was never an indifferent Spectator of the Misery or Happiness of any one; and he felt either the one or the other in greater Proportion as he himself contributed to either' (XV, viii).

Initially, to be sure, Fielding seems to align himself more closely with Shaftesbury. His book, a tribute to Lyttleton and Ralph Allen (the model for his 'Picture of a truly benevolent Mind', [Dedication]), is also a kind of tribute to Shaftesbury, whose image of the Deity has many of the features we discern in Allworthy: '. . . a Deity who is considered as worthy and good, and admired and reverenced as such, . . . In such a presence, 'tis evident that as the shame of guilty actions must be the greatest of any, so must the honour be of well-doing, even under the unjust censure of a world'.[1] But Fielding cannot sustain such confidence, as we may gather from his scepticism about the Gipsy King's benevolent despotism. As he says, it has the one defect that it is difficult to find 'any Man adequate to the Office of an absolute Monarch' (XII, xii). From the start, therefore, there is something unreal about Allworthy: 'a human Being replete with Benevolence, meditating in what Manner he might render himself most acceptable to his Creator, by doing most Good to his Creatures' (I, iv). We can hardly credit that this could be meant seriously, and Fielding does in fact give it an ironic twist: 'Reader, take Care, I have unadvisedly led thee to the Top of as high a Hill as Mr. *Allworthy*'s, and how to get thee down without breaking thy Neck, I do not well know. However, let us e'en venture to slide down together' (I, iv).

Allworthy has always seemed one of the puzzles of the book. Henry James Pye, writing in 1792, notes him as 'a character at opposition with himself, though more perhaps in general with that which the author tells you in his own person he is, than with his own conduct in those parts where the author suffers him to act from himself.' The trouble, as

[1] Op. cit., i, 268

Pye sees it, is that Allworthy, offered as 'a man of sense and discernment, with a benevolence almost angelic', is actually 'the dupe of every insinuating rascal he meets; and a dupe not of the most amiable kind, since he is always led to acts of justice and severity. The consequence of his pliability is oftener the punishment of the innocent than the acquittal of the guilty; and in such punishment he is severe and implacable.'[1] Andrew Wright sees more clearly that he could never have been intended as the 'moral centre' of the book[2] but errs, I think, in claiming that the existence in the novel of Western is 'the strongest of all reasons' for thinking so. No doubt Western is 'full of vitality, [and] also playful', but we need not conclude that either Fielding or the reader finds this combination of qualities 'irresistible'. There is surely some severity in Fielding's comment that 'Men over-violent in their Dispositions, are, for the most Part, as changeable in them' (XVIII, ix). Western is erratic, undependable and tyrannical. A full view of him must include the harsh ironies of Book VII, Chapter iv, in which his love for Sophia is measured against his hatred of his neglected and abused wife. Yet, it appears, Allworthy's detachment and impartiality are not in themselves a protection against profound error. One important way of establishing this is by comparison, not with Western or another character, but with the reader himself.

In Book IV, Chapter xi Allworthy is at first represented as somewhat arbitrary and harsh in his treatment of Molly Seagrim: 'I question, as here was no regular Information before him, whether his Conduct was strictly regular'. When Tom pleads for the girl, Allworthy's moral indignation is deflected ('I own, indeed, [the guilt] doth lie principally upon you, and so heavy it is, that you ought to expect it should crush you'). Allworthy fails to see how this rebuke

---

[1] *A Commentary Illustrating the Poetic of Aristotle* (London, 1792), reprinted in *Aristotle's Poetics and English Literature*, ed. E. Olson, pp. 39–40
[2] Op. cit., pp. 159–62

reflects on his judgment of Molly: should he not from the beginning have directed his anger against the principal offender? Fielding has insinuated, in any case, that the house of correction is an ineffectual punishment. And when he seems to wish to salvage Allworthy's reputation for impartiality it is with a curious effect: 'he was not so blinded by [the offence], but that he could discern any Virtue in the guilty Person, as clearly, indeed as if there had been no Mixture of Vice in the same Character'. This, Fielding asserts, indicates that he has come to 'the same Opinion of this young Fellow which, we hope, our Reader may have conceived'. But he has not in fact been encouraging us to estimate Tom in terms of this kind of 'moral arithmetic'. And its inadequacy emerges as soon as it is challenged. Thwackum, admittedly, cannot sway Allworthy. But Square, 'a much more artful Man', has no difficulty at all in persuading him that Tom's generosity is the mark of 'a depraved and debauched Appetite': 'he supported the Father, in order to corrupt the Daughter, and preserved the Family from starving, to bring one of them to Shame and Ruin'. To Allworthy these 'considerations' (not, we note, new evidence but a new interpretation of the evidence) are 'too plausible to be absolutely and hastily rejected' and stamp in his mind 'the first bad Impression concerning *Jones*'. His judgment throughout the episode is as wrong as it can be. If the arguments advanced by Square have any force, Allworthy should himself have reckoned with them in reaching his first judgment; if they do not, he should not have been affected by them. But his moral failure here is made more glaring by contrast with the kind of judgment Fielding expects from the reader. Before Square states his case, the reader is given the same evidence as Allworthy himself is given. 'The Reader must remember the several little Incidents of the Partridge, the Horse, and the Bible, which were recounted in the second Book.' They had first enlisted Allworthy's approval. 'The same, I believe, must have happened to him with every other Person who hath any Idea of Friendship, Generosity, and Greatness of Spirit; that is to say, who hath any Trace of Goodness in his Mind.' The reader will not easily forfeit his claim to such qualities, and Square's speech need not persuade him to do so. But Allworthy, by contrast, is blinded and confused; his very judiciousness saps his power to judge aright.

Furthermore, Allworthy's detachment and impartiality, fallible enough in themselves, all too often forsake him altogether. When he banishes Tom, for instance, we find him unexpectedly egocentric: it becomes obvious to the reader that what most sways him is Tom's supposed disrespect towards him. As this is just what he cannot admit openly, his censure of Tom looks motiveless: 'nay, indeed, (Tom) hardly knew his Accusation: for as Mr. *Allworthy*, in recounting the Drunkenness, *&c.* while he lay ill, out of Modesty sunk every Thing that related particularly to himself, which indeed principally constituted the Crime, *Jones* could not deny the Charge' (VI, xi). In fact his judgments are almost always prejudiced: 'the poor Game-keeper was condemned, without having any Opportunity to defend himself' (III, x); Molly was to be committed to Bridewell without a hearing; the evidence that Jenny might have given in support of Partridge 'would have deserved no Credit', and, when he continues to protest his innocence, 'Mr. *Allworthy* declared himself satisfied of his Guilt, and that he was too bad a Man to receive any Encouragement from him' (II, vi). Allworthy is quick to blame, more aware of guilt than innocence. Mrs Miller finds in Tom 'one of the most humane tender honest Hearts that ever Man was blessed with', though he is marred by 'Faults of Wildness and of Youth' (XVII, ii). Allworthy maintains rather that there are 'few Characters so absolutely vicious as not to have the least Mixture of Good in them' (XVII, vii). He is, accordingly, slow to see through Blifil, though quick to dismiss Tom.

Allworthy *should* have seen through Blifil. As Fielding says in his 'Essay on the Knowledge of the Characters of Men', 'the truth is, nature doth really imprint sufficient marks in the countenance, to inform an accurate and discerning eye' (*Works*, viii, p. 166). And in fact Mrs Miller's simplicity is more penetrating than Allworthy's deliberate and patient judgment: ' "Guilty!" ', she exclaims, on seeing the change in Blifil's face, ' "Guilty, upon my Honour! Guilty, upon my Soul!" ' (XVIII, v). With this in mind it is difficult not to suspect Fielding of irony when he appears to be defending Allworthy against possible criticism: 'Of readers who . . . condemn the Wisdom or Penetration of Mr. *Allworthy*, I shall not scruple to say, that they make a very bad and ungrateful Use of that Knowledge which we have communicated to them' (III, v). Must we take this to mean that there are no grounds for condemning Allworthy's judgments? Surely it is intended rather as a sharp reminder that but for Fielding's help we would fare no better ourselves. If Allworthy fails, his failure reflects no credit on us. It should in fact engage our admiration. There is something heroic in Allworthy. If Tom is the comic hero, always acting and always in the dark, Allworthy, never allowed to withhold judgment or to be less than his best, is the book's most admired yet poignant figure, its tragic hero in fact. It is through his high-minded failures that we gain some of our clearest impressions of the difficulty of judging well. Yet, in our respect for the stubborn excellence of Allworthy, we are not to reconcile ourselves to judging like him. We are expected to go 'behind the scenes', to do in fact what the author has been doing for us. There is no credit in ignorance.

## V

Not that Fielding simply recommends 'penetration' and keen discernment. Indeed it is obvious he likes the opposite qualities—the credulity of Mrs Miller, or the simplicity of Sophia. Mrs Western's penetration on the other hand, or the 'sagacity' of the reader, or the innkeeper who thought that Sophia was Jenny Cameron, are comical. Yet, as he argues elsewhere, 'Good-nature requires a distinguishing Faculty, which is another Word for Judgment, and is perhaps the sole Boundary between Wisdom and Folly; it is impossible for a Fool, who hath no distinguishing Faculty to be good-natured' (*The Champion*, March 27, 1740). Simplicity is not good-natured (and here we recall Partridge) unless it is combined with keen penetration. But, as we have seen, penetration is often a kind of blindness and folly. We can perhaps resolve the dilemma by recalling the distinction Fielding makes between the two degrees of suspicion. One, arising from the heart, imagines evil where none exists; the other, arising from the head, the understanding, is 'no other than the Faculty of seeing what is before your Eyes, and of drawing Conclusions from what you see' (XI, x). Whilst this is a way of detecting guilt, the former can only harm the innocent. But again this is a rather mechanical formula. To see a more vital connection between good nature and understanding, simplicity and discernment, we must turn to Tom.

Tom's good nature is described in terms which ought to apply to Allworthy; the moral principle which governs his conduct is a judicial one, 'like the LORD HIGH CHANCELLOR of this Kingdom in his Court; where it presides, governs, directs, judges, acquits, and condemns according to Merit and Justice; with a Knowledge which nothing escapes, a Penetration which nothing can deceive, and an Integrity which nothing can corrupt' (IV, vi). And this is an 'active Principle', not arbitrating in remote detachment, not content 'with Knowledge or Belief only', but prompting good actions and restraining from bad. Here, surely, is the hub of the book's meaning. All that Fielding has to show of the nature of judgment centres here, in these rare moral qualities. They place before us, as a constant point of reference in the book, the high ideal which, in Butler's sermons, is called conscience.

> But there is a superior principle of reflection or conscience in every man, which distinguishes between the internal principles of his heart, as well as his external actions: which passes judgment upon himself and them; . . . which, without being consulted, without being advised with, magisterially exerts itself, and approves or condemns him the doer of them accordingly: . . . It is by this faculty, natural to man, that he is a moral agent, that he is a law to himself.[1]

Thus our approval of Tom is meant to lead us to challenging moral issues. There is much more to him than a good heart and a healthy appetite. What we are to appreciate in his nature is something like the discernment and judgment we ourselves are expected to display in our reading of the novel. The book, by making us conscious of ourselves as readers, by exercising our critical faculties, is contributing no less than Butler himself to a philosophical process. Indeed the terms in which the eighteenth century derived its ethical principles, from the earlier reactions to Hobbes,[2] are strikingly relevant to the novel. Thus Richard Cumberland in 1672, in the act of refuting Hobbes, anticipates many of Fielding's remarks:

> Shall I not reckon among the perfections of the human understanding, that it can *reflect* upon it self? *Consider* its habits, as dispositions arising from past actions? *Remember* and *recollect* its own dictates, and compare them with its actions? *Judge* which way the mind inclines? And *direct* it self to the pursuit of what seems fittest to be done? Our mind is conscious to it self of all its own actions, and both can, and often does, observe what counsels produced them; it naturally sits a *judge* upon its own actions,

[1] *Works*, ii, 59
[2] See B. H. Baumrin, the New Introduction to Selby-Bigge, *British Moralists* (New York, 1964), pp. x et seq.

and thence procures to it self either *tranquillity* and joy, or *anxiety* and sorrow. In this power of the mind, and the actions thence arising, consists the whole force of *conscience*, by which it *proposes* laws to it self, *examines* its past, and *regulates* its future conduct.[1]

Here, as Baumrin points out, we find the 'terms and ideas which will become part of the conceptual hardware of rationalism';[2] Fielding not only shows himself familiar with them, he takes full possession of them in the imaginative world of his novel. And the reader, whose role in that world is so important, is in a position to possess them in the same way.

It may seem, in fact, that it is only in this way and not through the rendering of character and behaviour that such a meaning is established. Though Tom's moral sense certainly becomes more urgent as the story unfolds, yet his conduct with Lady Bellaston, for instance, calls for more self-reproach than he can command, and its moral implications remain unresolved. Yet Fielding does drive the narrative to a conclusion where Tom comes face to face with conscience. However lightly, Fielding at last indicates that the book has a religious dimension. Sophia demands of Tom this kind of awareness: ' "Sincere Repentance, Mr. *Jones*," answered she, "will obtain the Pardon of a Sinner, but it is from one who is a perfect Judge of that Sincerity" ' (XVIII, xii). After what we have seen of Fielding's sustained attention to the question of judgment, this ultimate appeal does not seem forced. It provides a way of estimating Allworthy's Shaftesburyan benevolence, and it anchors Tom's conduct firmly to the tougher principles of conscience: 'conscience naturally and always of course goes on to anticipate a higher and more effectual sentence, which shall hereafter second and affirm its own'.[3]

---

[1] *De Legibus Naturae* (1672), Ch. 2, Section 12, cited in Selby-Bigge, *British Moralists*, p. xxiii

[2] Ibid., p. xxiv

[3] Butler, op. cit., ii, 59

Yet after all it is by no means because he is morally impeccable that Tom is to be set against Allworthy. Fielding needs someone who can do wrong in order to bring out the hollowness of Allworthy's rectitude. A man who cannot act badly has no business to be judging others. It is in fact Tom, his own affairs tangled and squalid, who is able to persuade Nightingale to do what is right. It seems absurd that he should now 'preach', just as earlier Allworthy had read him 'a very severe Lecture on Chastity'. Nightingale is ready to scoff: 'Thou wilt make an admirable Parson' (XIV, iv). But it is because Tom is what he is that he can reply with authority and force: ' "Lookee, Mr. *Nightingale*," said *Jones*, "I am no canting Hypocrite, nor do I pretend to the Gift of Chastity, more than my Neighbours. I have been guilty with Women, I own it; but am not conscious that I have ever injured any—nor would I, to procure Pleasure to myself, be knowingly the Cause of Misery to any human Being." ' Not even, we are sure, to procure the pleasure of being in the right.

'Judge not, that ye be not judged': the injunction is often in Fielding's mind. *Tom Jones* shows, though, that we cannot choose not to judge. Nor can we avoid being judged, however 'prudent' our lives. But we can and should learn to judge with knowledge, that is with full experience and full sympathy; above all we have to learn how to forgive. The last thing to learn is that all this is part of a great comedy: if Fielding anywhere sets out his intentions in the book it is in his invocation to his genius, the genius of comedy:

> Teach me, which to thee is no difficult Task, to know Mankind better than they know themselves. Remove that Mist which dims the Intellects of Mortals, and causes them to adore Men for their Art, or to detest them for their Cunning in deceiving others, when they are, in Reality, the Objects only of Ridicule, for deceiving themselves. . . . fill my Pages with Humour; 'till Mankind learn the Good-Nature to laugh only at the Follies of others, and the Humility to grieve at their own. (XIII, i)

# CHAPTER 7

# Tristram Shandy *(i)*:
# *The Reader as Author*

## I

STERNE'S genius was for story-telling. He was a preacher, he knew the value of a story. In his sermon on the prodigal son he observed that 'lessons of wisdom have never such power over us, as when they are wrought into the heart, through the ground-work of a story which engages the passions'.[1] And another sermon concerns the way a story may penetrate the listener's self-approval; it is preached on the text '*And Nathan said unto David thou art the Man*'. Nathan's story strikes home to David's conscience:

> The story, though it spoke only of the injustice and oppressive act of another man—yet it pointed to what he had lately done himself, with all the circumstances of its aggravation—and withal, the whole was so tenderly addressed to the heart and passions, as to kindle at once the utmost horror and indignation.[2]

*Tristram Shandy* is a story too, and a story with this kind of concern for the reader. It is meant to implicate him, to draw him into a situation in which he can know himself better. But this 'situation' includes something more than the story that is to be told. In other words the story of this novel, as everyone knows, is in part the story of its telling. If the reader is to discover himself it will be by collaborating in the telling. Sterne wants the reader to see himself as in some

[1] *Sermons*, iii, V    [2] *Sermons*, i, IV

ways an author also. He wishes to bring the reader's creative imagination alive.

*Tristram Shandy* is a novel about the creative imagination. Dorothy Van Ghent says that the reader is 'never allowed to forget that the activity of creation, as an activity of forming perceptions and maneuvering them into an expressive order, *is itself the subject*'.[1] That is to say, Sterne is concerned not just with how to get a story told, not just with technique and the processes of fiction, but beyond these with the mysterious and profound sources of delight that are found in inventing, in imagining the existence of things. He is asking about the reality of fiction. What is the reality of a world which need not exist, and which would not exist if we did not say that it did? Edwin Muir writes very well about this. Sterne, he says, 'invented for himself a void which only his own figure could fill, so that without him we feel that Mr Shandy, Uncle Toby, Trim and the others would remain in eternal silence and immobility, and never think of the things they say'.[2] But, as Muir observes, it 'still does not do justice to Sterne' to say that *he* invents these people. Sterne's business is to invent the conditions in which they can be invented: he thinks of the mind that can create them; he can imagine Tristram who imagines all the rest. This is to project an image of the act of creating. And since Tristram is always asking for the collaboration of his readers, and thus is creating partly through the imaginations of his readers, Sterne is in effect projecting an image of the creative act of reading. Tristram is, as we shall see, a reader of a kind as well as an author. Tristram's readers are meant to discover that reading is a kind of authorship.

The story, then, and the telling of the story are more important than the story-teller. Fluchère makes it clear that Tristram exists by virtue of the story he tells:

[1] *The English Novel*, p. 87
[2] *Essays on Literature and Society*, pp. 50–1

His reality consists in the fiction he generated, whose central figure was the complex pattern of people and things set in motion by his own brain, his picture of a hypothetical world where nothing happened except as he wished it. So he does not live on after the book stops.[1]

But, though in this sense the story can be said to be what 'happens in the mind of Tristram Shandy at the very moment that he writes',[2] I do not think it is right to conclude that 'Sterne substituted for story, plot and perhaps character as well, the vigil of the consciousness'.[3] It is true that Tristram says his story is, like Locke's *Essay*, 'a history-book, Sir, (which may possibly recommend it to the world) of what passes in a man's own mind' (II, ii). But it *is* the story that interests him; his claim is that the consciousness can be read as a story. If, as Dorothy Van Ghent asserts, we think of *Tristram Shandy* 'as a mind in which the local world has been steeped and dissolved and fantastically re-formed',[4] we also cannot help seeing that what fills Tristram's mind is a story. He is bound up in it; he lives most fully through the story of the past.

Stories relate what has passed. Forster was right, surely, to say that in *Tristram Shandy* 'the facts have an unholy tendency to unwind and trip up the past instead of begetting the future'.[5] Tristram lives in the past. Granted that he recreates it and gives it a significance that would never belong to mere chronology, this is not to say, as Fluchère does, that 'the only thing that can give it life is a living consciousness of the past as identified with the present—in other words, the sense of a personal duration that emerges through becoming'.[6] In fact neither Tristram nor his readers can quite square the past with the present. The stories, which contain the past, usurp the 'sense of a personal duration', they fill the present *with* the past. Indeed they

[1] *Laurence Sterne*, p. 347          [2] Ibid., p. 101
[3] Ibid., p. 88                        [4] *The English Novel*, p. 86
[5] *Aspects of the Novel*, p. 117      [6] Op. cit., p. 110

interrupt the present. Whilst a story is being told time slips on, things have gone on happening, the present has got lost:

> What a tract of country have I run!—how many degrees nearer to the warm sun am I advanced, and how many fair and goodly cities have I seen, during the time you have been reading, and reflecting, Madam, upon this story! (VII, xxvi)

Whilst we attend to the past, time passes. In this novel the significant time is the time given up to reading. Time has to be filled with the events of a story. It becomes an area cleared for narrative; it is the present vacated for the past.

In any case, if the past were to be identified with the present it would not be in any calm space of the consciousness. For the consciousness is oppressed by the vertiginous panic of the current moment. Tristram is in a hurry. What business, he asks, has the writer with

> the length, breadth, and perpendicular height of the great parish church, or a drawing of the fascade of the abbey of Saint Austreberte . . . your worships and reverences may all measure them at your leisures—but he who measures thee, Janatone, must do it now—thou carriest the principles of change within thy frame . . . (VII, ix).

The present is a race against time; it is always about to be lost for ever—'considering the chances of a transitory life, I would not answer for thee a moment' (Ibid.)—yet, as Tristram admits in a celebrated passage, his story will never be able to overtake the present. Instead of advancing he is 'just thrown so many volumes back'. At this rate, 'I should just live 364 times faster than I should write— . . . and . . . I perceive shall lead a fine life of it out of this self-same life of mine; or, in other words, shall lead a couple of fine lives together' (IV, xiii). His life in the present *must* be discontinuous with the past. And thus it is that that part of the novel concerned with Tristram's own life in the present has to be seen as a scaring interruption of a story:

Now there is nothing in this world I abominate worse, than to be interrupted in a story—and I was that moment telling Eugenius a most tawdry one in my way, of a nun who fancied herself a shell-fish, and of a monk damned for eating a muscle, and was shewing him the grounds and justice of the procedure—

'—Did ever so grave a personage get into so vile a scrape?' quoth Death. Thou hast had a narrow escape, Tristram, said Eugenius, taking hold of my hand as I finished my story— (VII, i)

Of course, the story contained in Book VII, the story of Tristram's flight from death, the true story of the present, this is the defiant story that is being told by the whole novel. It is implicit in every one of Tristram's frustrating encounters with the creaking mechanism of his narrative.

When the precipitancy of a man's wishes hurries on his ideas ninety times faster than the vehicle he rides in—woe be to truth! and woe be to the vehicle and its tackling (let 'em be made of what stuff you will) upon which he breathes forth the disappointment of his soul! (VII, viii)

Hence what looks like his perverse way of telling a story can be seen as part of the story he is telling, the story of a brush with death, and of the imagination that rejects death. Sterne has hardly reached the end of the first volume before he arrives at the black page, the ultimate effect of black on white, the point at which black print on the page ceases to carry speech and the signs of life. It appears to be the point at which all written stories must arrive. Stories end; the story of the past has already come to its conclusion. The book, though, is a struggle to keep the past alive. All of Tristram's will to live is focused on his story. The imagination, busy with the sequences of the past, reclaiming things from the dead, this is his answer to the present and the fear of death. And this life of the imagination is what he asks the reader to share; he offers him the challenge of a marbled page, a 'motly emblem of my work', the expressions of those intricate 'opinions, transactions, and truths which

K

still lie mystically hid under the dark veil of the black one'
(III, xxxvi).

The book displays, then, in Fluchère's words, 'the action
of the mind at grips with its fictional material'.[1] But this is
not to say that that mind is the subject of the book. Rather
it deals with the need to imagine, with the fictive power and
the kind of reality it sustains. It is a book about what
stories mean, and this depends to a large extent on what
the reader makes of them.

## II

This is why Sterne is so interested in the *form* of his narrative: he sees it as a rhetorical medium designed to enlist a
special kind of attention. The novel may be described as an
opportunity to put this medium to the test; it is in effect a
critique of rhetoric.

It is, I think, from this point of view that we should
consider Shklovsky's interpretation of *Tristram Shandy* as a
'parodying novel'. He maintains that the book's formal
disorder only draws attention to the formal principles
governing all fictional works. The disruption of the narrative
is not 'motivated' by anything but the need for the novel to
display its own laws. 'By delaying the action of a novel
without an introduction of disrupting motifs, for example,
but through a simple transposition of its parts, the artist
shows us the aesthetic laws which lie behind both com-
positional devices.'[2]

John Traugott, reprinting this essay, finds in its argument
some of the limitations of the formalist method. Shklovsky's
'purist aesthetic', he says, 'probably could not in any case
reach that grateful sense of life called Shandean', or take

---

[1] *Laurence Sterne*, p. 33

[2] 'A Parodying Novel: Sterne's *Tristram Shandy*', in *Laurence Sterne: A
Collection of Critical Essays*, ed. Traugott, p. 89

account of the personal experiences and attitudes which are 'strangely figured in the emotional design of the work'. An interpretation ought to keep open the negotiations between fiction and reality. Parody, yes; but, in Traugott's view, parody as possibly 'the only way we have of communicating our experiences—and perhaps the only way of thinking about ourselves'.[1] There is a lot in this. Shklovsky hardly is able to catch the characteristic blend of fun and distress. '—'Twas nothing,—I did not lose two drops of blood by it—'twas not worth calling in a surgeon, had he lived next door to us—thousands suffer by choice, what I did by accident.——' (V, xvii). Whether or not it was nothing is what the book is all about. Thus, what Shklovsky makes a critique of the novel may really be the criticism of an attitude to life. A. D. McKillop cites as a parallel the kind of novel described in *Les Faux-Monnayeurs*: ' "the subject of the book, if you must have one, is just that very struggle between what reality offers him [i.e. the novelist] and what he himself desires to make of it" '.[2]

Parody, then, is a way to deal with the confusing area in which art and reality overlap and interact. And with this in mind we may be able to re-assess the formalist reading of parody. What Shklovsky calls parody of the novel-form— the 'time-shifts', the delayed explanations, the ellipses— can also be explained as devices of rhetoric. For rhetoric is the point at which art enters life. To negotiate successfully between art and reality is to bring rhetoric to perfection. If this novel proposes a critique of life it does so primarily by testing the resources of rhetoric.

W. J. Farrell argues along these lines, perhaps too far along them. *Tristram Shandy*, he says, allows the worlds of art and nature to 'collide in carefully planned confusion'.[3] Rhetoric proves in the circumstances to be an inadequate

[1] Op. cit., p. 8    [2] *The Early Masters of English Fiction*, p. 192
[3] 'Nature versus Art as a Comic Pattern in *Tristram Shandy*', *ELH*, Vol. xxx, No. 1, 1963, p. 16

vehicle: the structure of the novel, he maintains, is determined by just those rhetorical devices which are made to look ridiculous when, for instance, Walter Shandy uses them. Tristram speaks of his father as a 'natural' orator, yet praises him in effect (as did the fellows of Jesus College) for his command of artificial procedures—'a sudden and spirited Epiphonema, or rather Erotesis', Sorites or Aposiopesis. Hence, Farrell argues, the book is a thorough-going parody of systems of rhetoric, and its structure can be explained as a critique of their inadequacy to life.[1]

But if the book might be, through parody, 'the most typical novel of world literature',[2] might it not also, by parodying rhetoric as a system, work towards the improvement of rhetoric? Sterne must have believed it could. As a preacher he knew the force of rhetoric, which need not at all 'collide' with natural feeling. 'Great is the power of eloquence,' he wrote; 'but never is it so great as when it pleads along with nature.'[3] And in *Tristram Shandy* he makes a clear distinction between rhetoric as an art, self-regarding and an end in itself, and the rhetoric that enters into life, and is a token of our need of each other.

For Walter Shandy rhetoric has a value in itself:

> —A blessing which tied up my father's tongue, and a misfortune which let it loose with a good grace, were pretty equal: sometimes, indeed, the misfortune was the better of the two; for instance, where the pleasure of the harangue was as *ten*, and the pain of the misfortune but as *five*—my father gained half in half, and consequently was as well again off, as [if] it had never befallen him. (V, iii)

He is Ciceronian to the point of inhumanity. At least the way he overcomes his grief on hearing of Bobby's death seems to Tristram to be Ciceronian:

> When *Tully* was bereft of his dear daughter *Tullia*, at first he laid it to his heart,—he listened to the voice of nature, and

---

[1] Op. cit., p. 30          [2] Shklovsky, op. cit., p. 89          [3] *Sermons*, iii, V

modulated his own unto it.—O my *Tullia*! my daughter! my child!— . . . —But as soon as he began to look into the stores of philosophy, and consider how many excellent things might be said upon the occasion—no body upon earth can conceive, says the great orator, how happy, how joyful it made me. (V, iii)

Trim's eloquence on the same subject has a very different motive and a different effect:

Are we not here now, continued the corporal, (striking the end of his stick perpendicularly upon the floor, so as to give an idea of health and stability)—and are we not—(dropping his hat upon the ground) gone! in a moment!—'Twas infinitely strik-ing! *Susannah* burst into a flood of tears.—We are not stocks and stones.—*Jonathan*, *Obadiah*, the cook-maid, all melted.— The foolish fat scullion herself, who was scouring a fish-kettle upon her knees, was rous'd with it.—The whole kitchen crouded about the corporal. (V, vii)

It is true that Tristram makes even Trim look comical sometimes. Farrell notes that the 'attitude in which he read the sermon', the attitude he strikes on this occasion also, is a parody of the orator's stance. Tristram seems not to know how to describe or explain eloquence which is not calcu-lated and stiff. Yet he acknowledges that Trim speaks feelingly and makes a powerful effect. The sermon went very well after all: 'I should have read it ten times better, Sir, answered *Trim*, but that my heart was so full.—That was the very reason, *Trim*, replied my father, which has made thee read the sermon as well as thou hast done . . .' (II, xvii). And on the occasion of Bobby's death we are asked to notice the difference between Trim's rightness of feeling and Walter Shandy's impertinent display of wit.

My father was a man of deep reading—prompt memory— with *Cato*, and *Seneca*, and *Epictetus*, at his fingers ends.—

The corporal—with nothing—to remember—of no deeper reading than his muster-roll—or greater names at his finger's end, than the contents of it.

The one proceeding from period to period, by metaphor and

allusion, and striking the fancy as he went along, (as men of wit and fancy do) with the entertainment and pleasantry of his pictures and images.

The other, without wit or antithesis, or point, or turn, this way or that; but leaving the images on one side, and the pictures on the other, going strait forwards as nature could lead him, to the heart. O *Trim*! would to heaven thou had'st a better historian!—would!—thy historian had a better pair of breeches!— O ye criticks! will nothing melt you? (V, vi)

The story is leading us to a choice of styles. But it may also be the result of a choice, an achievement of rhetoric. For it seems natural for rhetoric to take the form of a story. Sterne's own sermons, as we have seen, gravitate towards narrative. 'It would be a pleasure to a good mind', he writes in his charity sermon on Elijah and the widow of Zarephath, 'to stop here a moment, and figure to itself the picture of so joyful an event.—'[1] The transition to story is characteristic:

Here then let us stop a moment, and give the story of the Levite and his Concubine a second hearing: like all others much of it depends upon the telling; and as the Scripture has left us no kind of comment upon it, 'tis a story on which the heart cannot be at a loss for what to say, or the imagination for what to suppose —the danger is, humanity may say too much.[2]

In the novel it is Trim, rather than the preacher Yorick, who is regarded as the story-teller, indeed even as the preacher. But there is an affinity between them. Trim reads Yorick's sermon, and we have seen him adopting his 'sermon' attitude for an 'oration upon death'. Later, one of his stories becomes associated with another of Yorick's sermons. Actually this is a story he is prevented from telling, and in fact it becomes part of *Tristram's* story. There occurs a significant mix-up of story and sermon.

Trim has been moralizing on Bobby's death and goes on to recollect the story of the death of Le Fever. But just as

[1] *Sermons*, i, V    [2] *Sermons*, iii, III

Trim is beginning the story Tristram breaks off the narrative. 'Fool that I was!' he says much later; 'nor can I
recollect, (nor perhaps you) without turning back to the
place, what it was that hindered me from letting the corporal
tell it in his own words;—but the occasion is lost,—I must
tell it now in my own' (VI, v). Trim's story has thus got
into the fabric of the novel, a significant transition. The
story of a story, which would have been an episode for the
reader to observe, turns into rhetoric—a story, that is,
which continues the narrator's dialogue with his reader.
Oddly enough in that case, it is told much more objectively
than other stories in this book. The narration is undemon-
strative; it does not draw attention to itself. For once, the
reader is left alone with the tale. Yet it also strikes one as the
sentimental apex of the book; and sentiment, as Mayoux
points out, implies 'the necessary intercessor, the tender
witness'.[1] Undoubtedly this 'objective' narrative is an
extreme example of rhetoric. As if to confirm this, Sterne
goes on to describe Yorick's funeral sermon for Le Fever.
But this does not get itself into the novel; we know nothing
about it except what Yorick thought of it. And the interesting thing is that Sterne so arranges things that it is to the
story of Le Fever that Yorick's modest self-approbation
seems to apply. This story and the sermon on Conscience
seem to show through the fictional veil. We seem to detect
Sterne himself behind the *personae* of Trim or Yorick, and
to hear Sterne's discreet voice in that cancelled '~~BRAVO~~',
'resembling rather a faint thought of transient applause,
secretly stirring up in the heart of the composer, than a
gross mark of it, coarsely obtruded upon the world' (VI, xi).
     What a charming transition this is, from the vigorous
comedy of Walter Shandy's vanity to this merest hint of
self-approval in the author's own voice heard just outside
the novel and 'more like a *ritratto* of the shadow of vanity,

---

[1] 'Laurence Sterne', in *Laurence Sterne: A Collection of Critical Essays*,
ed. Traugott, p. 111

than of VANITY herself' (VI, xi). It is in such ways that the novel traces the fluctuating values of rhetoric. It is not tolerant of display, though it accepts that a part of the beauty of rhetoric is in its self-consciousness. Thus the book works as a critique of rhetoric through parody, and as a model of rhetoric in the eloquent art of its story which survives parody. This is a book which expects and exercises the self-consciousness of both reader and author. It asks for the co-operation of both in getting closer to the truth of feeling.

## III

Of course, at the lowest estimate, the purpose of rhetoric both for the novelist and the preacher is to make sure that the auditor stays awake. This is the most obvious reason for the devious, erratic form of the narrative. Tristram deals summarily with what Bagehot was to declare 'an imperative law of the writing-art that a book should go straight on'.[1] 'I may arrive hereafter', he writes at the end of the volume we have been discussing, 'at the excellency of going on even thus;

---

which is a line drawn straight as I could draw it, by a writing-master's ruler, (borrowed for that purpose) turning neither to the right hand or to the left' (VI, xl). But this 'right line', 'the emblem of moral rectitude' (ibid.) is also the best line for cabbage-planters. It is the line of simplicity and sincerity, as in Trim's 'oration upon death', but it is not the line Tristram can follow. How, he asks, did it come to be confused with the 'line of GRAVITATION'? How could it fail to be? It is the line of unswerving mediocrity ('Shadwell never deviates into sense'). The 'lowest and flattest compositions pass off very well', Tristram says, provided

[1] *Collected Works*, ii, 289

that they keep in tune with themselves (IV, xxv). It is the stupid who rely on the straight line, the level road, and an air of gravity. Gravity is 'no better, but often worse, than what a *French* wit had long ago defined it,—*viz. A mysterious carriage of the body to cover the defects of the mind*' (I, xi). This was Yorick's opinion. 'In the naked temper which a merry heart discovered, he would say, There was no danger,—but to itself:—whereas the very essence of gravity was design, and consequently deceit . . .' (ibid.)

The rule of gravity is, for Tristram, a kind of opacity and the medium of impenetrable dullness or pretentious cant. It is impervious; it defeats the intentions of language.

> I hate set dissertations,—and above all things in the world, 'tis one of the silliest things in one of them, to darken your hypothesis by placing a number of tall, opake words, one before another, in a right line, betwixt your own and your readers conception,— . . . (III, xx)

Things should seem natural, unforced, unsystematic like good talk. Virginia Woolf writes of 'the gap which [Sterne's] astonishingly agile pen has cut in the thick-set hedge of English prose. . . . The order of the ideas, their suddenness and irrelevancy, is more true to life than to literature.' His writing has the 'sound and associations of the speaking voice'; 'we are as close to life as we can be'. Also, she observes, we are close to the author. 'The usual ceremonies and conventions which keep reader and writer at arm's length disappear.'[1] It is more than talk—after all, the man who *talks* is a bore—it is conversation. And that is a better word than 'rhetoric' to describe what Sterne is after. He is trying to define a style which will be a kind of relationship. Walter Shandy's rhetoric, his echoing vanity, is a mockery of this style. But Tristram's book, which seems so often to lose itself in admiration of such rhetoric, is always working towards a better understanding between author and

[1] *Collected Essays*, i, 95–6

reader: 'Writing', says Tristram, 'when properly managed (as you may be sure I think mine is) is but a different name for conversation' (II, xi).

But if the novel is a conversation it is a conversation about the failure of conversations. It is a prolonged contradiction of its own material. Such a character as Mrs Shandy frustrates everything the novel stands for. Hers is a life of pure function; words are irrelevant to her. 'She contented herself with doing all that her godfathers and godmothers promised for her—but no more; and so would go on using a hard word twenty years together—and replying to it too, if it was a verb, in all its moods and tenses, without giving herself any trouble to enquire about it' (IX, xi). All conversations with her have the same ending; they all converge on one or other of her mindless preoccupations, and on the silence that is so unnerving to her husband. Here they are talking about the widow Wadman and Uncle Toby:

> ... Unless she should happen to have a child—said my mother——
> —But she must persuade my brother Toby first to get her one——
> —To be sure, Mr. Shandy, quoth my mother.
> —Though if it comes to persuasion—said my father—Lord have mercy upon them.
> Amen: said my mother, *piano*.
> Amen: cried my father, *fortissimè*.
> Amen: said my mother again—but with such a sighing cadence of personal pity at the end of it, as discomfited every fibre about my father—he instantly took out his almanack; ...
> ... The first Lord of the Treasury thinking of *ways and means*, could not have returned home, with a more embarrassed look. (IX, xi)

On one notable occasion Mrs Shandy is even more frustrating, but this is when she has already put a stop to talk: 'Pray, what was your father saying?—Nothing' (I, i). So she is really responsible for the whole story.

Walter Shandy, for all his brilliance, is defenceless against his wife. His exasperation may explode into an unanswerable pun at her expense. But her simplicity insulates her. It is she after all who is unanswerable. She represents stupidity raised to the power of wit. Her lack of words becomes in the end a reflection on Walter Shandy. And so does Uncle Toby's 'Lillabullero'. But between Walter and Toby there is at least the illusion of talk. In fact their continuing conversation is for a large part of the book what constitutes the 'action'. Tristram's birth, the accident to his nose, the adventure with the sash-cord, these are all matters that the two brothers talk about. And if their talk is the action, the plot is in their persistent misunderstandings and the conflict of their separate preoccupations. It is in this respect, as John Traugott has shown, that the two brothers enact the 'skeptical possibilities of Locke's *Essay*'.[1] Their conversations are all at cross-purposes.

> Talk of what we will, brother,—or let the occasion be never so foreign or unfit for the subject,—you are sure to bring it in: I would not, brother *Toby*, continued my father,—I declare I would not have my head so full of curtins and horn-works.— That, I dare say, you would not, quoth Dr. *Slop*, interrupting him, and laughing most immoderately at his pun. (II, xii)

Dr Slop's pun, touching on Walter Shandy's private anxieties, plots the point where two personal obsessions meet. But Toby is not to be deflected: '. . . the curtins my brother *Shandy* mentions here, have nothing to do with bed-steads. . . .' And it is not long before Walter Shandy too has 'got into his element' and is launched into a 'dissertation upon trade' (II, xiv). But he is interrupted by the arrival of Trim with the volume of Stevinus from which is to fall the copy of Yorick's sermon.

No sooner has the conversation begun again after Trim's

---

[1] *Tristram Shandy's World*, rep. *Laurence Sterne: A Collection of Critical Essays*, ed. Traugott, p. 132

reading than it takes another lurch into Toby's private
world: 'I wish, quoth my uncle *Toby*, you had seen what
prodigious armies we had in *Flanders*' (II, xviii). At this
point, near the end of Volume II, the book itself gets in the
way of the conversation. Toby's words are left hanging in
the air and will not be answered until the publication of
Volume III a year later. When Toby then resumes, 'I *wish*
Dr. *Slop* . . .', the dialogue runs into new difficulties. Slop is
speechless, Walter struggling to get his handkerchief from
his pocket. Not until six chapters later can he reply, and
then Toby's final response is to whistle *Lillabullero*.

The beauty of such a sequence, as John Traugott indicates, is that it suggests the brothers are never out of
sympathy, perhaps not even out of touch. The comedy of
the scene is tinged with sentiment. The real comedy of this
collapse of dialogue is that it can be taken as the entry into a
finer dialogue of the heart. Toby bears no resentment when
he hears his Hobby-horse insulted; he looks up into Walter's
face 'with a countenance spread over with so much good
nature;—so placid;—so fraternal;—so inexpressibly tender
towards him;—it penetrated my father to his heart: . . .'
(II, xii).

Thus Walter Shandy is again thwarted by an impulse
towards an unspoken conversation of deeper meaning and
truer feeling than any that depends on words. Both Mrs
Shandy and Uncle Toby stand for something which contradicts his itch to talk. But they also introduce into the book a
continuing centre of comic frustration. They are not immune
from ridicule. But all these people and their vain attempts at
discourse are the subject of yet another conversation, which
is carried on between reader and author. This contains both
comedy and sentiment, and goes beyond them. It brings
into the book, not only comedy, the cause of laughter, but
gaiety, in which the reader and the author can rejoice
together. This is the kind of conversation to which the
whole story aspires.

## IV

If Tristram avoids being laughed at, it is because he is willing to play the fool: '. . . if I should seem now and then to trifle upon the road,—or should sometimes put on a fool's cap with a bell to it, for a moment or two as we pass along,—don't fly off,—but rather courteously give me credit for a little more wisdom than appears upon my outside' (I, vi). This is a way, as C. J. Rawson observes, to 'get the reader intimately involved'. He adds that there is, in this as in everything concerning Tristram, an element of parody; but it is not alienating as it would be in Swift. Tristram (no less than Sterne himself) enjoys his character 'as a rich fact of human nature. . . . Sterne's irony is one of fond permissive indulgence; the egotism, though mocked, is freely played with, and the reader offered hospitality within it.'[1] All this seems to me very well said. It admirably brings out what it is in Tristram's attitude that none of the characters in his story can rise to. Tristram can offer, as Rawson puts it, 'real tokens of relationship'.[2] Not that this produces a 'real' relationship, of course; for what does Tristram know of his readers? As we shall see, they are not there: he has to invent them. Here is, in effect, the fiction of sharing, and an imagined way of meeting. In this respect the proposed relationship, which will contain the story, is at the same time a paradigm for all the situations within that story. If, as Northrop Frye says, there could hardly be 'a more elementary critical principle than the fact that the events of a literary fiction are not real but hypothetical events',[3] this conversational narration may be taken to be the central hypothesis of the whole story. It is more than a framework for the events; it adumbrates the area within which they become conceivable, and, indeed, significant.

[1] 'Gulliver and the Gentle Reader', in *Imagined Worlds*, pp. 53–4
[2] Ibid., loc. cit.    [3] *Anatomy of Criticism*, p. 84

For this reason it seems to me that when John Stedmond points out that 'for all the apparent attempt to produce dialogue, the book is for the most part monologue',[1] he is giving a wrong emphasis to the facts. If the 'conversation' is a rhetorical device 'close to that of the pedagogue, or the preacher',[2] this is because Sterne is taking the measure of such rhetoric. The rhetoric of his narration has to be able to contain images of friendship, to bring into being a kind of symbolic relationship with a (perhaps symbolic) reader. It has to be able to postulate a conversation.

But it is true that it relates to the art of preaching. For a conversational style is meant to stand for something more than good company. It should be a way to break down the reader's fence of self-interest, as we have seen that the sermons try to do. It should urge on him an enlargement of sympathy, and encourage the enhanced sense of reality that springs from being able to go beyond the 'real'. It asks us to be capable of reaching out into the lives of others, or, more exactly, to be capable of imagining them. Ben Lehman has written excellently of the way in which Tristram detaches himself from the lonely, meagre 'reality' endured by his characters, and extends the area of his personal freedom and creativeness:

> Each of the other figures, deeply and greatly different as they are, shows itself shut up in its own world. No matter how warm their animal fellow feeling, at best they understand one another only by fits and starts. A pervasive loneliness is at the core of each, as in life itself. But Tristram understands them all, and the power of imagination that makes that possible dissolves the loneliness in him, makes him by so much less real to us because nothing in our own experience has prepared us to imagine him.[3]

But, as these last few phrases imply, it is the reader also who has to be redeemed from 'reality'; he too will wish to

[1] *The Comic Art of Laurence Sterne*, p. 62    [2] Ibid., loc. cit.
[3] 'Of Time, Personality, and the Author', in *Laurence Sterne*, ed. Traugott, pp. 27–8

move into an 'imagined world [which] has more reality than a stripped and ordered account', and he will find himself able to do so when he

> identifies himself with the observing reporter, takes on his state of mind and fancies himself moving selectively among the inexhaustible data of experience, prompted by the associations native to that state of mind.[1]

Lehman makes it clear that in asking for an ideal 'conversation' Sterne is defining the scope and meaning of 'the imagining reader-mind'.[2]

This is the real importance of the 'conversation' that Sterne looks for. In this light the distinction between reading and writing loses its edge. The reader, it is true, cannot assume that his imagination will be unrestricted: it must play over a 'given' body of material. But, as we shall see, the writer in his turn wishes to persuade us (and perhaps also himself) that he is confronted with a 'given' world, of which his representation is in effect a 'reading'. There is certainly a high gain in authenticity when the writer acts as the reader of what already exists. Equally it is easy to see that the entirely passive reader, who does not in some way invent what he reads, is not a reader at all. Essentially Sterne's rhetoric is designed to urge on the reader the need to be creative.

## V

This in particular was what Sterne meant when he made Tristram speak of a 'conversational' style. Let us return to that passage:

> Writing, when properly managed (as you may be sure I think mine is) is but a different name for conversation: As no one,

[1] 'Of Time, Personality, and the Author', in *Laurence Sterne*, ed. Traugott, p. 29

[2] Ibid., p. 30

who knows what he is about in good company, would venture to talk all;—so no author, who understands the just boundaries of decorum and good-breeding, would presume to think all: The truest respect which you can pay to the reader's understanding, is to halve this matter amicably, and leave him something to imagine, in his turn, as well as yourself. (II, xi)

'Imagine!'—this is an exhortation heard often in Sterne's sermons. 'Imagine how a sudden stroke of such impetuous joy must operate . . .' says Sterne after relating how Elijah brought the widow's child back to life.[1] 'Let us imagine';[2] 'send forth your imagination, I beseech you';[3] ' 'tis no unnatural soliloquy to imagine', he says of the words he gives to the men who fell among thieves.[4] And later in the same sermon he writes ' 'tis almost necessary to imagine' what could have prompted the good Samaritan's actions. Similarly, in the novel, especially in the opening chapters where he particularly needs to catch the reader's attention, the narrator keeps intimating that the story will be real only as long as the reader is capable of imagining it. 'Imagine to yourself a little, squat, uncourtly figure of a Doctor *Slop*, . . .' (II, ix); 'You will imagine, Madam, . . .' (I, xxi); 'My father, as any body may naturally imagine, . . .' (I, xvi).

But Sterne builds a larger expectation on such passages as these. It is not enough for the reader to be responsive, he should be really inquisitive; not merely attentive but full of curiosity. Imagining is only a step away from guessing. Why did Yorick get no credit for helping the midwife? 'Lay down the book, and I will allow you half a day to give a probable guess at the grounds of this procedure' (I, x). Why was the affair of 'my great aunt Dinah' so disturbing to Walter and Toby?

It will seem very strange,—and I would as soon think of dropping a riddle in the reader's way, which is not my interest to do, as set him upon guessing how it could come to pass, that an

---

[1] *Sermons*, i, V      [2] *Sermons* iii, VIII
[3] *Sermons*, iii, IX      [4] *Sermons*, i, III

event of this kind, so many years after it had happened, should
be reserved for the interruption of the peace and unity, which
otherwise so cordially subsisted, between my father and my uncle
*Toby*. (I, xxi)

In fact this cannot be explained until we know the reasons
for Toby's modesty: 'You will imagine, Madam, that my
uncle *Toby* had contracted all this from this very source; . . .
I wish I could say so' (I, xxi).

Thus the story appears to grow out of the reader's desire
to know more. Evidently its structure is only in part
determined by the way Tristram's mind works. Quite as
important is this reader whose curiosity it can hardly cope
with. The preacher may feel he has to use all his skill to
penetrate the massive indifference of his parishioners. But
the novelist can hardly be inventive enough. In one matter
especially his readers are likely to leave him standing; when
it comes to double meanings, innuendoes, indecent puns
and the like, their imaginations race:

> —Fair and softly, gentle reader!—where is thy fancy carrying
> thee?—If there is truth in man, by my great grandfather's nose,
> I mean the external organ of smelling, or that part of man which
> stands prominent in his face,—and which painters say, in good
> jolly noses and well-proportioned faces, should comprehend a
> full third,—that is, measuring downwards from the setting on
> of the hair.—
> —What a life of it has an author, at this pass! (III, xxxiii)

Sterne's insincerity is glaring: the reader affords the
flimsiest of excuses. Fluchère, indeed, thinks it 'annoying or
irritating' to be used like this, as a stalking-horse for
Sterne's obscenity. But if that is so, it hardly seems right to
urge, as he does, 'the salutariness of the obscenity that
Sterne sets in ambush round every corner'.[1] For his shifti-
ness, the rhetorical disclaiming of responsibility, is the
equivalent of a snigger. It converts the obscene into smut.

[1] *Laurence Sterne*, p. 232

L

This is what Mayoux cogently argues. The imaginary dialogue, he claims, does not proceed 'with honest openness'. In fact Sterne forces on the reader 'relations of complicity'. Thus, Mayoux continues, the reader is made 'to compromise himself to the point of becoming a responsible actor', and the situation contains 'a curious and subtle exhibitionism'. It is not a sign of freedom that Sterne should play with the reader's responses in this way. Quite the reverse: it lets us see in Sterne a profound 'anxiety'. 'His jesting guise and curative obscenity is only a surface manifestation of the deeper emotions represented by the obsessive recurrence of these images.'[1]

One answer to this argument is that Sterne himself would have argued in the same way. Mayoux starts by challenging the basic premise of Sterne's art but does not stick to this. His essay contains a strange *volte face* from 'complicity' to 'conversation' and from 'anxiety' to 'genius'. And, actually, his starting-point, that the obscenity allows only a pseudo-relationship, and that this forbids free play of the imagination to either narrator or reader, is also, as it happens, Sterne's starting-point. That is to say, Sterne uses the story, and in particular Tristram's way of telling it, to pursue the implications of an argument like Mayoux's. He is concerned, we have been discovering, with the terms on which the imagination operates, and he knows quite well that above all they consist in the ability to achieve a true relationship. He therefore allows the book to contain the possibility of a false one. Is it his own anxiety that keeps jerking the talk back to noses and whiskers and 'things'? I think it is rather that they keep suggesting themselves as 'specimens', as varieties of the imagination which pose a question about its reality. They are part of his subject; they function as a 'motif', an arrangement of tones which he has to set in motion and 'develop'. Of course, it is perfectly conceivable

[1] 'Laurence Sterne', in *Laurence Sterne: A Collection of Critical Essays*, ed. Traugott, pp. 109–10

that since he chooses these motifs so often, and not others, he is impelled by something like anxiety. But his treatment of them is objective, almost theoretical. At least, to the extent that it *is* objective, it speaks of his freedom to pursue his design as an artist.

That is to say, it will seem less likely that Sterne's imagination is obsessed with such images when it appears that a part of his subject is the obsessed imagination. His story of frustrated conversations is also a story of the imagination frustrated. His characters are not free, as we have seen; their minds run in their 'metalled ways' to their own foregone conclusions. So it is with Toby when he hears of the bridge that is being made for Tristram's nose: 'You must know, my uncle *Toby* mistook the bridge as widely as my father mistook the mortars;— . . .' (III, xxiii). His mistake makes him transparent; the lines laid down for his imagination show through:

> Had my uncle *Toby's* head been a *Savoyard's* box, and my father peeping in all the time at one end of it,—it could not have given him a more distinct conception of the operations of my uncle *Toby's* imagination, than what he had; . . . (III, xxvi)

But now another sort of imagination comes into play. Walter Shandy is seen here in a position similar to that of the reader. Like the reader he feels that Toby has made a richly comic exhibition of his true nature. But like the reader he is himself helping to create the portrait: the comedy which he relishes is the comedy he has found there. For he thinks Toby's hobby-horse 'the most ridiculous horse that ever gentleman mounted': 'it tickled my father's imagination beyond measure', says Tristram (III, xxiv). And this 'affair of the bridge' kindles his imagination:

> [he] would exhaust all the stores of his eloquence (which indeed were very great) in a panegyric upon the BATTERING-RAMS of the ancients,—the VINEA which Alexander made use of at the siege of *Tyre*.—He would tell my uncle *Toby* of the CATAPULTAE

of the *Syrians* which threw such monstrous stones so many hun-
dred feet, and shook the strongest bulwarks from their very
foundation;— . . .—But what are these, would he say, to the
destructive machinery of corporal *Trim*?— (III, xxiv)

This is a joke in which the reader shares. It is not long
before he finds himself doing the same thing and reading
double meanings into the descriptions of the new bridge:
one design, for instance, 'empowered my uncle *Toby* to raise
it up or let it down with the end of his crutch, and with one
hand, which, as his garrison was weak, was as much as he
could well spare,— . . .'; in another 'the whole might be
lifted up together, and stand bolt upright,— . . .' (III, xxv).
But here the narrator catches the reader in the act, and puts
him in his place in the same sentence as Walter Shandy:

> For a whole week after he [i.e. Toby] was determined in his
> mind to have one of that particular construction which is made to
> draw back horizontally, to hinder a passage; and to thrust for-
> wards again to gain a passage,—of which sorts your worship
> might have seen three famous ones at *Spires* before its destruc-
> tion,—and one now at *Brisac*, if I mistake not;—but my father
> advising my uncle *Toby*, with great earnestness, to have nothing
> more to do with thrusting bridges,—and my uncle foreseeing
> moreover that it would but perpetuate the memory of the cor-
> poral's misfortune,—he changed his mind. . . . (III, xxv).

The 'relations of complicity' are, let us note, with Walter
Shandy, not with Sterne or even Tristram. We *see* what the
indecent imagination looks like; we watch it vigorously at
work in Walter Shandy. And then we catch ourselves doing
the same thing. We are made conscious of what we are
doing. We are amused at our own amusement. The situation
is robbed of its furtiveness.

The same sort of thing happens when Tristram begins
to talk about noses. He himself creates the innuendo by
smirkingly claiming that there is none: 'I declare, by that
word I mean a Nose, and nothing more, or less' (III, xxxi).

('Less'?—is that likely?) But already Tristram has described a scene in which the reader can find an image of himself. Eugenius, without hesitation preferring the clean road to the dirty road, is easily made to look foolish when he hesitates over the two meanings of a word. He is reading the book in which we are reading about him. He is in *his* book, and it therefore seems almost that we are in ours; at least the act of reading is in our book.

> —Here are two senses, cried *Eugenius*, as we walk'd along, pointing with the fore finger of his right hand to the word *Crevice*, in the fifty-second page of the second volume of this book of books,— . . . (III, xxxi)

Suppose we turn back to that page and look for that word, *Crevice*. We shall then be imitating the action of the book, acknowledging that like Eugenius we are among Sterne's *dramatis personae*, and a part of his experiment. What is more, we shall begin to feel that the book and some of the words of the book are themselves part of the book's subject. What Eugenius is reading is the passage in which Toby is forced to acknowledge that he does not know the right end of a woman from the wrong:

> —Right end, quoth my uncle *Toby*, muttering the two words low to himself, and fixing his two eyes insensibly as he muttered them, upon a small crevice, formed by a bad joint in the chimney-piece.—Right end of a woman!—I declare, quoth my uncle, I know no more which it is, than the man in the moon;— . . . (II, vii)

This is a passage we have already read, no doubt with due recognition of the *double entendre*. Now we are to become aware of the way we had read it. And again the 'complicity' that emerges is with a character we have already been prepared to find amusing. When, therefore, Tristram himself takes up the question 'which is the right and which the wrong end of a woman' (IV, xxxii) we are prepared to take it as a kind of test case. It belongs to the 'chapter of THINGS',

which will lead ('in order to keep up some sort of connection in my works') to the chapter on WHISKERS. This
'dangerous chapter' on Whiskers turns out to be another
story about double meanings, another point at which the
obsessed imagination is displayed as a comic object. It
returns us to the word 'nose': it is a story about all such
words ('the word in course became indecent'):

> Does not all the world know, said the curate *d'Estella* at the
> conclusion of his work, that Noses ran the same fate some
> centuries ago in most parts of *Europe*, which Whiskers have now
> done in the kingdom of *Navarre*—The evil indeed spread no
> further then—, but have not beds and bolsters, and night-caps
> and chamber-pots stood upon the brink of destruction ever since?
> Are not trouse, and placket-holes, and pump-handles—and
> spigots and faucets, in danger still, from the same association?—
> Chastity, by nature the gentlest of all affections—give it but its
> head—'tis like a ramping and a roaring lion. (V, i)

This reads like an outrageous parody of Sterne's own book
and, as always, there is something ambivalent in the mockery
which is done with such relish. Yet the book which can
face itself like this and laugh (and ask the reader to laugh)
at its own preoccupations can hardly be said to be obsessed
by them.

   Thus the reader, like the narrator and like Sterne himself,
finds himself in a position to observe and so to appreciate
the humour of the obsessed imagination. Of course, Sterne
continues to claim that the reader himself 'creates' the
obscenities; in this sense they are simply the funniest
example of the imagining the reader has to do. And this
after all is their use. If they bring the reader and the author
into 'relations of complicity' these relations are in fact one
way of indicating the extent to which they both act as both
reader *and* writer. And it is by confronting the reader with
images of obsessed readers, people who are unable to resist
obscene meanings, that Sterne can liberate the reader's

imagination from such meanings. That is, he shows his reader how to imagine an imagination that is not free.

## VI

This, then, is a mischievous version of what Sterne is saying to the reader all the time—'imagine!'—not just 'imagine the other meaning', but 'imagine someone looking for another meaning, as you yourself were doing just now'. But there are naturally many other ways in which the success of the novel depends on what the reader can imagine. The story proceeds, as Shklovsky puts it, by 'a swarm of hints'. Because of the device of the 'time-shift', for instance, 'causes are given after effects, after deliberately implanted possibilities of false conclusions'.[1] The reader is expected, as it were, to piece the novel together out of what he imagines to be the meaning of unexplained events, unforeseen issues or riddling sequences. The reader has to make up the novel.

Fluchère makes a comment on this aspect of the work:

> The actual rigorousness of their sequence [i.e. of events and opinions] only reveals itself as we read on, which is as much as to say that Tristram succeeds in making us participate in his inventions, in making us adopt his intellectual activity as to some extent our own, though we are not given the right of introducing our own errors.[2]

Naturally Fluchère assumes that Sterne's rhetorical man-oeuvres are only a disguised form of telling. The reader *is* a reader: he must take what is given. Yet the fact is that in this novel the reader *is* free to make his own errors. At any rate there are occasions when he is required not only to guess at the meaning but even to supply the words themselves. Sterne, that is, does not merely leave things unsaid; at times he records that there is something he is not saying—not at

---

[1] 'A Parodying Novel', op. cit., p. 81    [2] *Laurence Sterne*, p. 76

all the same thing. Take for example the accident of the sash-cord:

> —The chamber-maid had left no ******* *** under the bed:
> —Cannot you contrive, master, quoth *Susannah*, lifting up the sash with one hand, as she spoke, and helping me up into the window seat with the other,—cannot you manage, my dear, for a single time, to **** *** ** *** ******? (V, xvii)

The asterisks spell out words which do not exist unless in the reader's imagination. In another way, however, they *are* there, waiting for the reader to voice them. The asterisks leave nothing out, they do not make a hole in the sentence. Elsewhere, in fact, Sterne does leave an empty space which he later proposes to fill with the asterisks of an unspoken word:

> . . . in selling my chaise, I had sold my remarks along with it, to the chaise-vamper.                    I leave this void space that the reader may swear into it, any oath that he is most accustomed to—For my own part, if ever I swore a *whole* oath into a vacancy in my life, I think it was into that—*** **** **, said I,—(VII, xxxvii)

It is true that this kind of thing is still within the compass of rhetoric, still only pretending to allow the reader to invent freely. Thus in Volume II, when Toby leaves a sentence unfinished, Tristram is quick to interpret it as a rhetorical trick:

> —'My sister, mayhap,' quoth my uncle *Toby*, 'does not choose to let a man come so near her ****.' Make this dash,—'tis an Aposiopesis.—Take the dash away, and write *Backside*,—'tis Bawdy.—Scratch Backside out, and put *Cover'd-way* in,—'tis a Metaphor; . . . (II, vi)

But often, when the asterisks seem to carry a definite meaning, a meaning which is firmly embedded in the sentence structure, it is impossible to be sure what that meaning is. What, for instance, do we make of the descrip-

tion of Widow Wadman's kick—'supposing \*\*\*\*\*\*\*\*\*\*
to be the sun in its meridian, it was a north-east kick'
(VIII, ix)? No one but the reader can say what exactly those
asterisks stand for; and he will never feel that he can say
precisely what the narrator left him to say. He has to
recognize his independence of the narrator. Whilst he can
still feel that he will know when he has guessed the 'right'
words, he must think of himself as 'reading' them. But here
he is aware that, though they exist, they can never be read;
in other words, he can read *into* the asterisks what he is
not able to read *in* them. And even when each letter of each
word is identified by an asterisk, when the words are *there*,
though not disclosed, the reader may still feel that he cannot
say for certain what the words are. What *did* Jenny say to
Tristram as he stood holding his garters, 'reflecting upon
what had not passed'?

—'Tis enough, Tristram, and I am satisfied, saidst thou,
whispering these words in my ear, \*\*\*\* \*\* \*\*\*\* \*\*\* \*\*\*\*\*\*;—
\*\*\*\* \*\* \*\*\*\*—any other man would have sunk down to the
centre—— (VII, xxix)

The asterisks, then, are a playful symbol of the reader's
sense of this book. They imply that the reader is both
receptive and creative, and that reading is sometimes equivalent to writing. And this is also what is implied by the
larger structural features of the novel. In some cases there is
nothing very subtle about what happens. When it comes to a
description of Widow Wadman, the narrator leaves a blank
page on which the reader can inscribe his own account:
'paint her to your own mind—as like your mistress as you
can—as unlike your wife as your conscience will let you—
'tis all one to me—please but your own fancy in it' (VI,
xxxviii). The blank page gives visual emphasis to a rhetorical
trick. It is in effect an illustration. But there are other
blank pages which do something more interesting. Chapters
Eighteen and Nineteen of Volume IX take up room, they

each occupy a page, they are there without question. Yet they contain no words, they are chapters of silence, or emptiness. Something similar has happened much earlier in the book. Chapter Twenty-three of Volume IV is followed directly by Chapter Twenty-five (and page '146' by page '156'). 'No doubt, Sir—there is a whole chapter wanting here—and a chasm of ten pages made in the book by it—' (IV, xxv). Tristram's explanation is that the chapter had been written and then torn out because its style was out of key with the rest of the volume. Chapter Twenty-five turns out, therefore, to be largely a summary and discussion of the missing Chapter Twenty-four. Sterne's subject here is something that did not get into the book, though clearly after all it *has* got in. He invents, as it were, the evidence of an 'anti-book' which consists of all the things that are the negation of this one. Or, rather, he is asking the reader to be able to imagine such material, which he himself only summarizes and describes. In Volume IX, however, the 'missing' chapters have a different effect. In fact they are *not* missing, but they do not contain anything, or rather they contain nothing. What is more, these two chapters of emptiness are followed by an inaudible dialogue in invisible words, thus:

### CHAPTER TWENTY

—　*　*　*　*　*　*　*　*　*
*　*　*　*　*　*　*　*　*　*
*　*　*　*　*　*　*　*　*　*
*　*　*　*　*　*
*　*　*　*　*　*　*　*
*　*　*　*　*　*　*　*　*
*　*　*　*　*　*　*　*　*　*
*　*　*____

—You shall see the very place, Madam; said my uncle Toby. (**IX**, xx)

Several pages later the narrator looks back to the two blank chapters: 'I look upon a chapter which has, *only nothing in it*, with respect' (IX, xxv). This is in Chapter Twenty-five, which he says had to be written before the eighteenth and nineteenth (the blank) chapters. And the reason must be that 'Chapter Twenty-five' is really made up of the words which had not been printed in the two empty chapters. Tristram has been playing a rather elaborate game with the sequence of the narrative. It is this trick in fact which Shklovsky takes as the starting-point for his discussion of 'displacement' in the novel. But it is not just a reshuffling of 'given' material, much more an experiment to test its materiality and to discover the relationship between what is and what has still be to created, between what can be read and what must be invented. Once more we are being asked to 'read' what has not yet been written, or more precisely, what has been written in the form of absence and silence. And what we later read is not, after all, Chapter Eighteen but **'The Eighteenth Chapter'**, not Chapter Nineteen but **'Chapter the Nineteenth'**. We almost begin to feel that we could compare the two forms. In any case these Gothic headings give the impression of material interpolated from another source. Are they *really* what the two blank chapters would have been? It is true that **Chapter the Nineteenth** would lead directly into Chapter Twenty, in which Trim is sent to fetch the map from the garret so that Mrs Wadman may 'see the very place' (IX, xx). But we find that it also leads directly into Chapter Twenty-six, where again Mrs Wadman asks her question, '—And whereabouts, dear Sir, quoth Mrs. Wadman, a little categorically, did you receive this sad blow?', and again Trim 'was detached into the garret to fetch [the map]', and again Mrs Wadman cannot 'explain the mistake' to Uncle Toby. Chapter Twenty-six, it appears, is an alternative version of Chapter Twenty. Does this not suggest that in an odd way the 'Gothic' chapters 18 and 19 are not simply what was *not there* earlier, but are themselves alternatives to whatever was there? It gives the impression that the author is adding a different version of the story that the reader has already 'written'. A procedure such as this creates an extraordinary effect, but it is not there just for the effect. Sterne is using it, like most of the procedures in the novel, to bring home to the reader the manifold ways in which he has to help create what he reads.

Sterne invites the reader to participate in the act of imagining the novel. He is working towards a kind of rhetoric that will permit a genuine conversation, and prompt the reader's imagination. Reading—this is the profound moral of the book—is a creative act, a discovery of the meaning of things. This is not to say that books lay out the meanings for the reader to pick up. Far from it. Reading is itself an activity which gives meaning:

> —Read, read, read, read, my unlearned reader! read, or by the knowledge of the great saint *Paraleipomenon*—I tell you before-hand, you had better throw down the book at once; for without *much reading*, by which your reverence knows, I mean *much knowledge*, you will no more be able to penetrate the moral of the next marbled page (motly emblem of my work!) than the world with all its sagacity has been to unravel the many opinions, transactions, and truths which still lie mystically hid under the dark veil of the black one. (III, xxxvi)

# CHAPTER 8

# Tristram Shandy (*ii*): *The Author as Reader*

## I

THERE is more to the comedy of *Tristram Shandy* than the comic. The cause of its laughter is joy, and the gaiety of the creative imagination. It asks the reader to share in the discovery of laughter and the freeing of the imagination. It has a Blakean innocence:

> Come live & be merry, and join with me,
> To sing the sweet chorus of 'Ha, Ha, He!'

It says that a man is what he is capable of imagining; and this, in turn, depends upon his capacity for laughter. This is a meaning worked out, as we have seen, in terms of the active participation of the reader. His imagination is certainly not meant to seem cramped or diminished by having to act within the circumference of the given story. Indeed Sterne evidently believes that stories stimulate the imagination: reading is an essentially creative act. There is a striking passage in one of the sermons in which he ponders the reasons for this. He has noted that Alexander, in real life a pitiless tyrant, 'at the bare representation of a tragedy which related the misfortunes of Hecuba and Andromache, ... was so touched with the fictitious distress which the poet had wrought up in it, that he burst out into a flood of tears'. The fiction made legible what his own experience had obscured:

> in *real* life he had been blinded with passions, and thoughtlessly hurried on by interest or resentment:—but here, there was no room for motives of that kind; so that his attention being first caught hold of, and all his vices laid asleep;—then NATURE awoke in triumph, and shewed how deeply she had sown the seeds of compassion in every man's breast; when tyrants, with vices the most at enmity with it, were not able entirely to root it out.[1]

Thus readers take possession of real life through a fiction. They lose themselves and find themselves in an imagined world. And that world is an affirmation; it is proposed, it asks for the reader's assent. If the reader has to collaborate with the author it is by giving definition and density to what has already been conceived. But when he says yes to this he is also, as Sterne shows, saying yes to the real world— 'then NATURE awoke in triumph'. Apparently reading too is, in a sense, a reading of unmediated experience, of 'reality'. And, if this is so, we should be able to talk of the *writer* as a reader; and then the world that is given to him in experience is what he reads. What he has had to invent, the *fictum*, is in some way what he knows already, a *datum*. The author invents by finding, just as the reader in assenting helps to create.

Admittedly, according to Sartre, we can properly talk of the writer only as a quasi-reader. 'The operation of writing', he says, 'implies that of reading as its dialectical correlative and these two connected acts necessitate two distinct agents.'[2] The writer *cannot* read in the way that the reader does: it is just his quasi-reading that makes real reading impossible. For, though the writer knows that his landscape really exists, that, as Sartre says, 'it is [there] before my eyes, and I can make *there be* being only if being already *is*',[3] yet he recognizes that he is free to make it become what he wishes.

[1] *Sermons*, i, V    [2] *What is Literature?* p. 37    [3] Ibid., p. 46

My freedom becomes caprice. . . . Because I have deeply re-
gretted that this arrangement which was momentarily perceived
was not offered to me by somebody and consequently is not *real*,
the result is that I fix my dream, that I transpose it to canvas
or in writing. Thus, I interpose myself between the finality
without end which appears in the natural spectacles and the gaze
of other men. I transmit it to them. It becomes human by this
transmission. Art here is a ceremony of the gift and the gift
alone brings about this metamorphosis.[1]

The reader can accept as art what the writer can understand
only as an appeal for art: what is not given as art is not
*given* at all.

All the same it is clear that some kinds of fiction want
to look like what *is*, what could not be otherwise, and what
can count as a 'given'. The novelist in particular wants
to create a world that looks unmodulated. He wishes to
encompass everything as it is; he aspires to be a reader. He
tries to become someone who, like a reader, 'is conscious of
disclosing in creating, of creating by disclosing'.[2] At any
rate this is the kind of creativity that Sterne is tracing in
*Tristram Shandy*. He is curious about the conditions of
realism, about the criteria for truth in fiction, about the
relation of fantasy to reality. We have seen that he is
interested in what the reader is capable of imagining. He
also fills the novel with people who in various ways wish to
remake the conditions of reality. His novel is about the fictive
imagination. It is a novel about authors and quasi-authors.

Many of the people in Tristram's story are in fact
incapable of imagining anything other than their own
destiny. Their element is gravity: they cannot imagine
wings. Mrs Shandy, especially, knows herself only in one
role. It is the one word 'wife' which, as it were, calls her
into existence:

My mother was going very gingerly in the dark along the
passage which led to the parlour, as my uncle *Toby* pronounced

---

[1] *What is Literature?* p. 47                [2] Ibid., p. 37

the word *wife*.— . . . my mother heard enough of it, to imagine
herself the subject of the conversation . . . (V, v)

She is as predictable as clockwork, and that absurd fact is, of
course, the point of departure for the whole novel. She is a
creature of pure reflex action: mention the word 'month'
and—'as my father pronounced the last word of the sentence
—my mother took a pinch of snuff' (VIII, xxxiii). Yet this
most rudimentary of all existences is the sweetest thing in
the book. It is delightful to see with what a pure instinct
she affirms the truth that so many of the others keep
stumbling over:

> —I think the procreation of children as beneficial to the
> world, said Yorick, as the finding out the longitude——
> —To be sure, said my mother, *love* keeps peace in the
> world——
> —In the *house*—my dear, I own——
> —It replenishes the earth; said my mother—— (ibid.)

She is at one with Yorick, we see, and seems to have a
wisdom she is unconscious of. At the same time, her wisdom
strikes us as ineffectual: it is purely an aspect of being and
therefore cannot act. She manifests it unwittingly; it is what
she is; she could hardly become aware of it without getting
confused. This is why she is so touching.

Uncle Toby has the same kind of charm. But he is unlike
her essentially. She is an innocent; he is a nostalgic myth of
innocence. Her simplicity is opaque and thing-like; his
simplicity is both radiant and troubled. She is a moral idiot,
she has no conception of virtue but is just true to her own
nature. He encourages us to value precisely those virtues
that seem unequal to the hard conditions of life. Mrs
Shandy is beautiful and funny because she is so perfectly
herself; but what is amusing and endearing about Toby is
his embarrassment, the incompatibility of his nature with
his dual role of soldier and lover. The beauty of it is that he
remains unaware of this: we sense that our amusement

glances off his complete trustfulness, and becomes a comment on some lack of merit in ourselves. He is in the most disarming way a satire on the reader. Fluchère brings out this aspect of his nature; he talks of the 'pure sincerity' with which Toby meets every situation, the 'absolute and joyful ... self-surrender to chance and illusion', and his 'extraordinary assurance' and 'crystalline solidity'.[1] These qualities Fluchère relates to his 'instinctive loyalty' to illusion and his 'power of being totally and unselfconsciously absorbed in make-believe'. But here, it seems to me, the book throws an ambiguity over Toby's nature and behaviour. What really, after all, makes him resemble Mrs Shandy is that he lacks the kind of imaginative belief Fluchère is talking about. Toby's games, he argues, console Trim and himself 'for their disability, their retirement, and in a certain sense for their common solitude'; their 'imaginary activity ... gives meaning to their past and incomparable zest to their present'.[2] But this is not all there is to it. Toby is not quite so uncomplicated. At least our feelings towards him are not. In fact it is just whether Toby has this capacity for 'belief and the happiness it brings'[3] that the book raises as a question.

## II

The first thing Tristram tells us about him prompts a question.

> My uncle TOBY SHANDY, Madam, was a gentleman, who ...
> possessed ... a most extream and unparallel'd modesty of nature;
> —tho' I correct the word nature, for this reason, that I may not
> prejudge a point which must shortly come to a hearing; and
> that is, Whether this modesty of his was natural or acquir'd.—
> (I, xxi)

---

[1] *Laurence Sterne*, p. 300     [2] *Laurence Sterne*, p. 301     [3] Ibid., p. 300
M

Characteristically Tristram believes that in asking this question he has got things out of order; but it is in fact one that is going to preoccupy him throughout the novel. And it leads to another question, whether Toby is fit to cope with reality. This is the real question about him. It hovers all the time over the talk about his 'modesty' and his 'wound'. His recovery, Tristram tells us, depended on 'the passions and affections of his mind' (II, iii). He would not be well again until he had become 'so far master of his subject, as to be able to talk upon it without emotion' (Ibid.). Until he can tell his story he must remain its victim. He needs the words that will give him control over his past. But a fortnight's work on 'Gobesius's military architecture and pyroballogy' does his wound 'no good' (II, iii): ' 'Twas not by ideas,—by heavens! his life was put in jeopardy by words' (II, ii). Trim's happy inspiration appears to solve the problem. The war, which will not be subdued to a science of fortifications and projectiles ('the parameter and semi-parameter of the conic section angered his wound', II, iv), can now be acted out in play.

> My uncle *Toby* blushed as red as scarlet as *Trim* went on;
> —but it was not a blush of guilt,—of modesty,—or of anger;—
> it was a blush of joy;—he was fired with Corporal *Trim's* project
> and description. (II, v)

Toby has discovered the imagination. He can now recreate the intractable realities in a way which will allow him to score off them. His game is 'one of the most refined satyrs upon the parade and prancing manner, in which *Lewis* XIV. from the beginning of the war, but particularly that very year, had taken the field' (VI, xxii).

On the other hand, Tristram makes it seem doubtful if Toby really has recovered from his wound. Even the desire to get well, Tristram says, appears to come from some 'crotchet . . . in my uncle *Toby's* head', rather than from 'the desire of life and health' or 'the love of liberty and enlargement' (II, iv). And actually, when the game is devised, his state of mind becomes hectic: '—The succession of his ideas was now rapid,—he broiled with impatience to put his design in execution' (II, v). What does this mean but that Toby has found his 'hobby-horse'? This is certainly what Tristram thinks: 'When a man gives himself up to the government of a ruling passion,—or, in other words, when his HOBBY-HORSE grows head-strong,—farewell cool reason and fair discretion!' (II, v). This looks remote from self-possession or an opening into reality.

In fact the words Tristram has used are a clear echo of the 'Digression concerning Madness'. Swift (or his 'modern' author) writes of the imagination as the choice of un-reality:

> When a Man's Fancy gets *astride* on his Reason, when Imagination is at Cuffs with the Senses, and common Under-standing, as well as common Sense, is kickt out of Doors; the first Proselyte he makes, is Himself, . . . 'tis manifest, what mighty Advantages Fiction has over Truth; and the Reason is just at our Elbow; because Imagination can build nobler Scenes, and produce more wonderful Revolutions than Fortune or Nature will be at Expence to furnish.[1]

Swift's narrator is himself astride his 'hobby-horse'. He is, in his own words, 'a Person, whose Imaginations are hard-mouth'd, and exceedingly disposed to run away with his *Reason*, which I have observed from long Experience, to be a very light Rider, and easily shook off'.[2] He is mad. It is madness to choose fiction rather tÿan fact.

Is Uncle Toby mad too? Of course, the novel would not tolerate the question. The slashing alternatives of *A Tale of a Tub* would have no meaning in Tristram's narration. Swift expects his madman's book to crash against something outside itself, some unseen snag of sanity. But Sterne

---

[1] *A Tale of a Tub*, p. 108
[2] *A Tale of a Tub*, p. 114

believes in the reality only of what can get imagined. As
Fluchère says,

> an invented character does not have to be related to some prob-
> lematic reality that is supposed to have preceded him. He has his
> own reality, his own truth. If you like he is true in relation
> to himself, and not in relation to some necessarily non-existent
> exterior model.[1]

The question that has to be asked must therefore be about
the authenticity of Toby's imagined world rather than its
sanity. What connection has it with reality, with the reality
imagined in the novel that is? And what, anyway, is the
relation of fiction to reality, or of reality to truth? What, in
other words, is the relation between making up fictions and
reading reality? These questions, which are meaningless in the
context of Swift's satire, are the substance of Sterne's novel.

Toby and Trim are at play. They are totally engrossed in
make-believe, in the kind of belief, that is, which rewards
and delights the imagination: '—What an honest triumph
in my uncle *Toby's* looks as he marched up to the ramparts!
What intense pleasure swimming in his eye as he stood over
the corporal, reading the paragraph ten times over to him,
. . .' (VI, xxii). 'Fiction is to the grown man', said Stevenson,
'what play is to the child; it is there that he changes the
atmosphere and tenor of his life.'[2] Has not Toby hit on that
discovery of the real world through play that we call fiction?
Certainly his game is a direct representation of the real
world. And this is really the trouble. His imagination is
quite literal. It is utterly enslaved to the facts. 'When the
duke of *Marlborough* made a lodgment,—my uncle *Toby*
made a lodgment too' (VI, xxii). If the Flanders mail is
delayed or the Gazette not to hand, the game collapses.
Its fascination is precisely that it calls for an exact alignment
with the real thing. What gives such 'intense pleasure' to
Toby is the need for unswerving accuracy: '. . . he stood

---

[1] *Laurence Sterne*, p. 286        [2] *Memories and Portraits*, p. 129

over the corporal, reading the paragraph ten times over to
him, as he was at work, lest, peradventure, he should make
the breach an inch too wide,—or leave it an inch too narrow'
(VI, xxii). Significantly, what they both appreciate is the
straight line, the 'cabbage-planter's' line in fact, the pattern
of parallels and right angles necessary to the game.

> . . . my uncle *Toby* and the corporal began to run their first
> parallel.—I beg I may not be interrupted in my story, by being
> told, *That the first parallel should be at least three hundred toises
> distant from the main body of the place,—and that I have not left
> a single inch for it*;—for my uncle *Toby* took the liberty of
> incroaching upon his kitchen garden, for the sake of enlarging
> his works on the bowling-green, and for that reason generally
> ran his first and second parallels betwixt two rows of his cabbages
> and his cauliflowers; . . . (VI, xxi)

A far cry, this, from Tristram's rambling progress. And
Toby's 'intense pleasure'—is not this equally remote from
the gaiety which animates Tristram's narrative? There is
something desperate in it. In a touching scene we eventually
see Toby's belief falter and the energy of his imagination
drain away. The peace of Utrecht is for him the time to
wake up to reality. He must plan the demolition of his
garrisons and his retreat; 'and having done that, corporal,
we'll embark for *England*.—We are there, quoth the
corporal, recollecting himself—Very true, said my uncle
*Toby*—looking at the church' (VI, xxxiv). This is their last
'delusive, delicious consultation' which allows them to hold
on to their game for a while longer;

> —still—still all went on heavily—the magic left the mind the
> weaker—STILLNESS, with SILENCE at her back, entered the soli-
> tary parlour, and drew their gauzy mantle over my uncle *Toby's*
> head;—and LISTLESSNESS, with her lax fibre and undirected eye,
> sat quietly down beside him in his arm-chair. (VI, xxxv)

The game was protecting Toby from reality, in particular
from the threat to his 'modesty'; '—and so naked and defenceless did he stand before you, (when a siege was out of

his head) that you might have stood behind any of our your
serpentine walks, and shot my uncle *Toby* ten times a day,
through his liver, if nine times in a day, Madam, had not
served your purpose' (VI, xxix). His imagination has been a
kind of refuge from reality, not because it was a fantasy, but
because it hardly could rise to fantasy. He has retreated into
the game, and his retreat has the look of sexual impotence:

> Never did lover post down to a belov'd mistress with more
> heat and expectation, than my uncle *Toby* did, to enjoy this self-
> same thing in private; . . . the idea of not being seen, did not
> a little contribute to the idea of pleasure preconceived in my
> uncle *Toby's* mind. (II, v)

After all, his imagination turns out to have been essentially
inert and uncreative. He has been slavishly dependent on
events and, in the end, is just as much at their mercy as ever
he was. Hence our mixed feelings about him. Like Mrs
Shandy, he represents a failure of the imagination. But this
is something she never even aspires to: even in her own eyes
she is an object. So her complete inability to transcend
herself hardly looks like a failure. Toby, however, is much
closer to us. He needs to be able to believe in an imagined
world. His fiction is important to him. We too want to
believe that it is important and could enhance the meaning of
the real world. We want to know about the chances of being
able to get closer to reality through fiction. Toby is putting
the reader's faith to the test, and it touches us when he
appears to fail. In this way he lets the reader down. But the
strange thing is that this is also what pleases us. There is
something unworldly about the way he makes no use of the
rich possibilities offered to him. He *chooses* to be inadequate.
He is a reproach to the gifted and to those who excel. He
really is 'one of the finest compliments ever paid to human
nature',[1] because he represents human nature as ineffectual
and *therefore* beautiful.

[1] Hazlitt, *Lectures on the English Comic Writers, Complete Works*, vi, 121

## III

It is a splendid thing that this book, full of laughter and creative energy, should address itself to this kind of failure. Toby's genius appears to be to confer distinction on those who are capable of celebrating him. Tristram is one of these, and so is Trim. Trim is really the creative partner in Uncle Toby's game, and his genius is certainly not diminished by being put at Toby's service. On the contrary it seems to improve through its constant resourceful attention to needs that Toby himself can hardly recognize. Trim keeps trying to mend the imagination which Toby keeps damaging. He keeps trying to protect Toby from his own will not to believe. He is a story-teller whose stories are needed but always frustrated, and in this way he is a prototype, in this book, of the author-figure.

His story of the King of Bohemia, which makes five vain attempts to get past the first sentence, naturally makes us think of Tristram's difficulty with *his* story. What is more important, it brings into play the central question of the novel about the relation of fact to fiction. Does action call for invention—making things up—or representation? Is it a discovery, a selection from what really exists, or is it a new creation? To what extent, that is, is fiction a *reading* of reality, to what extent a substitute for it? Toby's expectations, as we have seen, are that a story will tell truth. But this does not guarantee a foothold in reality. Trim's fanciful story is beyond him, and, since he does not know how to listen, it becomes an implicit criticism of him. On the other hand, its pure invention fades into untruth alongside his impregnable literal-mindedness. In this way a decision about the truth of what can be imagined depends on someone who hardly understands the imagination at all.

The story comes to grief, not because Trim cannot tell it but because Toby does not know how to take it. 'The eye of

Goodness espieth all things'; this is Tristram's interpretation of Toby's first reaction. But what Toby sees, as Trim is 'entering the confines of Bohemia', is only that he is not wearing his Montero-cap. The cap is getting worn out and prompts some moralizing which Toby prefers to the story: '—'Tis every word of it but too true, cried my uncle Toby, that thou art about to observe—"*Nothing in this world, Trim, is made to last for ever*" ' (VIII, xix). There follows a question about the date of the story, though 'chronology', Toby admits, would be useless to a soldier 'was it not for the lights which that science must one day give him, in determining the invention of powder' (Ibid.). The story has to be real in the way that history or geography is real: it cannot be allowed to envisage impossibilities—a giant alive in 1712 for instance. It must be governed by what is, not what may be. It is really unthinkable that Trim should be able to make up what is in fact true, 'there *happening*', for instance, 'throughout the whole kingdom of Bohemia, to be no sea-port whatever— How the deuce should there— Trim? cried my uncle Toby; for Bohemia being totally inland, it could have happen'd no otherwise—' (Ibid.)

The story collapses precisely at the point where it appears that things might happen otherwise, 'might happen, or not, just as chance ordered it'. It entirely fails to establish the reality of a world without necessity.

But it also leaves the way clear for quite a different kind story, a 'true' story, which is in fact an analogue of the one that Toby has never been able to tell. Trim, recollecting that he has 'often cried at his master's sufferings, but never shed a tear at his own' (ibid.), tells the story of *his* wound. He is talking now of real happenings, of events located in the memory and kept secure in experiences that have been lived through: 'Your honour remembers with concern, said the corporal . . .', 'your honour knows . . .'. This area of fact is paradoxically where Toby's imagination flourishes best: 'I see him galloping across me, corporal, to the left,

...—I see him with the knot of his scarfe just shot off, infusing fresh spirits into poor Galway's regiment—' (Ibid.). And what is more, Toby's response to this story, the story of the Beguine, though it is an involuntary reflection of his nature, looks comically like an act of the imagination; anyway it does not spoil the story:

> —my passion [Trim says] rose to the highest pitch—I seized her hand—
> —And then thou clapped'st it to thy lips, Trim, said my uncle Toby—and madest a speech.
> Whether the corporal's amour terminated precisely in the way my uncle Toby described it, is not material; it is enough that it contain'd in it the essence of all the love-romances which ever have been wrote since the beginning of the world. (VIII, xxii)

Trim's imagination and Toby's are here perfectly complementary. What, between them, they understand composes a definition of love that has the force of a discovery in the novel:

> I thought *love* had been a joyous thing, quoth my uncle Toby.
> 'Tis the most serious thing, an' please your honour (sometimes) that is in the world. (VIII, xx)

This is a story of real events, and it has real consequences —for Toby disastrous ones. Mrs Wadman has overheard it from her arbour, and now acts on it: 'the disposition which Trim had made in my uncle Toby's mind, was too favourable a crisis to be let slipped—'(VIII, xxiii). The story connects the past with the future; it allows the imagination to move from one area of knowledge to another, and to make experience accessible. It looks as if Trim was wrong to think of telling any other kind of story: '—thou hast seldom told me a bad one—', says Toby; '—Because, an' please your honour, except one of a *King of Bohemia and his seven castles*,—they are all true; for they are about myself—' (VIII, xix). The true story is best, because it appears to be a way of joining things in the real world and making things work. It is not subdued to literal truth: it has a truth extending beyond facts to meanings. Also it allows the story-teller, the maker, to present himself as an imitator, or a kind of reader. What happens in the story is not *made* to happen. His story will already have taken place, it will be in existence—at least potentially. Breathe on it and it will appear. The author-as-reader tells a story which could not be other than it is. It behaves like truth; it appears to be *there*, waiting for its author to read it.

On the other hand, it is not as a *story* that it is there. The story-teller does not transcribe fact as Toby and Trim attempted to do in their games on the bowling green. He sees in the facts some possibility which transfigures them. He has to be able to invent the truth.

IV

This is the kind of story Tristram has to tell. His self-consciousness as narrator, as we have seen, is often taken to indicate that he is responsible for his story, which is really the story of his consciousness. Yet he takes the view that there is something he is responsible *to*. If, for instance, we are to understand why Toby was wrong about the bridge for Tristram's nose, we ought to know what Toby had been doing; but 'the story, in one sense, is certainly out of its place here; . . . but then if I reserve it for either of those parts of my story,—I ruin the story I'm upon,—and if I tell it here—I anticipate matters, and ruin it there' (III, xxiii). Of course Tristram is in difficulties just because he understands that the mutually interfering narratives of real life do not fall into a story. A story has to be found in them, but where and how?

O ye POWERS! (for powers ye are, and great ones too)—which enable mortal man to tell a story worth the hearing,—that

kindly shew him, where he is to begin it,—and where he is to
end it,—what he is to put into it,—and what he is to leave out,—
how much of it he is to cast into shade,—and whereabouts he
is to throw his light!— . . . wherever, in any part of your
dominions it so falls out, that three several roads meet in one
point, as they have done just here,— . . . set up a guide-post,
in the centre of them, in mere charity to direct an uncertain
devil, which of the three he is to take. (III, xxiii)

But still Tristram is, as he says, 'a *biographical* freebooter';
he is narrating a life-story. Trim, in telling the story of the
King of Bohemia, was on the edge of a void out of which
he had to bring something into being. 'Take any date', says
Toby, 'in the whole world thou choosest, and put it to—
thou art heartily welcome— . . . [thus] had my uncle Toby
subjected this vast empire of time and all its abysses at his
feet' (VIII, xix). But Tristram's story, if he can get it told,
will be one which he had first been able to read. In fact to
tell it will be in a sense to read it. Tristram is the author in
the sense that he is the discoverer, the first reader, of his
story.

What this means is that 'story' is the significance which
the present gives to the past. Fluchère, we recall, spoke of
the past being appropriated to the present, but Tristram
does not swallow the past. He represents an attitude
towards it, a point of view from which the past takes on the
appearance of a story. He creates his material by standing
away from it.

The story exists in the way that Tristram reads it. And
this means, of course, that he must detach himself from it.
In some ways, it is true, Tristram appears to be the victim
of his own story: everything he relates has a fateful meaning
for him. 'I am lost myself!—', he says, '—But 'tis my
father's fault; and whenever my brains come to be dissected,
you will perceive, without spectacles, that he has left a large
uneven thread, as you sometimes see in an unsaleable piece
of cambrick, running along the whole length of the web, . . .'

(VI, xxxiii). Yet he is wonderfully self-effacing; it is his father's sufferings that concern him: 'When the misfortune of my NOSE fell so heavily upon my father's head, . . .' (IV, xvii). Tristram is getting free of his story by telling it, the thing that Toby wished to do. Of course, though it is *his* story, it is not a story *about* him. It never gets beyond his fifth year, and it ends five years before his birth. Yet, in another sense, it is about nothing but him: it begins when he begins writing in 1759—one observation 'was struck out by me this very rainy day, *March* 26, 1759, and betwixt the hours of nine and ten in the morning' (I, xxi)—and ends in 1766 when he stops writing. It is the story, not so much of Tristram's 'consciousness', as of the writing of the book. Tristram is reading himself; that is, he is reading the story of writing his book, and that story is the record of how he discovers himself in the lives of others.

And this is also what Sterne is doing. He does not invent Tristram, he finds Tristram within himself. Yet what Edwin Muir says is right: '. . . by appearing only as his imaginative portrait in *Tristram Shandy*, he renounces the luxury of being himself.'[1] What a man is is what he is capable of imagining. True, what Sterne is imagining is in some ways what he actually is. At least he 'imagines' that rainy morning in March 1759, or the time in 1766 when he 'lost some four score ounces of blood . . . in a most un-critical fever' (IX, xxiv), or the journey to France in 1762. And then he goes on to imagine writing this book. Evidently such imagining is a kind of reading, since it is a record of what really happened. But to read his own life in this way Sterne must invent himself. He must become the person for whom all the fictional Shandys are real, and whose history is the preposterous Shandy story. It is through a complication of untruths that he has to discover the truth about himself.

The novel is made up of superimposed fictions, each one

[1] *Essays on Literature and Society*, p. 52

creating by disclosing another. At the base are the most transparently fictional stories: Slawkenbergius's tale, or the story of the Abbess of Andoüillets. Over this is laid the story Tristram is telling (which itself includes stories, like the one about Phutatorius and the hot chestnut, or the story of Le Fever, or of Tom and the Jew's widow). Here there is a distinct thickening of reality; we seem now to be in a region where stories can be told. But this itself is found to be a story told in the world where Tristram lives, with Eugenius and Jenny and, no doubt, the readers, 'your honours', 'Madam', 'your reverences'. And finally Tristram and his readers are understood as a fiction by Sterne and *his* readers. This means that at each level there is something that is to be understood as a fiction. At each level the significant experience is that of reading, and the last is no exception. Thus it is that the author of this book is able to read his own novel. His material is always both known and unknown to him, both subjective and objective. Sterne has devised a book about readers and he is therefore able to be the ultimate reader, who can see himself as an object in the world he is inventing, can indeed see the *imagining* of that world as an object.

## V

By building stories upon stories Sterne arrives at an air of truth. At each stage story-telling comes to look more like reading; at each stage there becomes less room for pure invention. Yet Sterne can hardly be wanting to lock the imagination onto a world which *has* to exist. In fact he keeps reminding us that the process of reading opens up a region of make-believe. It allows us, that is, to believe in a world we have to some extent invented ourselves.

There is a strange narrative sequence in Volume VI

which shows how this might happen. In Chapter Twenty-eight Tristram speaks like a reader himself:

> —My uncle *Toby* retired into the sentry-box with the pipe in his hand.—
>
> —Dear uncle *Toby*! don't go into the sentry-box with the pipe,—there's no trusting a man's self with such a thing in such a corner.

This makes us feel that what is narrated did happen. But the next chapter opens with an appeal to the reader that deliberately destroys that illusion:

> I beg the reader will assist me here, to wheel off my uncle *Toby's* ordnance behind the scenes,—to remove the sentry-box, and clear the theatre, *if possible*, of horn-works and half moons, and get the rest of his military apparatus out of the way;—

So it was all staged? All just pretending? Actually Tristram is also managing to confirm the impression that it is something we are all *watching*: it is artificial certainly, yet it is a representation, taking part of its significance from the way it is attended to. Also it is a representation in which the readers must collaborate, even collaborate as stage-managers. Is not the metaphor of scene-shifting a reminder of the primacy of the reader's power to imagine, to set the scene for himself? *He* must make it happen. ('Vain science! thou assists us in no case of this kind—and thou puzzlest us in everyone.') By the end of this chapter Tristram is again the narrator who is like a reader. 'There was, Madam, in my uncle Toby, a singleness of heart which misled him . . . But where am I going? these reflections crowd in upon me ten pages at least too soon, and take up that time, which I ought to bestow upon facts.' Like a reader he is drawing conclusions from the story, and is actually telling it in doing so.

The author and reader, in a passage like this, work together to bring the real into existence, though both think of it as already existing. Reading, for both of them, consists in making up what they read as they go along. The reader, we have seen, is kept guessing; and Tristram wants to give the impression that he hardly knows himself what is coming next. At the beginning of Volume VIII, he talks about 'ways of beginning a book'.

> ... I begin with writing the first sentence—and trusting to Almighty God for the second.
>
> . . .
>
> I wish you saw me half starting out of my chair, with what confidence, as I grasp the elbow of it, I look up—catching the idea, even sometimes before it half way reaches me——(VIII, ii)

The self-parody indicates a serious intention. Northrop Frye writes of Sterne as bringing to perfection a 'sense of literature as process', and this is surely what Tristram is talking about. He is describing a way of evading the sense (particularly strong, Frye maintains, in Augustan writers) of 'literature as a finished product'. In such literature 'the suspense is thrown forward until it reaches the end, and is based on our confidence that the author knows what is coming next'.[1] But, like Richardson, Sterne does not want us to think of a predestined conclusion for the book. Tristram is designed to suggest that the act of writing is, again in Frye's words, 'a continuous process from experience'.[2] We recognize in Tristram Shandy what Bagehot calls 'the *optional* world of literature'.[3] Sterne sees it as Blake would see it, as a way of keeping faith with the creative joy of the book: 'He who kisses the joy as it flies / Lives in eternity's sun rise.' 'VIVA LA JOIA!': the Gascoigne roundelay sets the tone.

> —Then 'tis time to dance off, quoth I; so changing only partners and tunes, I danced it away from Lunel to Montpellier —from thence to Pesçnas, Beziers—I danced it along through Narbonne, Carcasson, and Castle Naudairy, till at last I danced myself into Perdrillo's pavilion, where pulling [out] a paper of

---

[1] 'Towards defining an age of sensibility', *ELH*, June 1956, reprinted in *Eighteenth-Century English Literature*, ed. J. L. Clifford, p. 312
[2] Ibid., p. 313          [3] *Collected Works*, ii, 293

black lines, that I might go on straight forwards, without digression or parenthesis, in my uncle Toby's amours—

I begun thus—(VII, xliii)

But, as we have seen, everything in this book is set against the principle of the straight black line. The essence of the book is in the dance.

Tristram calls it 'a rhapsodical work' (I, xiii). It is not predictable: '. . . if I thought you was able to form the least judgment or probable conjecture to yourself, of what was to come in the next page,—I would tear it out of my book' (I, xxv). Nor is it tied to truth. A. A. Mendilow is quite severe about this. Sterne, he says, 'does stretch the truth considerably in making Tristram describe what he did not witness and could not possibly have learned from other sources'.[1] As he says, Sterne seems at first to want to establish Uncle Toby as a source for some of the anecdotes. 'Later, however, he abandons all pretence of coming by his information as limiting his powers too seriously, and with unclipped wings he soars into the convention of the omniscient author, a convention artificial in itself and accepted as compatible only with the third-person novel.' However, the book would have been 'fatally circumscribed' if he had done otherwise.[2]

True, it would. At the same time, we have seen that Sterne did want to keep up an illusion of the real existence of his people. Tristram has to appear to be describing what actually happened at Shandy Hall at the turn of the century; the stability of the whole book depends on it. Like Uncle Toby's hobby-horse his story keeps pace with history: it advances 'step by step with the allies' (VI, xxii), a history itself, with the kind of truth that is vouched for by the memory, though it has to be perpetually renewed in the imagination. And Tristram's narrative does often sound like this kind of history. On at least one occasion he can explain the process. Uncle Toby has at last caught the fly

---

[1] *Time and the Novel*, p. 185     [2] Ibid., p. 186

which has been annoying him at dinner; but he releases it;
'—go poor Devil, get thee gone, why should I hurt thee?—
This world surely is wide enough to hold both thee and me'
(II, xii). Tristram tells us how the recollection of this has
stayed with him: 'I was but ten years old when this happened; but . . . this I know, that the lesson of universal
good-will then taught and imprinted by my uncle *Toby*, has
never since been worn out of my mind' (II, xii).

But this story does not really advance Tristram's narrative. He has introduced it in order to account for something
that took place, he maintains, many years earlier. Walter
Shandy had 'insulted' Toby's hobby-horse.

> Pray, Sir, what said he?—How did he behave?—Oh, Sir!—it
> was great: For as soon as my father had done insulting his
> HOBBY-HORSE,—he turned his head, . . . and look'd up into
> my father's face, with a countenance spread over with so much
> good nature, . . . it penetrated my father to his heart. (II, xii)

This took place on the night Tristram was born, yet he
talks like an eye-witness: 'Oh, Sir!—it was great.' It is
vividly realized. Nothing here is left for the reader to
imagine. It is personal testimony. Yet how can it be? It is
authenticated in the one way that must make us doubt its
authenticity.

Why did Sterne do this? Why not have Tristram relate
events at which he *was* present? As Fluchère sees it, if
Sterne needed Tristram to play the role of narrator he
could not also let him enter the action, 'to which he might
then have been obliged to contribute'. 'It is', Fluchère
continues, 'in fact, very difficult to be the narrator and the
character narrated at one and the same time—to be an actor
in a story one is telling oneself, to be the object of one's
own contemplation—without becoming an object pure and
simple'. Therefore the Tristram in the story must assume
'merely symbolic importance as the name, the fragment of
universal life, around which the Shandean comedy is

N

organised'.[1] If Fluchère is right then Sterne has really got into trouble: he cannot allow Tristram into the story, yet cannot without destroying its authenticity keep him out of it. But I wonder if the difficulty is what Fluchère thinks it is. It seems less likely that the narrator would become an 'object' in his story, than that the story would flow into the large expanse of the recording consciousness—as, in fact, Fluchère thinks it does. And in any case, if this were to seem real to us, we would have to be convinced of the reality of the story that fills it. Fluchère maintains in fact that Tristram 'records conversations he has heard and other people's memories that have since become his own, and he thus by re-thinking it re-lives as his own what was originally the experience of others'.[2] But Sterne, as we have seen, makes no effort to sustain this impression. It looks as if there must be some other reason for what he has done.

It is better, I think to regard him as making play with the dimensions of fiction. There is, as we have seen, the fiction which is a kind of reading, in which the writer discovers or discloses the significance of things. And there is also the kind of fiction which, like the story of the King of Bohemia, is all invention. A fiction is a representation and at the same time a new creation. In one sense a selection from the stuff of reality, it is also a creation out of nothing. For such a selection would have to be made from material which for the artist's purposes does not yet exist, and which, if it is not chosen, never will exist. The author creates by finding the being which is latent in non-being. This is the kind of creation Traherne celebrates in 'The Salutation':

> These little Limmes,
> These Eys and Hands which here I find,
> These rosie Cheeks wherwith my Life begins,
> Where have ye been? Behind
> What Curtain were ye from me hid so long!
> Where was? in what Abyss, my Speaking Tongue?

[1] *Laurence Sterne*, p. 337     [2] Ibid., loc. cit.

Between the real and the unreal, between literal truth and
pure fantasy, there is an area of the virtual which the
imagination must create, and which is then found to be
'true'.

This is the region Tristram is exploring. He has to create
his own past. He makes up a family for himself, 'my uncle
Toby', 'my father', 'my mother', even 'my grandmother'
and 'my grandfather'. Perhaps this is why there is that
curious discrepancy about the dates relating to his birth. He
was begotten, he is 'positive', 'in the night, betwixt the
first Sunday and the first Monday' in March 1718 (I, iv).
He was born on November 5th, eight months later—'as
near nine calendar months as any husband could in reason
have expected' (I, v). Yet his father had 'apprized Dr. *Slop*
but the week before, that my mother was at her full reckon-
ing' (II, x), though he had himself had sciatica in the
previous December, January and February. Who is
Tristram's father? Indeed who is Tristram's mother? We
recall that it was ruled 'that the mother is not of kin to her
child' (IV, xxix).

> —And pray, Yorick, said my uncle Toby, which way is this
> said affair of *Tristram* at length settled by these learned men?
> Very satisfactorily, replied *Yorick*; no mortal, Sir, has any con-
> cern with it—for Mrs. Shandy the mother is nothing at all akin
> to him—and as the mother's is the surest side—Mr. *Shandy*, in
> course, is still less than nothing—In short, he is not as much
> a-kin to him, Sir, as I am—
> —That may well be, said my father, shaking his head.
> (IV, xxx)

Tristram is not born of his parents; in a strange way they
are born of him. At least they seem often to exist by virtue
of the fiction itself: 'from the first moment I sat down to
write my life for the amusement of the world, . . . has a
cloud insensibly been gathering over my father' (III, xxviii).
When Tristram leaves his mother listening outside the
door she has to stay there until the story will allow her to

move again (V, xi). It takes two chapters to get the Shandy
brothers down one pair of stairs, and it will take the help of a
critic to get them to bed:

> Holla!—you chairman!—here's sixpence—do step into that
> bookseller's shop, and call me a *day-tall* critick. I am very willing
> to give any one of 'em a crown to help me with his tackling, to
> get my father and my uncle *Toby* off the stairs, and to put them
> to bed.— (IV, xiii)

It is what Tristram invents that has the most convincing
reality. The people and events exist in so far as Tristram
thinks them up. The vitality of their created life does not
spill out of the book. It is channelled into the story of
Tristram's inventive genius. In the same way the written
record has the power to turn all other written material into
fiction. The book becomes creative of other books—Hafen
Slawkenbergius *de Nasis*, for instance, or the bogus
*Lithopaedus Senonesis de Partu difficili*, which turns out to be
derived by a double mistake from the caption to 'a drawing
of a petrified child', i.e. *Lithopaedii Senonensis Icon* (II, xix).
It even begins to 'invent' the real words of real writers:
'Shall we for ever make new books, as apothecaries make
new mixtures, by pouring only out of one vessel into
another?' (V, i), Tristram asks, in words that are really part
of Burton's *Anatomy of Melancholy*. And above all, of course,
the book invents Sterne's own sermon on Conscience,
having first invented Yorick to be its author. At this point
the book makes room for real things by pretending that they
do not exist and have to be invented. Tristram, the fictional
author, turns real life, real books, real people (John Hall
Stevenson, for instance, or Dr Burton) into fictions. He
invents them, in just the way that he invents his own family,
to populate his fictional world. What is more, Tristram,
invented to be the author of Sterne's novel, turns Sterne
himself into the fictional Yorick. Sterne invents the conditions in which he can invent himself.

## VI

Sterne has been able to discover something of himself in Tristram. He is also in a position to discover what Tristram invents. He can be both creator and reader; he can stay cool and self-possessed behind his creative self. That is, he can assume the role, just as an actor does. Martin Price notices that Diderot's description of the actor fits Sterne: he is the artist who 'must be free of emotion in order to call up emotion in others'.[1] This is possible for Sterne because he can allow Tristram to be the author, and to invent Yorick. Thus he can do through Tristram what Tristram cannot do for himself: he can objectify himself in the narrative. In Yorick he can see himself as a fictional *character*, just as in Tristram he is a fictional *creator*.

Yorick is at once the most and least fictional character in the book. He 'is' Sterne but he is also what Hamlet's Yorick was—in Ben Lehman's good phrase, 'the absolute jester of the imagination'.[2] At first he exists, as O. P. James reminds us, only in the memory of a fictional character, as does Hamlet's Yorick.[3] And like him he enters the work through his death. Fluchère sees it as both a real and a symbolic death: real because Yorick's death 'brings out the moral implications of his life', symbolic because it allows the character to emerge into full fictional life.[4] He is thus the antithesis of Tristram whose imagination is engaged in trying to fend off death. Yorick is put beyond death. He becomes, in Fluchère's words, an 'unchanging a-temporal figure';[5] he is taken up into the calm region of fiction.

The same thing happens to his sermon. In the sequence

[1] *To the Palace of Wisdom*, p. 328
[2] 'Of Time, Personality, and the Author', in *Laurence Sterne*, ed. Traugott, p. 24
[3] *The Relation of Tristram Shandy to the Life of Sterne*, p. 92
[4] *Laurence Sterne*, p. 347            [5] Ibid., p. 348

of the novel it comes after his death. It falls out of a real book into a fictional situation, and it is read by a fictional character before a fictional audience. Its very first sentence provokes an imaginary conversation and a story, Trim's story of his brother Tom and the Inquisition. The story belongs to the lives of these fictional characters: '—O, Sir! the story will make your heart bleed,—as it has made mine a thousand times;—but it is too long to be told now;—your Honour shall hear it from first to last some day when I am working besides you in our fortifications;—' (II, xvii). Trim does tell it again towards the end of the book. It becomes one of those stories which are both part of the book and part of the story: it is there in the text for *us* to read and also in the action where the characters themselves attend to it:

> The Corporal was just then setting in with the story of his brother Tom and the Jew's widow: the story went on—and on —it had episodes in it—it came back, and went on—and on again; there was no end of it—the reader found it very long——
> (IX, x)

This story of a story contributes something substantial to the book. If Yorick's sermon is to be a real thing in the same way it too will have to become fiction. And in fact it is related to Trim's story; it turns towards the end to a description of the Inquisition:

> 'To be convinced of this, go with me for a moment into the Prisons of the inquisition.' [God help my poor brother *Tom*.]— 'Behold *Religion*, with *Mercy* and *Justice* chained down under her feet,—there sitting ghastly upon a black tribunal, propp'd up with racks and instruments of torment. Hark!—hark! what a piteous groan!'—[Here *Trim's* face turned as pale as ashes.] —'See the melancholy wretch who uttered it'—— (II, xvii)

Martin Price thinks that Trim's extreme reactions here 'show us the folly of the obsessive imagination'.[1] They

[1] *To the Palace of Wisdom*, p. 324

certainly bring pulpit rhetoric to the verge of self-parody.
All through, indeed, the reactions of these fictional listeners
keep threatening to push the sermon into absurdity. The
sermon is at the mercy of the novel. It has to be shown
capable of living up to the quite superior reality of the
fictional world in which it finds itself. Reality has to take
on the posture of fiction:

> I tell thee, *Trim*, again, quoth my father, 'tis not an historical
> account,—'tis a description.—'Tis only a description, honest
> man, quoth *Slop*, there's not a word of truth in it.—That's
> another story, replied my father.—— (II, xvii)

The sermon follows the account of Yorick's death, and
this makes it look like a posthumous work. In fact, of
course, Trim's reading is supposed to take place in 1718, on
the evening of Tristram's birth, which is about thirty years
before Yorick's death ('About ten years ago', says Tristram
in 1759, he 'left his parish, and the whole world at the same
time behind him', I, x). Yet after the reading, Tristram tells
us of an actual occasion when the sermon was preached:

> Can the reader believe, that this sermon of *Yorick's* was
> preached at an assize, in the cathedral of *York*, before a thousand
> witnesses, ready to give oath of it, by a certain prebendary of that
> church, and actually printed by him when he had done,—and
> within so short a space as two years and three months after
> *Yorick's* death.—*Yorick*, indeed was never better served in his
> life!—but it was a little hard to male-treat him after, and plunder
> him after he was laid in his grave. (II, xvii)

Here a fictional date (the date of Yorick's death) is used
to establish a real one (the preaching of Sterne's sermon).
Fiction is called on to substantiate fact. At this point, where
Sterne enters the novel in his own person, reality seems to be
subordinated to fiction. It looks quite impoverished and
attenuated in the fictional context. So that, if we speak of
Sterne finding himself, it is hardly in this shadowy, marginal
figure that he does so. The fictional roles of Tristram and

Yorick tell him more about himself than the real 'prebendary' of York Cathedral. The fictional characters, the inventions of himself, are symbolic portraits: they embody all the energy of his creative life. But this 'gentleman' is Sterne robbed of his genius, diminished, an alien in his own book.

How can he be said to be the 'true' Sterne? Could the creator of Tristram and Yorick be beyond the compass of his own creative life? Could he be marginal to his own creation? There is a striking parallel here with a picture by Hogarth. When he was in France in 1748 he was caught making sketches of the English gate at Calais, and arrested as a spy. In 'O the Roast Beef of Old England'[1] he records this incident. He represents himself on the edge of the scene, watching and sketching; a soldier's hand reaches into the picture from behind him and grasps his shoulder. 'My own figure in the corner with the soldier['s] hand upon my sholder is said to be tolerably like', he wrote in his *Autobiographical Notes*.[2] He has made himself and the setting life-like. But the other figures on the scene are characters in a symbolic fiction. It is a story of 'a farcical pomp of war, parade of riligion and Bustle with little with very little business [—] in short poverty slavery and Insolence ⟨with an affectation of politeness⟩'.[3] A fat friar is 'blessing' a huge sirloin of beef; in the distance behind him a priest carries the sacrament among kneeling people. In the left foreground the fishwives laugh at their own likeness in a leathery flat-fish, on the right an exiled Scot lies in listless despair; they are all in the shadow of the gate, their hands clasped in a parody of prayer. Ragged soldiers with their meagre rations of soup hardly seem equal to their grotesquely large muskets and bayonets and swords. On all sides are prison-like walls and chains and spikes of the gate.

It is a theatrical scene, carefully stage-managed and

---

[1] See the frontispiece.
[2] Quoted in Paulson, *Hogarth's Graphic Works*, i, 203     [3] Ibid., loc. cit.

posed. It might seem that Hogarth's presence in the picture
would be necessary to connect it with an actual scene. Like
Sterne, Hogarth wedges a bit of fact into his design, but as
in the novel, only with the effect of making it seem inadequate to the rich possibilities of the imagined world. The
picture speaks with all the force of Hogarth's prejudices
and loyalties. But the 'Hogarth' shown in the corner is an
innocent character, an observer merely, no spy but only an
artist. He does not in fact see the picture quite as we see it,
but from the 'wings'. And he looks smaller than the reality
it represents, just the Hogarth who could *not* have painted
the picture. In both cases, in both the book and the picture,
the artist, the creator, is left *uncreated* and external to the
scene. It is in the fictions he is capable of that the artist
really must find himself. When he puts 'himself' into the
area of his own fictions he creates in effect yet another
fiction. For he divests himself of the ability to create: he
reverts to a nostalgic fiction of his own artistic innocence.

At the same time, of course, he *is* the artist. Part of the
meaning of Hogarth's story is in that hand reaching out to
arrest him. The incident shown in the picture is the story of
the creation of the picture. Hogarth's presence alters, in a
sense it creates, the scene. Similarly the prebendary of
York cathedral has preached, has even printed, the sermon
which is now printed in Tristram's book. Both Sterne and
Hogarth are portraying someone who bears responsibility
for the work. And it is noteworthy that they represent him
as being nothing in himself. What they discover about the
artist is that his effective identity can only be that which is
made manifest in the substance of his work. Any part of him
which is not *in* the work must appear inert, just as anything
he does not select from the full range of the possible must
be considered not yet to have come into existence. This
means, of course, that, in placing himself thus in the
margins of his work, Sterne is asking his fictional world to
make room for the non-fictional, for the evidence of that

non-being which it really contradicts. He is able to envisage the uncreated possibilities against which the novel stands; or, rather, he can understand that the fictional realities emerge from this inchoate region. But the fiction is all he can believe in. For, like the reader, he finds himself enlarged and enriched in this world. The act of reading and the act of imagining, both collaborate in life. What Sterne's novel triumphantly demonstrates is that fiction, both for author and reader, is an entry into a more abundant world. Edwin Muir puts it like this:

> It is a world which can be thrown open only by complete masquerade or disguise, for disguise is a magical art. It not only enables us to do things which, with our own features presented to the world, we would not permit ourselves to do, or dare not do; it not only gives us licence to be irresponsible, undignified, outspoken; it sets free in us a new personality with a suppleness and daring of movement which seems to belong to the dream-world.[1]

This makes it sound as if fiction is being valued as an 'escape' from reality. This is not quite what Sterne is driving at: Uncle Toby's hobby-horse is what fiction comes to look like when it is conceived as no more than an escape. But Sterne is deeply concerned to get us to *believe* in fiction, to accept gratefully the generous provisions of that imagined world, and to allow that it may be preferable to the real. He wants the reader to be able to imagine, that is the point. Or, rather, he wants the reader to understand that imagining, the writer's imagining for instance, is really a way of reading the meaning of things. He asserts the gaiety of the imagination; he shows the reader how to imagine life as a comedy. He wonderfully establishes, in defiance of chronology, what Dorothy Van Ghent calls 'the atemporal time—the "timeless time"—of the imagination, where the words of Toby and Mr Shandy echo in their plenitude'.[2] But it is not,

[1] *Essays on Literature and Society*, pp. 52-3
[2] *The English Novel*, p. 92

as she maintains, the 'apparent timelessness of consciousness' that he arrives at, but the world of fiction; this exists
just in so far as there are readers capable of conniving at its
creation. On the one hand is death, and *'Freeze-land, Fog-
land*, and some other lands I wot of'; on the other, as he
writes in the first chapter of Volume VIII,

> . . . this clear climate of fantasy and perspiration, where every
> idea, sensible and insensible, gets vent— . . . this fertile land of
> chivalry and romance, where I now sit, unskrewing my ink-
> horn to write my uncle Toby's amours, and with all the meander-
> ings of JULIA's track in quest of her DIEGO in full view of my
> study window—
>
> . . .
>
> What a work it is likely to turn out!
> Let us begin it.

# CHAPTER 9

# Coda: The Reader as Actor

## I

THERE is another way in *Tristram Shandy* of representing the reader, and it is one which may usefully stand as a kind of coda to this whole account of the reader's role in eighteenth-century fiction. For Sterne, more even than the other writers we have been considering, is interested in the reader and wants to get him into the novel. That is to say, he deals more boldly and creatively with the difficulty that any writer is in. Writing has to be read: it implies, as Sartre says, 'the operation . . . of reading as its dialectical correlative. . . . It is the conjoint effort of author and reader which brings upon the scene that concrete and imaginary object which is the work of the mind. There is no art except for and by others'.[1] It has to be a conversation, as Sterne thinks; but with whom? The very act of writing seals off the writer from his audience. The reader cannot be anywhere but on the far side of the written words. It looks as if a written story must be addressed to no one in particular, for otherwise the reader will not feel that it is meant in particular for him. An epistolary novel, for instance, shows us the readers as well as the writers of letters. But if these readers are *only* readers, if they do not enter into a quasi-dramatic dialogue, they will only damage the relationship between the text and the reader. They stand in the reader's light, an intrusive Rev. Mr Villars or a Wilhelm. They rob the reader of 'his' book. The writer therefore is unable to

---

[1] *What is Literature?*, p. 37

project his reader as a part of the book. He really has to admit that his reader is just out of sight. All novels reach out, like *Doctor Faustus*, to some 'future reader' who is barely conceivable:

> ... at this moment there exists not the smallest prospect that my manuscript will ever see the light unless, by some miracle, it were to leave our beleaguered European fortress and bring to those without some breath of the secrets of our prison-house. (Ch. 1)

All novels are a comparable act of faith.

This is a situation which Defoe, perhaps fortuitously, is able to turn to his own advantage. He is calling in question the reader's ability to speak truth, and he can do this because the reader might be anybody. Defoe hardly concerns himself with anything but the *irony* inherent in this situation. But Richardson was acutely conscious of the situation itself and of the paradox that it is at once the most intimate and the most remote kind of relationship. Even the letter-writer, who chooses her reader, is really choosing to be alone: '—Retired, the modest Lady, happy in herself, happy in the Choice she makes of the dear Correspondent ... uninterrupted; her Closet her Paradise, her Company, herself, and ideally the beloved Absent; ...'[1] Writing both idealizes and negates the reader—'ideally the beloved Absent'. Fielding, it is true, can welcome the reader into the fiction, and seems to be on easy terms with him. Yet he projects him in surprisingly impersonal terms, usually as '*the* reader', not so often 'my' or 'our' reader, still less often 'thee'. 'The reader will be pleased to recollect', 'the reader will be apt to conceive', 'the reader must remember', or 'the reader has seen'; it is all rather formal and remote. In fact Fielding cannot *see* the reader: 'we cannot possibly divine what Complexion our Reader may be of' (*Tom Jones*, I, ix). And actually he is not particularly interested in the person,

[1] *Selected Letters*, p. 68.

rather in the function, the fact that there must be a reading. He can therefore quite often use abstract terms: 'it may be wondered . . .', 'it may be objected . . .', 'it may be imagined . . .'. Thus the reader, who only matters to Fielding in so far as he *is* a reader, is being defined by what the book will demand of him.

It seems as if this must be so. The reader's role is to be the watcher, the witness. He stands for the inability to take part. He cannot get into the story. Yet he may well find that the story itself concerns him and reflects his predicament as a reader. The book will create the kind of reader it wants; it will ask to be read in certain ways. 'The particular attention of such of the Fair Sex, as are more apt to read for the sake of amusement than instruction, is requested to this Letter of Mr Lovelace' (*Clarissa*, II, 50; ii, 35). 'Oh let none read this Part without seriously reflecting on the Circumstances of a desolate State, and how they would grapple with mere want of Friends and want of Bread' (*Moll Flanders*, p. 220). Such passages tell the reader fairly bluntly who he is to be and where he is to stand. But so also do passages where he is apparently ignored: the novels may be said to be creating their readers by implication. Moll's narration, as we have seen, is an ironic manoeuvre against an unspecified reader. In *Tom Jones* irony is used, as Robert Alter puts it, 'to implicate [the reader] in a particular relationship with the narrator and the material narrated'.[1] The writer, who can hardly tell his story if he does not feel sure that some one will read it, is impelled to imagine a reader. Or, in other words, the way in which he tells his story may be taken as envisaging its reader. But it seems as if the reader can at best only be deduced from the book. Even Fielding's friendly approach to the reader does not create a picture of him within the novel. The representations of 'readers', the world's upper gallery, the pit, the boxes, for instance, really create a distraction from the process of *read-*

[1] 'Fielding and the Uses of Style', *Novel*, Fall 1967, p. 56

*ing.* They create situations analogous to reading, but more social: the reader is in the audience at a play, or in the jury box.

Yet, in *Tristram Shandy*, Sterne does make room for the reader in the act of reading. The text itself describes its own writing and reading. It forms the basis for a relationship: it is what reader and narrator share. As we have seen, they collaborate in making it; it only exists whilst they are able to work together, and it is only together, through the text and for it, that they can work. Fielding imagines situations for the reader: Sterne imagines the *only* situation for the reader. And the text of the novel is that situation.

> —How could you, Madam, be so inattentive in reading the last chapter? I told you in it, *That my mother was not a papist.*— Papist! You told me no such thing, Sir. Madam, I beg leave to repeat it over again, That I told you as plain, at least, as words, by direct inference, could tell you such a thing.—Then, Sir, I must have miss'd a page.—No, Madam,—you have not miss'd a word. Then I was asleep, Sir.—My pride, Madam, cannot allow you that refuge.—Then, I declare, I know nothing at all about the matter.—That, Madam, is the very fault I lay to your charge; and as a punishment for it, I do insist upon it, that you immediately turn back, that is, as soon as you get to the next full stop, and read the whole chapter over again. (I, xx)

In a passage like this the reading process becomes part of the story. The lady leaves the text in order to re-read Chapter Nineteen. She is left behind, the narration goes on without her. She becomes, therefore, legible herself, a part of the story that has been read. 'I have imposed this penance upon the lady, neither out of wantonness or cruelty; but from the best of motives; and therefore shall make her no apology for it when she returns back' (Ibid.). She was after all not *the* reader, because here is Sterne talking to the reader about her. Yet Sterne obviously wants her to stand *for* the reader, and to be an example to us all: '—'tis to rebuke a vicious taste which has crept into thousands besides herself,—of reading straight forwards, more in quest of adventures, than of the deep erudition and knowledge which a book of this cast, if read over as it should be, would infallibly impart with them'. (Ibid.) When she goes back we should go back as well, though, of course, we are also going forward with the narrative. We should learn to be as free with the material as Tristram is. The story, as he says, 'is digressive and it is progressive too,—and at the same time,' (I, xxii). The text is both a process, the onward movement of the conversation between writer and reader, and a product, the substance of that conversation. Thus the reader is both inside and outside it. He is helping forward the imagining of a world in which he can then see this imagining reflected as a story. Thus the more he loses himself in the pursuit of the fiction, the more likely he is to be able to believe in his identity within that fiction. Sterne is bringing the reading situation into the compass of the book; he is asking us to see it as something discovered by the imagination, whilst at the same time it is work for the imagination to do. Reading is not trying to be not-reading. It opens up a new sense of the self, the sense that it can create other kinds of existence for itself.

## II

*Tristram Shandy*, it has often been said, is a novel about writing a novel. It is also, as now appears, a novel about reading one. Sterne invents not only the novel but the readers whose reactions nudge it into shape. The novel will not be quite finished until it is read as being read in *this* way by *these* readers. It asks the reader to see who the readers are that are to be deduced from it. In effect it is asking him to imagine new roles for himself. John Traugott writes about this:

> . . . the reader is always viewing himself in character. How many personae are there? As many as the reader may care to discover. He discovers for one thing that even his sex is doubtful: 'Madam,'

'Sir,' 'Your Worship'. 'Unmistrusting ignorance' may be shot
from ambush 'ten times a day . . . if nine times a day, Madam,
had not served your purpose.' And the reader will come to believe
that not only his sex but his sexuality is in question.[1]

Traugott sees this as confirming that Sterne as a preacher
had a 'vested interest in dramatic rhetoric'. 'It was', he
points out, 'precisely as a preacher that Sterne insisted that
his parishioners doubt themselves and discover themselves
as all the personifications of his sermons'.[2] But it goes
further than this. We have seen already how the reader is
expected to 'imagine' the situations and the people in the
book, and in this way he can help along that ideal conversation which is the book's rhetoric. Now we discover that he
must imagine himself: he must understand who he would
have to be to do the imagining; or, rather, since the readers
are mostly found to be unsatisfactory, who he would not
have to be.

It is not just that Sterne addresses him directly. If he
says 'Sir', or 'Madam', or 'friend', or 'good folks', or 'my
fellow-labourers and associates in this great harvest of our
learning . . .' (I, xxi), it is because he still has to admit that
he cannot identify the reader, who might be anybody:

> I told the Christian reader—I say *Christian*—hoping he is
> one—and if he is not, I am sorry for it—and only beg he will
> consider the matter with himself, and not lay the blame entirely
> upon this book,——
> I told him, Sir—— (VI, xxxiii)

Sterne invokes the anonymous 'Sir' in order to share with
him a joke about the still more indeterminate 'Christian
Reader'. He is not so much creating a reader in this way as
inoculating himself against possible bad ones, especially
the worst kind of all, the critics:

> . . . in the first place, I have left half a dozen places purposely
> open for them;—and, in the next place, I pay them all court,——

---

[1] *Tristram Shandy's World*, rep. *Laurence Sterne*, ed. Traugott, p. 126
[2] Ibid., loc. cit

o

> Gentlemen, I kiss your hands,—I protest no company could
> give me half the pleasure,—by my soul I am glad to see you,—
> I beg only you will make no strangers of yourselves, but sit down
> without ceremony, and fall on heartily. (II, ii)

Here, surely, are the accents of Fielding's inn-keeper; here
again is the mock invitation to a feast. But Sterne takes it
further: he brings the critic himself into the text:

> —How, in the name of wonder! could your uncle *Toby*, who,
> it seems, was a military man, and whom you have represented
> as no fool,—be at the same time such a confused, pudding-headed,
> muddle-headed fellow, as—Go look.
> So, Sir Critick, I could have replied; but I scorn it.—'Tis
> language unurbane,—and only befitting the man who cannot
> give clear and satisfactory accounts of things, or dive deep enough
> into the first causes of human ignorance and confusion. (Ibid.)

There is here a curious oscillation between present and past
tense, between a story told to one reader and a drama
enacted with another. But Sterne soon begins to blur the
two identities. It becomes difficult to disentangle the critic
from the reader. At any rate the former drops out of the
conversation for a time, and therefore what is said to him
begins to sound as if it is said directly to the reader. For the
time being the reader seems to be put in the critic's place:

> Gentle critick! when thou hast weigh'd all this, and con-
> sider'd within thyself how much of thy own knowledge, discourse,
> and conversation has been pestered and disordered, at one time
> or other, by this, and this only:— . . . thou wilt not wonder at
> my uncle *Toby's* perplexities,—thou wilt drop a tear of pity upon
> his scarp and counterscarp;—his glacis and his covered-way;—
> his ravelin and his half-moon: 'Twas not by ideas,—by heaven!
> his life was put in jeopardy by words. (II, ii)

In this kind of sequence Sterne draws the reader into a
situation and then leaves him to act it out. He has begun to
attach a personality to the word 'Sir'; the reader begins to
feel that an identity has been chosen for him. In fact, all

through the novel, the vague outline of the second person, the 'you', keeps sharpening into a definite character, a figure on the scene. And this is particularly true when the reader is addressed as 'Madam'. She is a much more intrusive reader than the 'critic'. She is inquisitive and incautious, and her responses are entirely transparent: 'Was it a true nose?', she asks (IV, i). And when Tristram asserts that Jenny is a 'friend', it is she who takes him up: 'Friend!— My friend.—Surely, Madam, a friendship between the two sexes may subsist and be supported without—Fy! Mr. *Shandy*.' (I, xviii.) The lady-reader is quite as much a character within the book as Jenny herself. In some ways she is more of one. Jenny plays her part off-stage; she is oblivious of the book Tristram is writing; she belongs to that part of his life which is hidden from us by the book. But the lady does not exist apart from her interest in the story. Jenny advances the meaning of the book really by her ignorance of it: she stands for the life that is going on all round the book; she is a point of contact with a world that does not obey Tristram's imagination. This, one would think, is how the reader should appear if he is to be brought into the book. But the lady-reader has all the features of a character *within* the fictional world. Her business is to read, to attend, to be absorbed in the book. She gets all her personality from the way she reacts to the events narrated. She exists only as a reader. And as a reader she may be said to be created by the book she reads, or even within it, like one of its characters. She is totally engrossed in the fiction.

So Tristram can tease the lady with the image she is expected to have in the book in relation to the other characters:

> Which ever way my uncle *Toby* came by it [i.e., his modesty] 'twas nevertheless modesty in the truest sense of it; and that is, Madam, not in regard to words, for he was so unhappy as to have very little choice in them,—but to things;—and this kind of modesty possessed him, and it arose to such a height in him,

as almost to equal, if such a thing could be, even the modesty of a woman: that female nicety, Madam, and inward cleanliness of mind and fancy, in your sex, which makes you so much the awe of ours. (I, xxi)

The ironies contribute to the definition of character. The lady is expected not only to understand Toby better, but to compare herself with him. She is not outside the situation. And in the same way the critic, 'Sir', is implicated, and takes on a definite personality. What, for instance, does he think of Walter Shandy's theory of names? Can he afford to laugh at it?

> I own [it] has an air more of fancy than of solid reasoning in it;—and yet, my dear Sir, if I may presume to know your character, I am morally assured, I should hazard little in stating a case to you,—not as a party in the dispute,—but as a judge, and trusting my appeal upon it to your own good sense and candid disquisition in this matter;—you are a person free from as many narrow prejudices of education as most men;—and, if I may presume to penetrate further into you,—of a liberality of genius above bearing down an opinion, merely because it wants friends. Your son!—your dear son,—from whose sweet and open temper you have so much to expect.—Your BILLY, Sir!—would you for the world, have called him JUDAS? (I, xix)

But Sterne not only proposes an identity, or several identities, for the reader, he asks the reader to impersonate them. He gives him a part to play and lines to speak:

> —Why, 'tis a strange story! Tristram.
> —Alas, Madam, had it been upon some melancholy lecture of the cross— . . . —I wish I never had wrote it: but as I never blot any thing out— let us use some honest means to get it out of our heads directly. —Pray reach me my fool's cap—I fear you sit upon it, Madam—'tis under the cushion—I'll put it on—
> —Bless me! you have had it upon your head this half hour.— (VII, xxvi)

Elsewhere the reader's part in the dialogue is to ask

questions: 'Pray, what was your father saying?—Nothing'
(I, i); '—But pray, Sir, What was your father doing all
*December,—January,* and *February?* (I, iv); and, when
Tristram talks of water-drinking:

> —'And in perfect good health with it?'
> —The most perfect,—Madam, that friendship herself could
> wish me—'And drink nothing!—nothing but water?' (VIII, v)

## III

Thus there are occasions when Sterne literally dramatizes
the processes of reading; he writes dialogue for the reader;
at least, he writes words for some of the parts the reader has
to play. And in this way he very effectively symbolizes the
reader's essential relationship to what he reads: he is in
effect defining the reader as a kind of actor.

It is not just that he asks the reader to take *these* parts and
speak *these* words. But in doing so he draws attention to
the characteristic situation of a reader. For these imagined
readers, the lady and the critic, by no means eclipse the
reader; they stand for him, but they do not usurp him. They
are, as we have seen, embedded in the fiction; but the reader
is not. He is still outside it, and they are what he is reading
about. Any attempt to write the reader into the story will
have this result, for the reader has to be the person for whom
all the rest is written. He cannot be shown in the work, for it
is to him that everything must be shown. Yet reading does
seem like entering a new world, the world of the novel, and
Sterne's imaginary readers help to show how this can happen.
They are an invitation to the reader to act out different
versions of himself; they allow him to assume various
identities within the fiction. This is not to say that he
identifies himself with these characters. At least, if he does
so, it is without losing his own identity. Sterne is proposing
a controlled and deliberate commitment to the fictional

roles. He wants the reader to be able to 'play' another character and yet remain himself.

In fact he should be capable of the simultaneous involvement and detachment that Diderot sees as the paradox of acting. He must be two people at once, the one immersed in his role and the other coolly observant and critical outside it. These are the terms in which Diderot describes 'la Clairon': once she has come into possession of her part, 'elle se répète sans émotion'.

> Nonchalamment étendue sur une chaise longue, les bras croisés, les yeux fermés, immobile, elle peut, en suivant son rêve de mémoire, s'entendre, se voir, se juger et juger les impressions qu'elle excitera. Dans ce moment elle est double: la petite Clairon et la grande Agrippine.[1]

According to Diderot the actor needs judgment, not sensibility; he must be in command of himself all the time: 'moi, je lui veux beaucoup de jugement; il me faut dans cet homme un spectateur froid et tranquille.'[2] As we have seen,[3] Sterne himself can be described in this way, and it is clear that Diderot regards the actor as a creative artist. 'Les grands acteurs' are linked with 'les grands poètes' and 'les grands imitateurs de la nature'—all of them 'les êtres les moins sensibles': 'nous sentons, nous; eux, ils observent, étudient et peignent.'[4] But, as these last few words suggest, Diderot conceives of the writer in the terms we have been considering, that is, as a kind of reader: 'les grands poètes dramatiques surtout sont spectateurs assidus de ce qui se passe autour d'eux dans le monde physique et dans le monde moral.'[5]

Of course, both actor and reader lack the writer's freedom of movement, after all they serve his purpose. Their business is to apprehend 'le modèle idéal' imagined by the writer. They are responsible to the text. Their world is defined for

---

[1] *Paradoxe sur le Comédien, Diderot's Writings on the Theatre*, pp. 255–6
[2] Ibid., pp. 253–4   [3] See p. 189   [4] Ibid., p. 257   [5] Ibid., p. 256

them. They can do no more than be faithful to what they are given. But there is something rewarding in this. The actor is taken beyond himself. For the time being he moves in a more ample world, he rises to 'le vrai de la scène',

Qu'est-ce donc que le vrai de la scène? C'est la conformité des actions, des discours, de la figure, de la voix, du mouvement, du geste, avec un modèle idéal imaginé par le poète, et souvent exagéré par le comedien. Voilà le merveilleux. Ce modèle n'influe pas seulement sur le ton; il modifie jusqu'à la démarche, jusqu'au maintien. De là vient que le comédien dans la rue ou sur la scène sont deux personnages si différents, qu'on a peine à les reconnaître. La première fois que je vis M$^{lle}$ Clairon chez elle je m'écriai tout naturellement: «Ah! mademoiselle, je vous croyais de toute la tête plus grande.»[1]


# IV

The same is true of the reader. Like the actor he has to help the writer's work into existence. We have been looking at some of the ways this can happen. In fact we have been considering the possibility that the special quality of some novels consists in what they expect the reader to do, and I am inclined myself to consider the further possibility that a lot of the satisfaction of reading comes from this. It is not so much the quality of what is revealed or displayed that matters, as the quality, the character, of our encounter with it. Reading, especially reading fiction, is good practice for the imagination. It is like being in the hands of a good director, who can make us capable of excelling ourselves. We become, like the actor, a head taller.

Presumably all books provide this opportunity for us, all works of the imagination that is. We are talking about reading, not just 'reading good books'. Whatever we read gives us a unique kind of experience in a unique way.

[1] *Paradoxe sur le Comédien, Diderot's Writings on the Theatre*, p. 263

C. S. Lewis describes this kind of experience in terms that come close to many of the things we have been discovering about the reader of fiction:

> Good reading, therefore, though it is not essentially an affectional or moral or intellectual activity, has something in common with all three. In love we escape from our self into one other. In the moral sphere every act of justice or charity involves putting ourselves in the other person's place and thus transcending our own competitive particularity. . . . Obviously this process can be described either as an enlargement or as a temporary annihilation of the self. But that is an old paradox; 'he that loseth his life shall save it.'
>
> We therefore delight to enter into other men's beliefs (those, say, of Lucretius or Lawrence) even though we think them untrue. . . .
>
> It is not a question of knowing . . . It is *connaître* not *savoir*; it is *erleben*; we become these other selves. Not only nor chiefly in order to see what they are like, but in order to see what they see, to occupy, for a while, their seat in the great theatre, to use their spectacles and be made free of whatever insights, joys, terrors, wonders or merriment those spectacles reveal. . . .
>
> This, so far as I can see, is the specific value or good of literature considered as Logos; it admits us to experiences other than our own.[1]

Lewis writes here of 'good' reading; he is trying to defend his argument that 'good literature' may be defined as 'that which permits, invites, or even compels good reading; and bad, as that which does the same for bad reading'.[2] But, in the way Lewis means it, this is an empty statement. It means only that good literature permits a reader to say that it *is* good literature: good reading is the recognition of good literature. But Lewis does not really wish to limit the value of reading to the reading of 'good' books; indeed he says that it is the 'literary experience' itself which 'heals the wound without undermining the privilege of individuality'.[3]

[1] *An Experiment in Criticism*, pp. 138–9    [2] Ibid., p. 104
[3] Ibid., p. 140

At the same time he does not wish to be caught saying that there is no difference between good books and bad. He seems to want to say both that reading is valuable in itself and that it is really a means of access to things of value.

He is in this dilemma, I think, because he does not recognize reading as a creative act. It 'admits' us, that is all, 'to experiences other than our own'; its value must therefore depend on the values it makes available. But the novels we have been studying ask the reader to help create new experiences, and new values. They expect the reader to complete the design. They show how the process of reading can be part of the fabric, and hence part of the value of a work of art. The 'work', that is, is partly the work done by the reader, and the value of the 'work' is inseparable from the value of *that* work. The literature we value most will thus be that which has given us the most valuable work to do. Taken like this I think it makes sense to say that good literature 'permits, invites, or even compels good reading'. It does so because it expresses in its form the form of its reading. An essential index of its quality will be the quality of the reading it expects; its special character will be found at least partly in the particular configuration it gives to the reading experience.

This, at any rate, is the point of view from which we have been looking at some eighteenth-century novels. What seems to me to give each of them real merit is the subtlety and intricacy of the reading situation it establishes. These are not primitive works, though some of them tend to look primitive when only their psychological or formal realism is considered. It is true that they use a more deliberate and unconcealed rhetoric than later English novels; they invoke the reader, they make him appear, they do not disguise the dialogue. But just for this reason they make it easy to find out about what may be called a rhetoric of reading. The eighteenth-century English novelists were pushing forward the possibilities of the novel and were therefore in effect

o*

asking for a different kind of reader. Their professed contempt of the 'critic' was not just a conventional joke. It was part of the process of remaking a reader, who would have to be capable of sustaining a much more complex and challenging situation than the mere 'critic'. What this may be and how it may be manifested in particular novels are matters for the kind of interpretations I have been proposing. But if any one image of the reader can be thought to emerge from such interpretations it will surely be the one suggested by Sterne's novel, the reader as actor.

What these novelists are doing (perhaps what all novelists do) is to project as one of the resources of their fiction an appropriate role for the reader. At their best they will be assisting the reader to be at his best; they will in effect be creating the pattern of an ideal assumption of the role. What they demand of the reader and what they help him to achieve can be summed up in what Goethe writes in *Wilhelm Meister's Apprenticeship* about the qualities needed in a good actor:

'I have noticed,' answered Serlo, 'that as easily as you may set in motion the imaginations of men, gladly as they listen to your tales and fictions, it is yet very seldom that you find among them any touch of an imagination you can call productive. In actors this remark is strikingly exemplified. Any one of them is well content to undertake a beautiful, praiseworthy, brilliant part; and seldom will any one of them do more than self-complacently transport himself into his hero's place, without in the smallest troubling his head whether other people view him so or not. But to seize with vivacity what the author's feeling was in writing; what portion of your individual qualities you must cast off, in order to do justice to a part; how by your own conviction that you are become another man, you may carry with you the convictions of the audience; how by the inward truth of your conceptive power, you can change these boards into a temple, this pasteboard into woods; to seize and execute all this is given to very few. That internal strength of soul, by which alone deception can be brought about; that lying truth, without which nothing will affect us rightly, have by most men never even been imagined.

'Let us not then press too hard for spirit and feeling in our friends! The surest way is first coolly to instruct them in the sense and letter of the piece; if possible, to open their understandings. . . . And among actors, as indeed in all cases, there is no worse arrangement than for any one to make pretensions to the spirit of a thing, while the sense and letter of it are not ready and clear to him.' (V, vi)

# BIBLIOGRAPHY

## I. TEXTS

1. DANIEL DEFOE:
*Moll Flanders* (1st ed.), 1722.
    In quotations from the novel I use the text of the first edition, but, for ease of reference, I give the page numbers of the World's Classics edition (Oxford, 1961) which is a modernized version of the first edition.
*An Essay upon Projects* (1st ed.), 1697.
*A Hymn to the Pillory*, from *A Second Volume of the Writings of the Author of the True-born Englishman*, 1705.
*Serious Reflections . . . of Robinson Crusoe*, a reprint (1925) of the first edition, 1720.
*The Political History of the Devil* (6th ed.), 1770.

2. SAMUEL RICHARDSON:
*Clarissa* (4th ed.), 1751.
    In quotations I use the text of the seven-volume edition (octavo). I give references first to the volume and letter number of this edition, and then to the volume and page number of the Everyman Library edition in four volumes (1932), e.g.: (IV, 14; ii, 440).
*Clarissa: Preface, Hints of Prefaces, and Postscript*, ed. R. F. Brissenden, Los Angeles, 1964.
*Sir Charles Grandison* (7th ed.), 1781.
*The Correspondence of Samuel Richardson*, ed. A. L. Barbauld, 1804.
*Selected Letters of Samuel Richardson*, ed. J. Carroll, Oxford, 1964.

3. HENRY FIELDING:
*Tom Jones* (3rd ed.), 1749.
*The Champion*, 1741.
*An Apology for the Life of Mrs. Shamela Andrews*, ed. S. W. Baker, Los Angeles, 1953.
*The Works of Henry Fielding*, ed. A. Murphy, 1771.

4. LAURENCE STERNE:
   *Tristram Shandy* (1st ed.), 1760–7.
   *The Sermons of Mr. Yorick*, 1760–9.

## II. WORKS REFERRED TO IN THE TEXT

ALTER, ROBERT, 'Fielding and the Uses of Style', *Novel*, I, 1, 1967.
——, *Rogue's Progress*, Harvard, 1964.
ANDERSEN, H. H., 'The Paradox of Trade and Morality in Defoe', *Modern Philology*, xxxix, 1942.
AUERBACH, ERICH, *Mimesis*, tr. Willard Trask (Anchor Books ed.), 1957.
BAGEHOT, WALTER, *Collected Works*, ed. N. St. John-Stevas, 1965.
BARTHES, ROLAND, *Writing Degree Zero*, tr. A. Lavers and C. Smith (Cape Editions), 1967.
BAUMRIN, see SELBY-BIGGE.
BEER, GILLIAN, 'Richardson, Milton, and the Status of Evil', *Review of English Studies*, xix, 75 (NS), August 1968.
BISHOP, JONATHAN, 'Knowledge, Action and Interpretation in Defoe's Novels', *Journal of the History of Ideas*, xiii, 1952.
BLAKE, WILLIAM, *Poetry and Prose*, ed. Keynes, 1956.
BOOTH, WAYNE C., *The Rhetoric of Fiction*, Chicago and London, 1961.
BRADBROOK, FRANK W., 'Samuel Richardson' in FORD, q.v.
BRISSENDEN, R. F., *Samuel Richardson*, 1958.
BURTON, ROBERT, *The Anatomy of Melancholy* (6th ed.), 1632.
BUTLER, JOSEPH, *Works*, ed. Gladstone, Oxford, 1896.
CAMUS, ALBERT, *The Fall*, tr. Justin O'Brien (Penguin Books), 1963.
CLIFFORD, J. L., ed., *Eighteenth-Century English Literature*, New York, 1959.
CRANE, RONALD S., 'The Concept of Plot and the Plot of *Tom Jones*', *Critics and Criticism, Ancient and Modern*, Chicago, 1952.
CUMBERLAND, RICHARD, *De Legibus Naturae*, 1672, rep. in SELBY-BRIGGE, q.v.
DIDEROT, DENIS, *Paradoxe sur le Comédien*, rep. in GREEN, q.v.
DOBRÉE, BONAMY, *English Literature in the Early Eighteenth Century*, Oxford, 1959.
DONOGHUE, DENIS, 'The Values of *Moll Flanders*', *Sewanee Review*, lxxi, Spring 1963.
EHRENPREIS, IRVIN, *Fielding*: Tom Jones, 1964.

ELIOT, T. S., *Selected Essays*, 1951.

EMPSON, WILLIAM, 'Tom Jones', *The Kenyon Review*, xx, Spring 1958, rev. and rep. in PAULSON, q.v.

FARRELL, WILLIAM J., 'Nature versus Art as a Comic Pattern in *Tristram Shandy*', *ELH*, xxx, 1963.

——, 'Fielding's Familiar Style', *ELH*, xxxiv, March 1967.

FLUCHÈRE, HENRI, *Laurence Sterne: From Tristram to Yorick*, tr. and abridged by Barbara Bray, 1965.

FORD, BORIS, ed., *The Pelican Guide to English Literature*, IV, *From Dryden to Johnson*, 1963.

FORSTER, E. M., *Aspects of the Novel*, (Pelican Books), 1962.

FRYE, NORTHROP, *Anatomy of Criticism*, New York, 1966.

——, 'Towards Defining an Age of Sensibility', *ELH*, June 1956, rep. in CLIFFORD, q.v.

GOETHE, WOLFGANG VON, *Wilhelm Meister's Apprenticeship*, tr. Carlyle (Everyman Library) n.d.

GOLDEN, MORRIS, *Richardson's Characters*, Michigan, 1963.

GREEN, F. C., ed., *Diderot's Writings on the Theatre*, Cambridge, 1936.

GREGOR, IAN, see MACK.

HARDING, D. W., 'Psychological Processes in the Reading of Fiction', *British Journal of Aesthetics*, ii, April 1962.

HAZLITT, WILLIAM, *Complete Works*, ed. P. P. Howe, 1931.

HILL, CHRISTOPHER, 'Clarissa Harlowe and her Times', *Essays in Criticism* v, Oct., 1955, rep. in SPECTOR, q.v.

HILLES, F. W., ed., *The Age of Johnson, Essays presented to Chauncey Brewster Tinker*, Yale, 1949.

HUTCHENS, ELEANOR N., *Irony in* Tom Jones, Alabama, 1965.

JAMES, HENRY, *The Art of the Novel*, intr. by R. P. Blackmur, 1947.

JAMES, OVERTON P., *The Relation of Tristram Shandy to the Life of Sterne*, The Hague, 1966.

JEFFREY, FRANCIS, *Contributions to The Edinburgh Review*, 1844.

JOST, FRANÇOIS, 'Le Roman Épistolaire et la Technique Narrative au XVIIIe Siècle', *Comp. Lit. Studies*, iii, 1966.

KEARNEY, ANTHONY, '*Clarissa* and the Epistolary Form', *Essays in Criticism*, xvi, 1966.

KERMODE, FRANK, 'Afterword' to *Tom Jones* (Signet Classics edition), 1963.

——, *The Sense of an Ending*, New York, 1967.

KETTLE, ARNOLD, *An Introduction to the English Novel*, 1951.

KOONCE, HOWARD L., 'Moll's Muddle: Defoe's Use of Irony in *Moll Flanders*', *ELH*, xxx, Dec., 1963.

LAING, R. D., *The Divided Self* (Pelican Books), 1965.

LEAVIS, F. R., *The Great Tradition*, 1948.

LE BOSSU, R., *Traité du Poëme Epique*, Paris, 1693.

LEHMAN, B. H., 'Of Time, Personality, and the Author: a study of Tristram Shandy', *Studies in the Comic*, Berkeley, 1941, rep. in SPECTOR, q.v. and TRAUGOTT, q.v.

LEWIS, C. S., *An Experiment in Criticism*, Cambridge, 1961.

LUBBOCK, PERCY, *The Craft of Fiction* (Travellers' Library), 1926.

MCKILLOP, A. D., *The Early Masters of English Fiction*, 1962.

MACK, MAYNARD and GREGOR, IAN, ed., *Imagined Worlds, Essays on Some English Novels and Novelists in Honour of John Butt*, 1968.

MANN, THOMAS, *Doctor Faustus*, tr. H. T. Lowe-Parker (Penguin Books), 1968.

MAYOUX, JEAN-JACQUES, 'Laurence Sterne' tr. J. Traugott, rep. in TRAUGOTT, q.v.

MENDILOW, A. A., *Time and the Novel*, 1952.

MUIR, EDWIN, *Essays on Literature and Society*, 1965.

NOVAK, M. E., 'Defoe's *Shortest Way with the Dissenters*: Hoax, Paradox, Fiction, Irony and Satire', *Modern Language Quarterly*, xxvii, 1966.

O'CONNOR, WILLIAM V., ed., *Forms of Modern Fiction*, Minneapolis, 1948.

OLSON, ELDER, *Aristotle's Poetics and English Literature*, Chicago, 1965.

ORTEGA Y GASSET, JOSE, *On Love . . . Aspects of a Single Theme*, tr. Toby Talbot (Cape Editions), 1967.

PAULSON, RONALD, ed., *Hogarth's Graphic Works*, New Haven and London, 1965.

——, ed., *Henry Fielding: A Collection of Critical Essays*, New Jersey, 1962.

POULET, GEORGES, *Études sur le temps humain*, Paris, 1950.

PRICE, MARTIN, *To the Palace of Wisdom* (Anchor Books), New York, 1965.

PYE, HENRY JAMES, *A Commentary Illustrating the Poetic of Aristotle*, 1792, rep. in OLSON, q.v.

RAWSON, C. J., 'Gulliver and the Gentle Reader', in *Imagined Worlds*, ed. MACK, q.v.

ROUSSET, JEAN, *Forme et Signification*, Paris, 1964.

SALE, W. M., 'From *Pamela* to *Clarissa*' in HILLES, q.v. also rep. in SPECTOR, q.v.

SARTRE, JEAN-PAUL, 'Camus's *The Outsider*', *Situations* I, rep. in *Camus: A Collection of Critical Essays*, ed. G. Brée, New Jersey.

——, *What is Literature?*, tr. Wallace Fowlie, New York, 1965.

SCOTT, WALTER, *Lives of the Novelists*, ed. G. Saintsbury (Everyman Library), 1910.

SELBY-BIGGE, L. A., *British Moralists*, new introduction by B. H. Baumrin, New York, 1964.

SEYLAZ, JEAN-LUC, *Les Liaisons Dangereuses et la Création Romanesque chez Laclos*, Paris, 1958.

SHAFTESBURY, ANTHONY ASHLEY COOPER, 3rd Earl of, *Characteristics*, ed. J. M. Robertson, 1900.

SHERBURN, GEORGE, 'Fielding's Social Outlook', *Philological Quarterly*, Jan., 1956, rep. in CLIFFORD, q.v.

SHINAGEL, MICHAEL, *Daniel Defoe and Middle-Class Gentility*, Harvard, 1968.

SHKLOVSKY, VIKTOR, 'A Parodying Novel: Sterne's *Tristram Shandy*', tr. George Isaak in TRAUGOTT, q.v.

SPECTOR, ROBERT D., ed., *Essays on the Eighteenth Century Novel*, Indiana, 1965.

STARR, GEORGE A., *Defoe and Spiritual Autobiography*, Princeton, 1965.

STEDMOND, J. M., *The Comic Art of Laurence Sterne*, Toronto, 1967.

STEPHEN, LESLIE, *Hours in a Library*, 1909.

STEVENSON, R. L., 'A Gossip on Romance', rep. in *Memories and Portraits*, 1924.

STEVICK, PHILIP, 'Fielding and the Meaning of History', *PMLA*, lxxix, 1964.

SWIFT, J., *A Tale of a Tub*, ed. H. Davis, Oxford, 1957.

TAINE, H., *History of English Literature*, tr. H. Van Laun, Edinburgh, 1873.

TATE, ALLAN, 'Techniques of Fiction', *The Sewanee Review*, lii, 1944, rep. in O'CONNOR, q.v.

THORNBURY, ETHEL MARGARET, *Henry Fielding's Theory of the Comic Prose Epic*, Wisconsin, 1931.

TRAUGOTT, JOHN, *Tristram Shandy's World: Sterne's Philosophical Rhetoric*, Cambridge, 1955.

——, ed., *Laurence Sterne: A Collection of Critical Essays*, New Jersey, 1968.

VAN GHENT, DOROTHY, *The English Novel: Form and Function* (Harper Torchbook), New York, 1961.

WATT, IAN, *The Rise of the Novel*, 1957.

WOOLF, VIRGINIA, *Collected Essays*, 1966.

WORK, JAMES A., 'Henry Fielding, Christian Censor', in HILLES, q.v.

WRIGHT, ANDREW, *Henry Fielding, Mask and Feast*, 1965.

# INDEX

219